CW00504309

CYCLING LONDON TO PARIS

THE CLASSIC DOVER/CALAIS ROUTE
AND THE AVENUE VERTE

740007305285

About the Author

Mike Wells is an author of both walking and cycling guides. He has been walking long-distance footpaths for 25 years, after a holiday in New Zealand gave him the long-distance walking bug. Within a few years, he had walked the major British trails, enjoying their range of terrain from straightforward downland tracks through to upland paths and challenging mountain routes. He then ventured into France, walking sections of the Grande Randonnée network (including the GR5 through the Alps from Lake Geneva to the Mediterranean), and Italy to explore the Dolomites Alta Via routes. Further afield, he has walked in Poland, Slovakia, Slovenia, Norway and Patagonia.

Mike has also been a keen cyclist for over 20 years. After completing various UK Sustrans routes, such as Lôn Las Cymru in Wales and the C2C route across northern England, he then moved on to cycling long-distance routes in continental Europe and beyond. These include cycling both the Camino and Ruta de la Plata to Santiago de la Compostela, a traverse of Cuba from end to end, a circumnavigation of Iceland and a trip across Lapland to the North Cape. He has written a series of cycling guides for Cicerone following the great rivers of Europe.

Other Cicerone guides by the author

The Adlerweg
The Rhine Cycle Route
The Moselle Cycle Route
The Danube Cycleway Volume 1
The Danube Cycleway Volume 2
The River Rhone Cycle Route
The Loire Cycle Route

CYCLING LONDON TO PARIS

THE CLASSIC DOVER/CALAIS ROUTE AND THE AVENUE VERTE

by Mike Wells

JUNIPER HOUSE, MURLEY MOSS,
OXENHOLME ROAD, KENDAL, CUMBRIA LA9 7RL
www.cicerone.co.uk

© Mike Wells 2018
First edition 2018
ISBN: 978 1 85284 914 6

Printed in China on behalf of Latitude Press Ltd
A catalogue record for this book is available from the British Library.
All photographs are by the author unless otherwise stated.

Route mapping by Lovell Johns www.lovelljohns.com
© Crown copyright 2018 OS PU100012932.
Contains OpenStreetMap.org data © OpenStreetMap
contributors, CC-BY-SA. NASA relief data courtesy of ESRI.

Updates to this Guide

While every effort is made by our authors to ensure the accuracy of guide-books as they go to print, changes can occur during the lifetime of an edition. Any updates that we know of for this guide will be on the Cicerone website (www.cicerone.co.uk/914/updates), so please check before planning your trip. We also advise that you check information about such things as transport, accommodation and shops locally. Even rights of way can be altered over time.

The route maps in this guide are derived from publicly available data, databases and crowd-sourced data. As such they have not been through the detailed checking procedures that would generally be applied to a published map from an official mapping agency, although naturally we have reviewed them closely in the light of local knowledge as part of the preparation of this guide.

We are always grateful for information about any discrepancies between a guidebook and the facts on the ground, sent by email to updates@cicerone.co.uk or by post to Cicerone, Juniper House, Murley Moss, Oxenholme Road, Kendal, LA9 7RL, United Kingdom.

Register your book: To sign up to receive free updates, special offers and GPX files where available, register your book at www.cicerone.co.uk.

Front cover: Two iconic landmarks; the London Eye, start point of Avenue Verte (Ave Verte Stage 1) and the Eiffel Tower, finish point of the classic route (classic route Stage 11)

CONTENTS

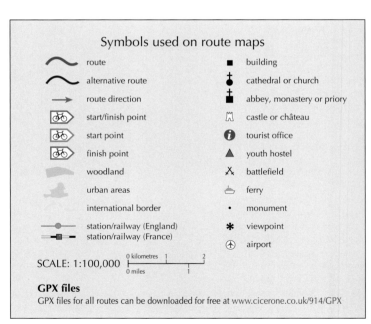

Symbols used on route maps

route
alternative route
route direction
start/finish point
start point
finish point
woodland
urban areas
international border
station/railway (England)
station/railway (France)

building
cathedral or church
abbey, monastery or priory
castle or château
tourist office
youth hostel
battlefield
ferry
monument
viewpoint
airport

SCALE: 1:100,000

GPX files

GPX files for all routes can be downloaded for free at www.cicerone.co.uk/914/GPX

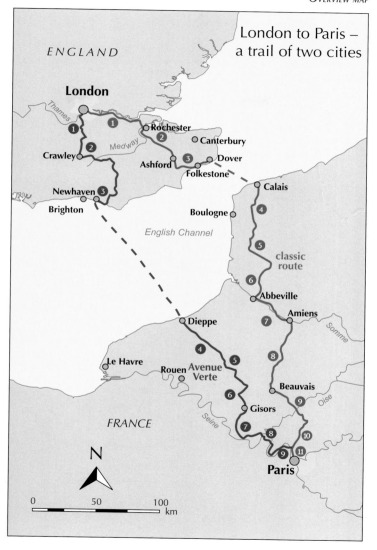

London to Paris –
a trail of two cities

ENGLAND

London

Thames

Medway

1

1

2

○ **Rochester**

2

○ **Canterbury**

Crawley ○

Ashford ○

3

○ **Dover**

Folkestone ○

Newhaven ○

3

○ **Calais**

4

Brighton

Boulogne ○

English Channel

5

classic
route

6

○ **Abbeville**

○ **Amiens**

○ **Dieppe**

7

Somme

Le Havre ○

4

5

8

Rouen ○

*Avenue
Verte*

6

○ **Beauvais**

9

FRANCE

Seine

○ **Gisors**

7

8

10

N

9

11

Paris

0   50   100
km

7

Mello château sits on a hilltop overlooking the town (classic route, Stage 9)

ROUTE SUMMARY TABLES

Stage	Start	Finish	Distance km (miles)	Page
Classic route				
1	London, Tower Hill station	Rochester bridge	50 (31)	42
2	Rochester bridge	Ashford, Henwood roundabout	47.5 (29.5)	56
3	Ashford, Henwood roundabout	Dover Eastern docks	49.5 (31)	67
4	Calais Gare Maritime	Desvres, Pl Léon Blum	41 (25.5)	82
5	Desvres, Pl Léon Blum	Hesdin, Pl d'Armes	49.5 (31)	94
6	Hesdin, Pl d'Armes	Abbeville fairgrounds	40 (25)	103
7	Abbeville fairgrounds	Amiens, Maison de la Culture	46.5 (29)	111
8	Amiens, Maison de la Culture	Beauvais cathedral	65 (40.5)	119
9	Beauvais cathedral	Chantilly, Pl Omer Vallon	46 (28.5)	133
10	Chantilly, Pl Omer Vallon	St Denis market	38.5 (24)	142
11	St Denis market	Paris, Eiffel Tower	16.5 (10.5)	150
Total	**London**	**Paris**	**490 (304.5)**	
Avenue Verte				
1	London Eye	Redhill station	40.5 (25)	158
2	Redhill station	Eridge station	49 (30.5)	171
3	Eridge station	Newhaven ferry terminal	62.5 (39)	184
4	Dieppe ferry terminal	Neufchâtel-en-Bray, old station	37 (23)	197
5	Neufchâtel-en-Bray, old station	Gournay-en-Bray, Pl Nationale	45 (28)	205
6	Gournay-en-Bray, Pl Nationale	Gisors, Pl de Blanmont	35.5 (22)	213
7	Gisors, Pl de Blanmont	Neuville-sur-Oise bridge	60.5 (37.5)	221
8	Neuville-sur-Oise bridge	St Denis station	44 (27.5)	232
9	St Denis station	Paris, Notre Dame cathedral	13 (8)	242
Total	**London**	**Paris**	**publicly available (240.5)**	

Façade of the old Carmelite abbey in
Forges-les-Eaux (Avenue Verte, Stage 15)

INTRODUCTION

The City of London skyline has many modernistic buildings (classic route, Stage 1)

Near the northern edge of Western Europe stand two great capital cities, London and Paris, undoubtedly two of the greatest cities in the world. Both were the capitals of worldwide empires that competed for domination around the world. This imperial past is long gone but has resulted in cosmopolitan populations with residents drawn from around the globe. Grand government buildings, important centres of worship and famous museums and galleries line world-renowned streets surrounded by popular parks and gardens. Everything one has, the other claims to match or better: Paris has the Eiffel tower, London has Tower bridge; Paris has Notre Dame cathedral, London St Pauls; Paris has the Louvre, London the National gallery; Paris has the Bois de Boulogne, London the Royal parks; the list is endless.

But these two cities are not isolated phenomena, both being surrounded by attractive countryside with rolling chalk downland, pastoral Wealden valleys and picturesque country towns. There are even two great cathedrals in the land that lies between them: Canterbury (off-route) is the mother church of the Church of England while Amiens (classic route, Stage 7) is the largest cathedral in France. Before the last ice age, which finished about 10,000 years ago, this

11

was one continuous landmass but as the ice melted and sea levels rose the two countries became separated by the English Channel. The opening of the Channel Tunnel in 1994 revolutionised travel between London and Paris. Frequent trains now make the journey in less than two and a half hours, speeding between London St Pancras and Paris Gare du Nord at up to 300kmph. Passengers have a brief glimpse of the countryside of southeast England and northern France as they rush past, but no time to explore or savour it.

A compensating breakthrough came in 2012. To celebrate the London Olympics (the choice of venue for which had resurrected old rivalries with a tight contest between the two cities before London was awarded the games) a waymarked cycle route was inaugurated running from centre to centre. Known as the Avenue Verte

(Green Avenue) this 387km route uses suburban streets, quiet country roads and cycle tracks along old railway lines to traverse Surrey and Sussex in England and Haute Normandy in France, crossing the English Channel between Newhaven and Dieppe. The route has become popular with cyclists, particularly French cyclists heading for London.

However, the Avenue Verte is not the only way of cycling from London to Paris. Traditionally the busiest route has always been via the short ferry link between Dover and Calais, indeed this is the preferred route for British cyclists riding to Paris, many of them undertaking sponsored rides to raise money for charity. This 490km ride (described here as the classic route) is not waymarked as a through journey, but can be ridden following NCN (National Cycle Network) routes through Kent to the English Channel,

Avenue Verte follows an old railway line from Neufchâtel-en-Bray to Serqueux (Avenue Verte, Stage 5)

and then quiet country roads, canal towpaths and dis-used railways across the Pas de Calais and Picardy to reach the Île de France and Paris.

While some cyclists are happy using just one of these routes to travel between London and Paris, making their return journey by Eurostar train or by plane, others seek to complete the round trip as a circular journey going out by one route and returning by the other. This guide provides detailed out and back descriptions for both routes, enabling cyclists to complete the return ride in either direction. Allowing for a few days sightseeing in the destination city, the 877km round trip makes an ideal two-week journey for average cyclists. There are many places to stay overnight in towns and villages along both routes, while places to eat include country pubs in England and village restaurants in France. Surely this is a more rewarding way to travel between London and Paris than flashing past at 300kph in a Eurostar train!

The first residents of the British Isles arrived from continental Europe before the last ice age when Britain was attached to the mainland. They probably followed the downland chalk ridges that run across what is nowadays northern France and south-east England, keeping above the then thickly forested and swampy valleys of rivers like the Medway and Somme. Traces of these routes still exist and are occasionally followed by the classic route in this guide.

Roman civilisation

By the time the Romans arrived in the first century BC, rising sea levels had split Britain from continental Europe,

Samara was the site of Caesar's winter camp when he conquered Gaul (classic route, Stage 7)

with both sides of the English Channel inhabited by Iron Age tribes of Gauls and Celts. Julius Caesar captured Gaul (most of modern France) between 58 and 51BC, but although he visited Britain, Roman occupation of England did not commence until AD43. The Romans involved local tribal leaders in government and control of the territory. With improvements in the standard of living, the conquered tribes soon became thoroughly romanised and tribal settlements became Romano-Gallic or Romano-British towns. Both London and Paris have their roots in the Roman Empire but while Londinium (London) was the capital of Britannia, Lutetia (Paris) was merely a provincial town in Gaul. The Romans built Watling Street, a road that linked the port of Dubris (Dover, the site of the best preserved Roman house in England) with London and the north. The towns of Canterbury and Rochester were built along this road, while Amiens and Beauvais were Roman towns in northern Gaul between Paris and the Channel. During the fourth century AD, the Romans came under increasing pressure from Germanic tribes from the east and by mid-fifth century had withdrawn their legions from both England and France.

Frankish and Anglo-Saxon settlement
After the Romans left there followed a period of tribal settlement. The Franks were a tribe that settled in northern France. From AD496 when Clovis I became their king and established a capital in Paris, the Frankish kingdom expanded by absorbing neighbouring states. After Charlemagne (a Frank,

Rochester castle was a Norman stronghold (classic route, Stage 2)

ruled AD768–814) temporarily united much of western Europe, only for his Carolingian empire to be split in AD843, the Franks became the dominant regional force. During the same period, southern England was settled by Saxons (from eastern Germany), with an area of Jutish (from Jutland in Denmark) settlement in Kent.

The Vikings from Scandinavia began migrating to the region in the early-ninth century AD. In France they settled in Normandy, while in England they initially occupied an area in the north known as the Danelaw. In 1015 the Viking king Canute defeated the Anglo-Saxons in southern England and extended Viking rule over the whole country. In 1066, a disputed succession caused the Normans from Normandy led by William the Conqueror to invade England and for the first time since the Romans left, unify England and northern France under one crown.

The Hundred Years' War

For nearly 500 years the Norman kings of England and their Plantagenet successors sought to consolidate and expand their territory in Britain and France. The main confrontation was the Hundred Years' War (1337–1453) fought between France and an alliance of England and Burgundy. For many years the English and Burgundians had the upper hand and success at Crécy in 1346 (classic route, Stage 6) led to the capture of large areas of France. The turning point came in 1429 when a French force led by 17-year-old Jeanne d'Arc (Joan of Arc) succeeded in lifting the siege of Orleans. By 1453 the English had been driven almost completely out of France, consolidating the French monarchy as the dominant force in the region. The last English stronghold at Calais (classic route, Stage 4) fell in 1558.

Religious influences and the rise of Protestantism

The Romans converted to Christianity in AD312 and this became the predominant religion in France. St Augustine brought Christianity to Anglo-Saxon England in AD597, establishing a church at Canterbury which later became the most important cathedral in the country. Following the murder of Thomas Becket (1170), Canterbury became a destination for pilgrims visiting Becket's grave. Many ventured further, with both English and French pilgrims continuing through France to Rome or Santiago. During the reign of Henry VIII (1509–1547), the Church of England split from the Catholic Church becoming Protestant. While there was a period of religious turmoil, the change stuck and Protestantism became the dominant force.

In France, the country's biggest Catholic cathedral was built at Amiens in the 13th century (classic route, Stage 7) and an even bigger one started at Beauvais (classic route, Stage 8), but this was never finished.

In the early 16th century the Protestant reformation reached France from Germany and Switzerland, rapidly taking hold driven by widespread perception of corruption among Catholic clergy. By mid-century many towns had substantial numbers of Protestant worshippers, known as Huguenots. This sparked violent reaction from devout Catholics led by the Duc de Guise and between 1562 and 1598 France was convulsed by a series of ferocious wars between religious factions. It is estimated that between two million and four million people died as a result of war, famine and disease. The wars were ended by the Edict of Nantes which granted substantial rights and freedoms to Protestants. However, this was not the end of the dispute. Continued pressure from Catholic circles gradually reduced these freedoms and in 1685 Louis XIV revoked the edict. Thankfully this did not provoke renewed fighting, many Huguenots choosing to avoid persecution by emigrating to Protestant countries (particularly Switzerland, Britain and the Netherlands), but it had a damaging effect on the economy.

The French Revolution

Both France and England were monarchies, although French kings ruled with more autocratic powers than English ones. This led eventually to violent revolution (1789–1799) which ended the ancien régime in France. The monarchy was swept away and privileges enjoyed by the nobility and clergy removed. Monasteries and religious institutions were closed while palaces and castles were expropriated by the state. Many were demolished, but some survived, often serving as barracks or prisons. In place of the monarchy a secular republic was established. The revolutionary mantra 'liberté, égalité, fraternité' is still the motto of modern day France. Chaos followed the revolution and a reign of terror resulted in an estimated 40,000 deaths, including King Louis XVI and his wife Marie Antoinette. The English novelist Charles Dickens described this period in A Tale of Two Cities:'it was the best of times, it was the worst of times'. A coup in 1799 led to military leader Napoleon Bonaparte taking control.

Napoleon Bonaparte

Despite ruling France for only 16 years, Napoleon (1769–1821) had a greater influence on the political and legal structures of the country than any other person. He made peace with the Catholic Church and allowed many exiled aristocrats to return, although with limited powers. In 1804, he declared himself Emperor of France and started a series of military campaigns which saw the French briefly gain control of much of western and central Europe. Feeling threatened by French aggression, Britain went to war with France. A legacy from this period can be found all along the south-east coast of England (classic route, Stage 3 and Avenue Verte, Stage 3) in the form

Napoleon is buried under the dome of Les Invalides in Paris (classic route, Stage 11)

of Martello towers, small defensive forts built to defend against French invasion. Napoleon was defeated in 1815 by the combined forces of Britain and Prussia, this being the last war between the British and French.

Agricultural and industrial revolutions

In Britain, political stability and an entrepreneurial environment allowed industry to develop and grow, fermenting the late 18th-century industrial revolution. Agricultural mechanisation caused millions of workers to leave the land and take jobs in factories producing textiles and iron goods which were distributed by a network of canals and railways and exported by a growing merchant fleet. This industrialisation was primarily in the north, with agriculture continuing to dominate the downland and Wealden valleys of south-east England. Indeed, the pre-19th-century iron industry in the Sussex Weald was unable to compete and ceased to exist.

French industrialisation came later, but by the mid-19th century the French economy was growing strongly based upon coal, iron and steel, textiles and heavy engineering. Coalfields developed in the Nord-Pas de Calais region and textile mills could be found across northern France.

Twentieth-century wars

The fields of northern France were the scene of much fighting during the First World War (1914–1918), with British and French armies engaged for over four years in trench warfare against an invading German army.

17

The frontline lay east of the classic route, with some of the heaviest fighting in the Somme valley near Amiens (classic route, Stage 7). Despite being on the winning side, the French economy was devastated by the war and the depression of the 1930s. Invasion by Germany in the Second World War (1939–1945) led the French army to surrender and the British army to retreat across the Channel, with the Germans occupying northern France for four years. Defensive works spread along Britain's south coast to defend against an expected German attack that never materialised. An allied invasion of France through Normandy (1944) lifted this occupation with Paris being liberated on 25 August.

European integration

After the war, France was one of the original signatories to the Treaty of Rome (1957) which established the European Economic Community (EEC) and led to the European Union (EU). Economic growth was strong and the French economy prospered. Political dissent, particularly over colonial policy, led to a new constitution and the establishment of the Fifth Republic under Charles de Gaulle in 1958. Subsequent withdrawal from overseas possessions has led to substantial immigration into metropolitan France from ex-colonies, creating the most ethnically diverse population in Europe. Since the 1970s, old heavy industry has almost completely disappeared and been replaced with

Tower bridge opens to allow ships into the pool of London (classic route, Stage 1)

high-tech industry and employment in the service sector.

Although not joining the EU until 1973 (and planning to leave in 2019), Britain's post-war path has been remarkably like that of France. Withdrawal from empire in the 1960s and a movement of people from former colonies has made London almost as cosmopolitan as Paris. Heavy industry has been replaced by light industry and services with London becoming the biggest financial centre in Europe. New and developing towns at Crawley (Avenue Verte, Stage 2) and Ashford (classic route, Stage 2) have attracted light industry.

THE ROUTES

Classic route

Historically this route started in Southwark at the southern end of London bridge and used the old Roman Watling Street (A2 in the British road numbering system) to reach Dover. It then followed Route National 1 (N1), a road created during Napoleonic times, from Calais to Paris where it ended at point zero, a bronze plaque set in the pavement in front of Notre Dame cathedral. Modern day traffic conditions have seen these roads change in character and the original route is nowadays not suitable for a leisurely cycle ride. In England, much of the A2 has been improved with up to four lanes of fast moving traffic in each direction, while in France the completion of the *autoroute* (motorway) network and transfer of responsibility for non-motorway roads from national to local government has led to a downgrading and renumbering of N1 to D901. Despite this, the largely unimproved D901 is a dangerous road with fast moving traffic.

To avoid these problems, this guide describes a route using mostly quiet country roads and rural tracks. It tries, wherever possible, to follow established cycle friendly routes with either separate cycle tracks or cycle lanes marked on the road, but there are a few short stretches on main roads. The geology of southeast England and northern France are similar with successive bands of chalk downland separated by river valleys at right angles to the direction of travel. The route attempts to minimise ascents, although some short climbs are inevitable.

There are a number of off-road sections. Most of these are well-surfaced with either 100 per cent asphalt or a mixture of asphalt and good quality gravel surfaces, usually on old railway trackbeds or along canal towpaths, and present no difficulties for cyclists. Two are rougher and are not suitable for bikes with smooth tyres. The 28km Pilgrims' Way in England (classic route, Stage 2) follows an ancient track along the North Downs. While this is part of the national cycle network, its use by agricultural vehicles can cause deep ruts to develop

Chantilly château was built in the 19th century after the original building was destroyed during the revolution (classic route, Stage 9)

and it can be difficult to traverse in wet weather. The 30km Coulée Verte in France (classic route, Stage 8) follows the route of an unsurfaced old railway line. In a dry period it is an easy ride, but during wet weather it becomes soft and muddy making it difficult to traverse. An alternative road route is described to avoid this part of Stage 8.

The cycled route runs from the Tower of London to the Eiffel Tower in Paris, giving a 'tower-to-tower' distance of 490km (excluding Channel crossing). In London, a network of cycle super-highways (dedicated cycle lanes alongside major roads) is under construction and one of these (CS4) is planned from London Bridge to Woolwich. While this was still in the planning

stage as this guide was being written, the beginning of Stage 1 from Tower Bridge Road to Woolwich follows the proposed super-highway. After Woolwich, a waymarked local cycle route (LCN18, part of the London Cycle Network) winds through suburban streets to the edge of Greater London where NCN1 (part of the British National Cycle Network) is joined and followed on dedicated cycle tracks parallel with the busy A2/M2 motorway to reach the Medway at Rochester. Stage 2 uses rural tracks to climb over the North Downs and then joins a cycle track following the ancient Pilgrims' Way along the shoulder of the downs to Ashford. After a short ride the route reaches the English Channel coast and this is followed (Stage 3) through olkestone (where an alternative route links with the Channel Tunnel erminal) then climbs over the iconic white cliffs to reach Dover ferry port.

After crossing the Channel, Stages –6 follow a canal and disused railway across the coastal plain, then undulate on minor roads through ownland, climbing in and out of a eries of pretty valleys, to reach the ver Somme at Abbeville. After a flat tage (Stage 7) following the towpath f the canalised Somme to Amiens, he Coulée Verte track along another ld railway is followed (Stage 8) up he Selle valley and over more downand before descending to Beauvais. o avoid more hills that lie across the oute to Paris, Stage 9 turns south-east own the Thérain valley to Chantilly nd then climbs over one last ridge

(Stage 10) to reach the Paris Basin. Most, but not all, of Stage 11 through Greater Paris to the Eiffel Tower is on cycle tracks. If you wish to end at point zero, an alternative route described under Avenue Verte Stage 9 takes you to Notre Dame cathedral.

Avenue Verte

To celebrate the 2012 Olympics in London, cycling organisations in Britain and France developed a new cycle route between the London Eye and Notre Dame in Paris. They chose a route which crossed the Channel between Newhaven and Dieppe. Although this gives a longer and less frequent crossing, the 387km cycled is just over 100km shorter than the classic route. The route was designed to make maximum use

Much of the route across the Vexin plateau is on gravel cycle tracks (Avenue Verte, Stage 7)

of Sustrans off-road cycle tracks in England and *voies vertes* (rural cycle routes) in France, which resulted in long stretches along disued railway track beds in both countries. Most of the route is complete, although in England part of the route following the Cuckoo Trail in Kent (Stage 3) has proved difficult to realise due to land ownership problems, while in France the Forges-les-Eaux–Gisors sector (Stages 5–6) became unavailable when a previously closed railway was reopened and the route now follows local roads over chalk downland to by-pass this problem.

When inaugurated, the route out of London (Stage 1) followed city streets to reach the Wandle Trail. Since then a cycle super-highway (CS7) has been built between central London and Merton and the route described follows this to join the Wandle Trail rather than the more complicated waymarked route. Quiet roads are then used to leave London and climb over the North Downs into the Sussex Weald. After passing Gatwick airport, Stage 2 follows a disused railway east along the mid-Wealden ridge then turns south again (Stage 3) along another disused railway. Minor roads are taken through a gap in the South Downs to the port of Newhaven.

Once in France, a disused railway trackbed takes the route (Stages 4–5) from near Dieppe through the Bray (the French Weald) to Forges-les-Eaux then undulates over downland (Stage 6) before dropping into the Epte valley at Gisors. Another ol railway (Stage 7) and a climb ont the Vexin plateau bring the route t the new town of Cergy-Pontoise o the edge of the Paris basin. Stage crosses St Germain forest then follow river and canalside towpaths and cit streets into Paris. The final leg (Stag 9) uses more canal towpaths and cit streets to reach Notre Dame cathedra in the heart of the city.

Physical geography

Prior to the last ice age, south-eas England and Northern France wer part of the same landmass and a a result share the same geologica structure. After the ice age, sea leve rose cutting England off from cont nental Europe but leaving a series c chalk and limestone anticlinal ridge and clay and gravel filled synclina depressions that cross both countrie from west to east. These are a resu of compression caused approx mately 30 million years ago whe the African and European tectoni plates collided and pushed up th Alps. Where erosion has removed th upper layers between ridges this ha revealed sandstone bedrock (Mic Wealden ridge in England) and cre ated fertile agricultural land know as the Weald in England and the Bra in France. At the northern and south ern ends of the route, both Londo and Paris sit in artesian basin bounded by chalk downland or limestone plateaux.

On both sides of the Channel rivers flow through the valleys between the ridges; including the Medway and Stour in England and the Canche, Somme, Oise and Epte in France. These valleys are mostly filled with tertiary deposits and have been extensively quarried for aggregates leaving large areas of water-filled gravel pits.

Wildlife

While several small mammals and reptiles (including rabbits, hares, squirrels, voles, water rats and snakes) may be seen scuttling across the track, this is not an area inhabited by larger animals with a few exceptions. Foxes are common in England, particularly in London where they can be seen foraging even by day, while many of the forests passed through have roe deer, fallow deer or muntjac populations. Boar can be found in French forests and there are some in southeast England although these are rarely seen. Badgers are common, but as nocturnal animals are unlikely to be encountered.

When to go

The routes can be cycled at any time of year, but they are best followed between April and October when the days are longer, the weather is warmer and there is no chance of snow.

Sauf cyclistes *(cyclists excepted)* shows contra-flow cycling allowed on a one-way street

How long will it take?

Both routes have been broken into stages averaging just under 50km per stage. A summary of stage distances can be found in the route summary tables. A fit cyclist, cycling an average of 80km per day should be able to complete the eleven stages of the classic route in six days and the nine stages of Avenue Verte in five days. Allowing time for exploring Paris, the round trip can be accomplished in two weeks. A faster cyclist averaging 100km per day could complete the round trip in nine days, whereas those preferring a more leisurely pace of 60km per day would take about 17 days. There are many places to stay along both routes making it possible to tailor daily distances to your requirements.

What kind of cycle is suitable?
Most of the route is on asphalt cycle tracks or along quiet country roads. However, there are some stretches with gravel surfaces and, although most are well graded, there are some rougher sections, particularly on the Pilgrims' Way (classic route, Stage 2) and Coulée Verte (classic route, Stage 8), which are not passable on a narrow tyred racing cycle. The most suitable type of cycle is either a touring cycle or a hybrid (a lightweight but strong cross between a touring cycle and a mountain bike with at least 21 gears. Except for the off-road Coulée Verte (classic route, Stage 8, which has an on-road alternative), there is no advantage in using a mountain bike. Front suspension is beneficial as it absorbs much of the vibration. Straight handlebars, with bar-ends enabling you to vary your position regularly, are recommended. Make sure your cycle is serviced and lubricated before you start, particularly the brakes, gears and chain.

As important as the cycle, is your choice of tyres. Slick road tyres are not suitable and knobbly mountain bike tyres not necessary. What you need is something in-between with good tread and a slightly wider profile than you would use for everyday cycling at home. To reduce the chance of punctures, choose tyres with puncture resistant armouring, such as a Kevlar™ band.

GETTING THERE AND BACK

The start and end points in London and Paris are in city centre locations. Regular fast Eurostar trains connect London St Pancras and Paris Gare du Nord stations enabling you to start or end your ride in either city. See Appendix D for a list of useful transport details.

Getting to the start
Main line, suburban and overground trains in London carry cycles. On underground trains in central London, cycles are permitted on sub-surface lines (Circle, District, Hammersmith & City, Metropolitan) but not on deep-tube lines (Bakerloo, Central,

	UK Nat Grid	Geographic	UTM
Tower Hill	TQ336807	00°04'35"W, 51°30'35"N	30U 700031E, 5709709N
London Eye	TQ307799	00°07'04"W, 51°30'11"N	30U 702873E, 5710563N
St Pancras	TQ300832	00°07'38"W, 51°32'00"N	30U 699243E, 5713049N
Eiffel Tower		02°17'39"W, 48°51'31"N	31U 448228E, 5411979N
Notre Dame		02°20'56"W, 48°51'12"N	31U 452237E, 5411356N
Gare du Nord		02°21'17"W, 48°52'56"N	31U 452695E, 5414559N

ubilee, Northern, Piccadilly, Victoria, Waterloo & City). On all lines prohibitions apply during weekday rush hours.

The Tower of London is in front of Tower Hill underground station served by the Circle and District lines, both of which carry cycles, and is only a short ride from Cannon Street, Fenchurch Street, Liverpool Street and London Bridge railway stations and Aldgate on the Metropolitan line.

The London Eye is on the South Bank of the Thames close to Waterloo station. Although main line and suburban trains can be used to reach Waterloo, none of the underground lines that serve the station carry cycles. The nearest cycle-permitted underground stations are both on the other side of the river: Westminster (cycle over Westminster bridge and

turn left into Belvedere Road) and Embankment (take your cycle by lift to the walkway beside Hungerford railway bridge and walk it over the river). Both these stations are served by the Circle and District lines.

St Pancras Eurostar station is served by Circle, Hammersmith & City and Metropolitan lines which carry cycles (and Northern, Piccadilly and Victoria lines which do not). It is also served by main line and suburban trains at Kings Cross and St Pancras stations and is only a short ride from Euston (main line, suburban and overground services).

Crossing the Channel
The classic route crosses the English Channel at its narrowest point between Dover or Folkestone in England and Calais in France. There

Up to 40 ferry sailings per day connect Dover and Calais (classic route, Stages 3–4)

are two ways of making this crossing, by ferry from Dover or by shuttle train through the Channel Tunnel.

Up to 40 ferry sailings operate daily (depending on the season) between Dover Eastern docks and Calais Gare Maritime ferry port operated by two companies, P&O (www.poferries.com) and DFDS (www.dfdsseaways.co.uk). Crossing time is 90 minutes. As these are vehicular ferries there is ample capacity on board for cyclists without the need for reservations, although lower prices are available by advance booking online.

Although up to four vehicle shuttles run every hour through the Channel Tunnel between Cheriton terminal near Folkestone and Coquelles near Calais, only two departures daily carry cycles. These are transported in a specially contracted vehicle, equipped to carry six cycles, which picks up from Cheriton Holiday Inn hotel at 0800 and 1530 and deposits you opposite the CIFFCO building near the Coquelles terminal. Return journeys pick-up in Coquelles at 1230 and 1800. Reservations must be made at least 48 hours in advance on tel +44 1303 282201. This service is provided as a requirement in Eurotunnel's operating license and is heavily subsidised, but as it is not promoted by the company it is little used. For more information see www.eurotunnel.com. Directions to Cheriton and Coquelles are given in Stages 3 and 4 of the classic route.

The Channel Tunnel cycle shuttle is slightly cheaper and slightly faster than the ferries and saves 17km of cycling from Folkestone to Dover. However, as this must be booked in advance with only two services per day it is considerably less flexible than the Dover ferries which run frequently throughout the day and night, providing a turn-up-and-go service.

The Avenue Verte crosses the Channel using a ferry operated by DFDS between Newhaven and Dieppe. There are two or three sailings daily depending upon season which take four hours. Reservations are not normally needed for cycles although as prices vary between sailings advance booking may enable you to obtain the best price.

Intermediate access

There are international airports at Gatwick (Avenue Verte, Stage 2) and Beauvais (classic route, Stage 8). The English part of the classic route (Stages 1–3) and the first half of Avenue Verte as far as Three Bridges (Stages 1–2) are closely followed by railway lines, as are Stages 7 and 9 of the classic route (Abbeville–Amiens and Beauvais–Chantilly) in France. Stations en route are listed in the text. Between Serqueux–Gisors (Avenue Verte, Stages 5–6) a previously closed railway has been reinstated for freight trains and a limited passenger service has started, but only a few stations have reopened.

High-speed Eurostar trains cover the distance from London to Paris in under two and a half hours

etting home

his book hopes to encourage you to ycle home by using a different route that taken on your outward jour- ey. However, if time is at a premium r you are too exhausted to cycle ack, it is possible to return by public ansport.

The easiest way to return home om Paris to London with your cycle by train. Eurostar services that ke under two and a half hours run pproximately hourly throughout the ay between Paris Gare du Nord– ondon St Pancras using the Channel unnel. Cycles booked in advance avel in dedicated cycle spaces in e baggage compartment of the ame train as you. Bookings, which pen six months in advance and cost 30 single, can be made through urodespatch (tel +44 344 822 5822)

in London or Geoparts (tel +33 1 55 31 58 33) in Paris. Cycles must be checked in at Geoparts luggage office in Gare du Nord (follow path to L of platform 3) at least 60 minutes before departure. There are two dedicated places per train for fully assembled cycles and four more places for dis- assembled cycles packed in a spe- cial fibre-glass box. These boxes are provided by Eurostar at the despatch counter, along with tools and packing advice. Leave yourself plenty of time to dismantle and pack your bike. After arrival in St Pancras cycles can be collected from Eurodespatch Centre beside the bus drop-off point at the back of the station. More information can be found at www.eurostar.com.

By air, Paris's three airports have flights to worldwide destina- tions, including frequent services to

London's six airports. These are operated by several airlines, the main ones
being BA (Charles de Gaulle and Orly
to Heathrow), Air France (Charles de
Gaulle to Heathrow), EasyJet (Charles
de Gaulle to Gatwick, Luton and
Southend), Cityjet (Orly to City) and
Flybe (Charles de Gaulle to City).
These airlines, and Ryanair (who fly
from Beauvais, classic route, Stage
8), also operate services to other
UK airports. Airlines have different
requirements regarding how cycles
are presented and some, but not all,
make a charge which you should pay
when booking as it is usually greater
at the airport. All require tyres par-
tially deflated, handlebars turned
and pedals removed (loosen pedals beforehand to make them easier
to remove at the airport). Most will
accept your cycle in a transparent
polythene bike-bag, although some
insist on use of a cardboard bike-box.
These can be obtained from cycle
shops, usually for free. You do, however, have the problem of how you get
the box to the airport.

NAVIGATION

Waymarking
In England, the classic route follows
a series of local and national waymarked cycle trails. In France, the
only waymarking is on parts of Stages
4, 7 and 8. Avenue Verte is waymarked throughout, often coinciding
with other routes.

*The British NCN waymark with AV
symbol added; the French Avenue
Verte waymark; the French yellow
provisional waymark where the final
route is still being considered;*

Both routes in France often follow
local roads. These are numbered
as départemental roads (D roads).
However, the numbering system can
be confusing. Responsibility for roads
in France has been devolved from
national to local government with
responsibility for many former routes
nationales (N roads) being transferred to local départements. This has
resulted in most being renumbered as
D roads. As départements have different numbering systems, these D road
numbers often change when crossing
département boundaries.

Maps
While it is possible to cycle both
routes using only the maps in this

Summary of cycle routes followed

Classic route		
CS4	Cycle Superhighway 4	Stage 1 (planned)
LCN18	London Cycle Network 18	Stage 1
NCN1	National Cycle Network 1	Stage 1
NCN177	National Cycle Network 177	Stage 1
NCN17	National Cycle Network 17	Stage 2
NCN2	National Cycle Network 2	Stage 3
V30	Somme Canalisée towpath	Stage 7
CV	Coulée Verte	Stage 8
N–S	N–S Véloroute	Stage 11
Avenue Verte		
AV	Avenue Verte	Stages 1–9
CS7	Cycle Superhighway 7	Stage 1
NCN20	National Cycle Route 20	Stages 1–2
NCN21	National Cycle Route 21	Stages 1–3
NCN2	National Cycle Route 2	Stage 3
V33		Stage 7
N–S	N–S Véloroute	Stage 9

book (particularly the Avenue Verte which is waymarked throughout), larger scale maps with more detail are available, although these are not specifically cycle maps. Ordnance Survey Landranger 1:50,000 maps give excellent coverage of the English stages while either Michelin or IGN local maps are good for France. Street atlases might be useful for cycling in London and Paris.

Various online maps are available to download, at a scale of your choice. Particularly useful is Open Street Map (www.openstreetmap. org) which has a cycle route option showing British NCN routes, French voie verte and the Avenue Verte. The official website for the Avenue Verte is www.avenuevertelondonparis.co.uk which includes definitive route maps, details about accommodation and

	Classic route	Avenue Verte
OS Landranger (1:50,000)	177 East London	176 West London
	178 Thames Estuary	187 Dorking & Reigate
	189 Ashford & Romney Marsh	188 Maidstone & Royal Tunbridge Wells
	179 Canterbury & East Kent	199 Eastbourne & Hastings
		198 Brighton & Lewes (very small part)
Michelin (1:150,000)	301 Pas de Calais, Somme	304 Eure, Seine-Maritime
	305 Oise, Paris, Val d'Oise	305 Oise, Paris, Val d'Oise
IGN (1:100,000)	101 Lille/Boulogne-sur-Mer	107 Rouen/Le Havre (small part)
	103 Amiens/Arras	103 Amiens/Arras
	108 Paris/Rouen	108 Paris/Rouen

refreshments, points of interest, tourist offices and cycle shops.

Guidebooks

This is the only guidebook for the classic route and the only one which describes Avenue Verte in both directions. There are two other guidebooks for the Avenue Verte: one in English describing the route from London to Paris (*Avenue Verte*, published by Sustrans) and one in French for the route from Paris to London (*Paris–Londres à vélo*, published by Chamina Edition).

There are many guidebooks to London and south-eastern England and to Paris and northern France, including some specially aimed at cyclists. Most of these maps and guidebooks are available from leading bookshops including Stanford's, London and The Map Shop, Upton upon Severn. See Appendix D for further details. Relevant maps are widely available en route.

ACCOMMODATION

For most of the route there is a wide variety of accommodation. The stage descriptions identify places known to have accommodation, but are by no means exhaustive. Prices for accommodation in France are similar to prices in the UK. See Appendix D for a list of relevant contact details.

Hotels, guest houses and B&B

Hotels vary from expensive five-star properties to modest local establishments and usually offer a full meal service. Guest houses and bed and breakfast accommodation, known as *chambres d'hôte* in French,

An accueil vélos *(cyclists welcome) sign shows an establishment that provides facilities for cyclists*

generally offer only breakfast. Tourist information offices (see Appendix B) will often telephone for you and make local reservations. Booking ahead is seldom necessary, except in high season (mid-July to mid-August in France). Most properties are cycle friendly and will find you a secure overnight place for your pride and joy. Accueil Vélo is a French national quality mark displayed by establishments within 5km of the route that welcome cyclists and provide facilities including overnight cycle storage.

Youth hostels and gîtes d'étape
While there are several youth hostels in both London and Paris, there are only three hostels en route (Calais, Montreuil and Amiens; all on the classic route in France) and three just off-route (Medway, Eastbourne and

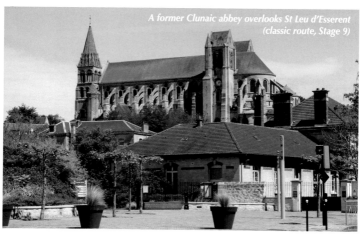

A former Clunaic abbey overlooks St Leu d'Esserent (classic route, Stage 9)

Southease in England). These are listed in Appendix C. English hostels managed by the YHA and FUAJ hostels in France are affiliated to Hostelling International. Other French hostels are managed by BVJ. Unlike British hostels, most European hostels do not have self-catering facilities but do provide good value hot meals. Hostels get very busy, particularly during school holidays, and booking is advised through www.hihostels.com.

Gîtes d'étape are hostels and rural refuges (shelters) in France mainly for walkers. They are mostly found in mountain areas, although there is one at Forges-les-Eaux (Stage 5) on Avenue Verte. Details of French gîtes d'étape can be found at www.gites-refuges. com. Do not confuse these with Gîtes de France which are rural properties rented as weekly holiday homes.

Camping

If you are prepared to carry camping equipment, this will probably be the cheapest way of cycling the route. Stage descriptions identify official campsites. Camping may be possible in other locations with the permission of local landowners.

FOOD AND DRINK

Where to eat

There are many places where cyclists can eat and drink, varying from snack bars, crêperies, pubs and local inns to Michelin starred restaurants.

Locations are listed in stage descriptions, but these are not exhaustive. Days and times of opening vary. When planning your day, try to be flexible as some inns and small restaurants do not open at lunchtime. In France, an auberge is a local inn offering food and drink. English language menus may be available in big cities and tourist areas, but are less common in smaller towns and rural locations.

When to eat

In England, breakfast in hotels, guest houses and B&B is usually a cooked meal while English pubs generally provide a wide variety of light snack and full meal options for both lunch and dinner.

In France, things are a little different. Breakfast (petit déjeuner) is continental: breads, jam and a hot drink. Traditionally lunch (déjeuner) was the main meal of the day, although this is slowly changing, and is unlikely to prove suitable if you plan an afternoon in the saddle. Most French restaurants offer a menu du jour at lunchtime, a three-course set meal that usually offers excellent value for money. It is often hard to find light meals/snacks in bars or restaurants and if you want a light lunch you may need to purchase items such as sandwiches, quiche or croque-monsieur (toasted ham and cheese sandwich) from a bakery.

For dinner (dîner) a wide variety of cuisine is available. Much of what is available is pan-European and will be easily recognisable. There are however national and regional dishes you may wish to try. Traditionally French restaurants offered only fixed price set menus with two, three or more courses. This is slowly changing and most restaurants nowadays offer both fixed price and à la carte menus.

What to eat

France is widely regarded as a place where the preparation and presentation of food is central to the country's culture. Modern day French cuisine was first codified by Georges Auguste Escoffier in *Le Guide Culinaire* (1903). Central to Escoffier's method was the use of light sauces made from stocks and broths to enhance the flavour of the dish in place of heavy sauces that had previously been used to mask the taste of bad meat. French cooking was further refined in the 1960s with

the arrival of nouvelle cuisine which sought to simplify techniques, lessen cooking time and preserve natural flavours by changing cooking methods.

Northern France and Normandy are not particularly well-known for gastronomy, although there are a few local specialities you may wish to try (or avoid!). *Andouillettes* are coarse sausages made from pork intestines with a strong taste and distinctive odour. Not a dish for the faint hearted. As in nearby Belgium, *moules et frites* (mussels and chips) are popular light meals while Dieppe (Avenue Verte, Stage 4) is famous for *hareng saur* (smoked herring). Local cheese includes Neufchâtel (Avenue Verte, Stage 4) while Camembert (from lower Normandy), Brie (from the Marne valley) and Maroilles (from Picardy) are produced nearby. All are soft, creamy

Neufchâtel cheese is a heart-shaped soft cheese from Neufchâtel-en-Bray (Avenue Verte, Stage 4)

cows' milk cheeses with blooming edible rinds. One way of serving cheese is *le welsh*, a northern French take on welsh rarebit consisting of ham and grilled cheese on toast often topped with an egg. Normandy and the Bray have orchards producing apples, pears and cherries from which fruit tarts such as *tarte tatin* are produced.

What to drink
Both England and France are beer and wine consuming countries. In England beer sales are declining but wine is growing, while in France wine is declining and beer growing.

Although France is predominantly a wine drinking country, beer (*bière*) is widely consumed, particularly in

In Normandy apples are used to produce cider

the north. Draught beer (*une pression*) is usually available in two main styles: blonde (European style lager) or blanche (partly cloudy wheat beer). Most of this is produced by large breweries such as Kronenbourg and Stella Artois but there are an increasing number of small artisanal breweries producing beer for local consumption. No wine is produced commercially in northern France, although wine from all French vineyard regions is readily available. *Cidre* (cider) and *calvados* (apple brandy) are produced in Haute Normandy, while Bénédictine liqueur comes from Basse Normandy.

All the usual soft drinks (colas, lemonade, fruit juices, mineral waters) are widely available.

AMENITIES AND SERVICES

For a breakdown of facilities en route, see Appendix A. This list is not exhaustive but provides an indication of the services available.

Grocery shops
All cities, towns and larger villages passed through have grocery stores, often supermarkets, and most have pharmacies. In France, almost every village has a *boulangerie* (bakery) that is open from early morning and bakes fresh bread several times a day.

Cycle shops
Most towns have cycle shops with repair facilities. Locations are listed in

the stage descriptions, although this is not exhaustive. Many cycle shops will adjust brakes and gears, or lubricate your chain, while you wait, often not seeking reimbursement for minor repairs. Touring cyclists should not abuse this generosity and always offer to pay, even if this is refused.

Currency and banks

The currency of France is the Euro. Almost every town has a bank and most have ATM machines which enable you to make transactions in English. However very few offer over-the-counter currency exchange. In London, Paris and port towns (Dover, Folkestone, Newhaven, Calais and Dieppe) there are commercial exchange bureau but in other locations the only way to obtain currency is to use ATM machines to withdraw cash from your personal account or from a prepaid travel card. Contact your bank to activate your bank card for use in Europe or put cash on a travel card. Travellers' cheques are rarely used.

Telephone and internet

The whole route has mobile phone coverage. Contact your network provider to ensure your phone is enabled for foreign use with the optimum price package. International dialling codes are +44 for UK and +33 for France.

Almost all hotels, guest houses and hostels, and many restaurants, make internet access available to guests, usually free of charge.

Electricity

Voltage is 220v, 50HzAC. Plugs in Britain are three-pin square while in France standard European two-pin round plugs are used. Adaptors are widely available to convert both ways.

WHAT TO TAKE

Clothing and personal items

Even though the route is not mountainous there are some undulating sections crossing chalk downland and consequently weight should be kept to a minimum. You will need clothes for cycling (shoes, socks, shorts/trousers, shirt, fleece, waterproofs) and clothes for evenings and days off. The best maxim is two of each, 'one to wear, one to wash'. Time of year makes a difference as you need more and warmer clothing in April/May and September/October. All of this clothing should be capable of being washed en route, and a small tube or bottle of travel wash is useful. A sun hat and sun glasses are essential, while gloves and a woolly hat are advisable except in high summer.

In addition to your usual toiletries you will need sun cream and lip salve. You should take a simple first-aid kit. If staying in hostels you will need a towel and torch (your cycle light should suffice).

Cycle equipment

Everything you take needs to be carried on your cycle. If overnighting in

A fully equipped cycle

accommodation, a pair of rear panniers should be sufficient to carry
all your clothing and equipment,
although if camping, you may also
need front panniers. Panniers should
be 100 per cent watertight. If in
doubt, pack everything inside a strong
polythene lining bag. Rubble bags,
obtainable from builders' merchants,
are ideal for this purpose. A bar-bag
is a useful way of carrying items you
need to access quickly such as maps,
sunglasses, camera, spare tubes,
puncture-kit and tools. A transparent
map case attached to the top of your
bar-bag is an ideal way of displaying
maps and guide book.

Your cycle should be fitted with
mudguards and bell, and be capable
of carrying water bottles, pump and
lights. Many cyclists fit an odometer
to measure distances. A basic tool-kit

should consist of puncture repair kit,
spanners, Allen keys, adjustable span-
ner, screwdriver, spoke key and chain
repair tool. The only essential spares
are two spare tubes. On a long cycle
ride, sometimes on dusty tracks, your
chain will need regular lubrication
and you should either carry a can
of spray-lube or make regular vis-
its to cycle shops. A strong lock is
advisable.

SAFETY AND EMERGENCIES

Weather
The whole route is in the cool temper-
ate zone with warm summers, cool
winters and year-round moderate
rainfall. Daily weather patterns are
highly variable.

Average temperatures (max/min °C)

	Apr	May	Jun	Jul	Aug	Sep	Oct
London	15/7	18/10	21/13	23/15	23/15	20/13	16/10
Paris	16/7	20/11	23/14	25/16	25/16	21/13	16/10

Average rainfall (mm/rainy days)

	Apr	May	Jun	Jul	Aug	Sep	Oct
London	43/16	50/15	43/13	41/14	48/13	49/15	71/15
Paris	25/14	26/12	24/11	22/11	21/10	16/11	25/13

Road safety

While in England cycling is on the left, in France it is on the right side of the road. If you have never cycled before on the right you will quickly adapt, but roundabouts may prove challenging. You are most prone to mistakes when setting off each morning.

France is a very cycle-friendly country. Drivers will normally give you plenty of space when overtaking and often wait patiently behind until space is available to pass. Much of the route is on dedicated cycle paths, although care is necessary as these are sometimes shared with pedestrians. Use your bell, politely, when approaching pedestrians from behind. Where you are required to cycle on the road there is often a dedicated cycle lane.

Many city and town centres have pedestrian-only zones. These restrictions are often only loosely enforced

Where there is no cycle lane, motorists and cyclists are urged 'partageons la route' (share the road)

Secure cycle storage facility in Gournay-en-Bray (Avenue Verte, Stage 5)

and you may find locals cycling within them, indeed many zones have signs allowing cycling. One-way streets in France often have signs permitting contra-flow cycling.

Neither England nor France require compulsory wearing of cycle helmets, although their use is recommended.

Emergencies

In the unlikely event of an accident, the standardised EU emergency phone number is 112. The entire route has mobile phone coverage. Provided you have an EHIC card issued by your home country, medical costs of EU citizens are covered under reciprocal health insurance agreements, although you may have to pay for an ambulance and claim the cost back through insurance.

Theft

In general, the route is safe and the risk of theft low. However, you should always lock your cycle and watch your belongings, especially in cities.

Insurance

Travel insurance policies usually cover you when cycle touring but they do not normally cover damage to, or theft of, your bicycle. If you have a household contents policy, this may cover cycle theft, but limits may be less than the actual cost of your cycle. Cycle Touring Club (CTC), www.ctc org.uk, offer a policy tailored to the needs of cycle tourists.

ABOUT THIS GUIDE

Text and maps

There are 20 stages, each covered by separate maps drawn to a scale of 1:100,000. The maps for the English stages 1–3 of both the classic route and Avenue Verte are based upon UK Ordnance Survey mapping and as a result differ slightly in style to those for the French stages. Detailed maps of city centres (including London and Paris) and major towns are drawn to 1:40,000. The route line (shown in red) is mostly bi-directional. Where outward and return routes differ, arrows show direction of travel. Some alternative routes exist. Where these offer a reasonable variant, usually because they are either shorter or offer a better surface, they are mentioned in the text and shown in blue on the maps.

Place names on the maps that are significant for route navigation are shown in **bold** in the text. Distances shown are cumulative kilometres within each stage and altitude figures are given in metres. Please note that 'signposted' is abbreviated to 'sp'. For each city/town/village passed an indication is given of facilities available (accommodation, refreshments, youth hostel, camping, tourist office, cycle shop, station) when the guide was written. This list is neither exhaustive nor does it guarantee that establishments are still in business. No attempt has been made to list all such facilities as this would require another book the same size as this one. For full accommodation listings, contact local tourist offices. Such details are usually available online. Tourist offices along the route are shown in Appendix B.

While route descriptions were accurate at the time of writing, things do change. Temporary diversions may be necessary to circumnavigate improvement works and permanent diversions to incorporate new sections of cycle track. This is particularly the case in London where on-going work to create a cycle super-highway network will affect Stage 1 of the classic route for a few years. Where construction is in progress you may find signs showing recommended diversions, although these are likely to be in the local language only.

GPX tracks

GPX files are freely available to anyone who has bought this guide on Cicerone's website at www.cicerone.co.uk/914/gpx.

Language

This guide is written for an English-speaking readership. In France, English is taught as a second language in all schools and many people, especially in the tourist industry, speak at least a few words of English. However, any attempt to speak French is usually warmly appreciated. In this guide, French names are used except for Normandie

Porte St Martin in Paris commemorates battle victories of Louis XIV (classic route, Stage 11/Avenue Verte, Stage 9)

and Picardie where the English Normandy and Picardy are used. The French word *château* covers a wide variety of buildings from royal palaces and stately homes to local manor houses and medieval castles.

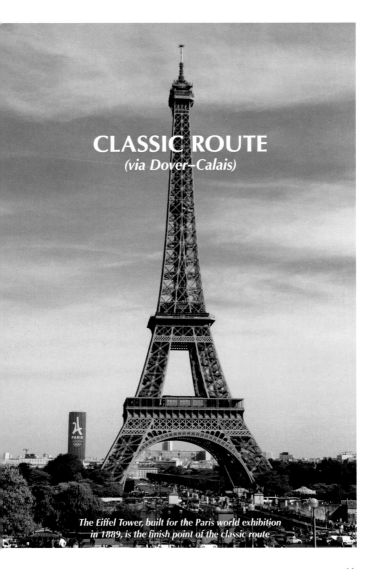

CLASSIC ROUTE
(via Dover–Calais)

The Eiffel Tower, built for the Paris world exhibition in 1889, is the finish point of the classic route

41

STAGE 1
Tower of London to Rochester

Start	Tower of London (18m)
Finish	Rochester bridge (4m)
Distance	50km (31 miles)
Ascent	207m
Waymarking	CS4 Southwark–Woolwich (under construction), LCN18 Woolwich–Barnes Cray, NCN1 Barnes Cray–Ebbsfleet, NCN177 Ebbsfleet–Strood

This stage starts with a level ride through suburban south-east London, mostly on cycle lanes beside minor roads but with some busier sections. After Dartford, it follows cycle tracks beside the old Roman Watling Street (now a busy motorway), climbing over two small outliers of the North Downs before descending to cross the Medway into Rochester. If you want to avoid cycling in London, Southeastern trains have frequent services from Charing Cross and London Bridge stations to Dartford.

THE TOWER OF LONDON

When it was built in 1078, the Tower of London was seen by the Anglo-Saxon English as a hated symbol of Norman oppression following William the Conqueror's invasion in 1066. However, over the centuries it became a cherished symbol at the heart of London, Britain and the British Empire. It is said that if the ravens that live there should ever leave, the kingdom will fall. The tower has been used as a fortress, royal palace, armoury, treasury, the home of the royal mint and is nowadays a museum holding important national collections including the British crown jewels. For over eight centuries (1100–1952) it also housed a prison, mostly for prisoners who had fallen foul of the monarch including the uncrowned king Edward V (imprisoned by his uncle Richard III who took the crown for himself), Anne Boleyn (second wife of Henry VIII) and Sir Walter Raleigh. The heart of the complex is the White Tower, the oldest and best-preserved Norman stone keep in Britain. This is surrounded by other buildings, two sets of encircling walls and a moat, which is nowadays dry. A poignant use of the moat in 2016 saw it filled with 888,246 ceramic poppies in commemoration of British and empire combatants killed during the First World War.

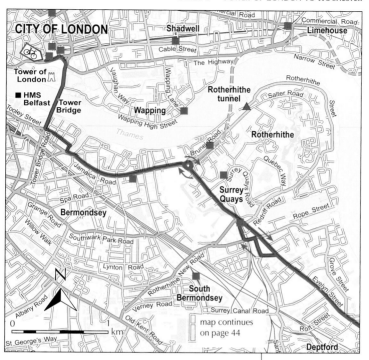

From Tower Hill on N side of **Tower of London** follow
Tower Bridge Approach S and cross Thames on **Tower
bridge**. Turn L (Queen Elizabeth St) and R at end (The

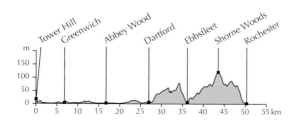

The classic route starts from the Tower of London

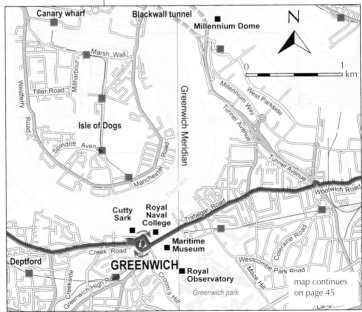

map continues on page 45

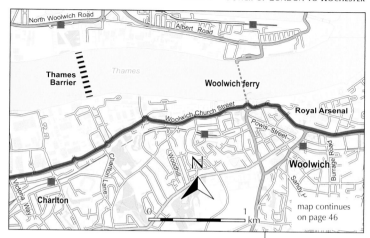

North Woolwich Road

Albert Road

Thames Barrier

Thames

Woolwich ferry

Royal Arsenal

Woolwich Church Street

Powis Street

Charlton Lane

Woodhill

Victoria Way

Charlton

Woolwich

Sandy Hill

Burrage Road

N

0   1 km

map continues on page 46

Shad) to reach T-junction. ▶ Turn L (Jamaica Rd, A200), using bus lane, to **Rotherhithe** roundabout. Turn R (third exit, Lower Rd, sp Greenwich) past **Surrey Quays** shopping centre L (3.5km, 3m) and continue on Evelyn St to **Deptford**. Go ahead (Creek Rd) over Deptford Creek to reach T-junction in **Greenwich** (7km, 6m) (accommodation, refreshments, tourist office, cycle shop, station).

Cycle Superhighway CS4 will be joined here.

> **Greenwich** (pronounced Gren-itch), which has a long maritime history, is synonymous with the zero meridian which passes close to the Royal observatory in Greenwich park. The former naval hospital designed by Christopher Wren, which became the Royal Naval college from 1873–1998, now houses the university of Greenwich; while the old naval asylum has been the National Maritime museum since 1934. The tea clipper *Cutty Sark*, preserved in a dry dock beside the Thames, was built in 1869 for the tea trade from China. This three-masted sailing ship held the record for the journey to Australia for 10 years before steam ships took over the route.

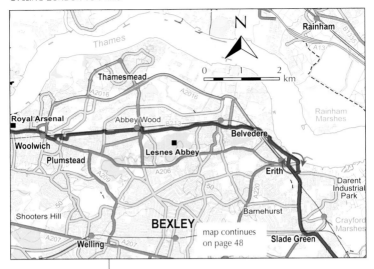

To visit the Cutty Sark, continue ahead on Church Street.

Turn L following one-way system and bear R (College Approach). ◀ Turn R again (King William Walk) in front of entrance to old Royal Naval College then L at cross-roads (Romney Rd, A206). Continue between old Royal Naval College L and National Maritime museum R (with Royal Observatory in Greenwich park rising behind) into Trafalgar Rd. Continue into Woolwich Rd then go ahead over roundabout beneath motorway and pass through **Charlton** (10km, 4m) (refreshments, cycle shop, station).

Go ahead over two roundabouts and at third, turn R (third exit, Woolwich High St, sp Woolwich ferry) to reach roundabout by ramp leading to **Woolwich ferry** L (12.5km, 6m) (accommodation, refreshments, cycle shop, station).

Go ahead past Waterfront leisure centre L and bear R at next roundabout (second exit, Beresford St). Pass modern development on site of former **Woolwich Royal Arsenal** L and continue on Plumstead Rd beside bus lane. Where road turns L, bear R across road and fork R on bus and cycle only lane past Plumstead bus garage L. Rejoin

The Royal Artillery's Firepower museum is in the former Woolwich Royal Arsenal

road and pass **Plumstead station** R (14km, 6m) (refreshments, station).

Turn first L (Heverham Rd) and at end turn R (Reidhaven Rd). Follow this bearing R and turn L at crossroads (Hartville Rd). Continue over crossroads to T-junction and turn L (Barth Rd) then follow this bearing R into Marmadon Rd. Road becomes Bracondale Rd and passes under road bridge, eventually becoming Abbey Grove. Where road ends, continue ahead on cycle track between houses 8–9. Turn L (Wilton Rd) and follow this bearing R past **Abbey Wood station** L (16.5km, 2m) (refreshments, station) and under road bridge.

Turn R (Florence Rd) then L at crossroads (Abbey Rd, B213) using cycle lane L. Pass **Lesnes Abbey** ruins R. ▶ Continue ahead into Gilbert Rd, becoming Picardy St and finally Lower Rd. Pass B&Q/Asda superstore L and fork L on cycle track dropping down to pass under roundabout in **Belvedere** (station). Rejoin main road, then pass over railway and road bridges and go ahead over two mini-roundabouts. Follow road bearing R into West St and go ahead over mini-roundabout into **Erith** (21.5km, 10m) (refreshments, station).

Lesnes abbey (built 1178) was closed by Cardinal Wolsey in 1525 and was one of the first abbeys pulled down during the dissolution of the monasteries in 1534.

47

At next roundabout bear L (first exit, Erith High St) to reach T-junction. Go ahead on dual use pedestrian/cycle track passing under bridge linking two parts of shopping centre and continue to reach roundabout. Turn R (James Watt Way, fourth exit) then L at traffic lights onto dual carriageway Queens Rd (A206). ◄ Follow this over small roundabout then pass under railway to reach second (larger) roundabout. Turn L (first exit) and immediately after roundabout use staggered crossing to reach other side of main road. Turn L on cycle track R of road then fork R past third roundabout and continue ahead over small fourth roundabout to reach Barnes Cray roundabout (25km, 8m).

Follow cycle track anticlockwise around roundabout and continue beside Thames Rd (A206) under railway bridge. Bear R past next roundabout then follow cycle track crossing to L of road and turn R (Burnham Rd, A2026). Turn L (Lawson Rd) and bear R at end (Priory Rd). Emerge on main road (Victoria Rd) and turn L. Go

Queens Road is a busy main road.

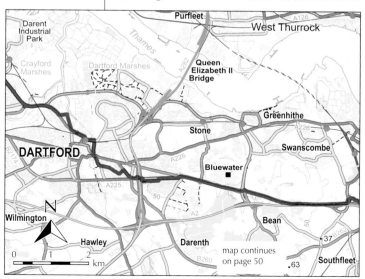

map continues on page 50

ahead over mini-roundabout past gasholder L then use cycle track L to pass next roundabout, continuing into Mill Pond Rd past back of **Dartford station** R (27km, 4m) (accommodation, refreshments, cycle shop, station).

Cross bridge over river Darent and turn R at traffic lights (Overy St), passing under railway bridge. Bear L at end and go ahead L over traffic lights into road reserved for buses, using cycle track L. Follow this uphill then bear L on cycle track continuing uphill onto parallel road (Darenth Rd). Fork L beside Ivy Leaf pub (Brent Lane) continuing uphill. Where road bears R, continue ahead (still Brent Lane) and turn immediately L (Downs Ave). Turn R at T-junction (Park Rd, A296) on cycle track R. Pass Hesketh Park L and cross to other side at central reservation. Continue to roundabout and bear L. Pass under footbridge and continue beside main road (Princes Rd, A296). Follow cycle track bearing R under next roundabout, then turn L on bridge over M25 motorway and R to pass under opposite side of roundabout. Turn sharply L, then L again through barriers and pass car park of Dartford Bridge pub L. Emerge onto Hesketh Ave and continue ahead on Fleet Rd. Turn L between houses 73–75 then R at T-junction (Princes Rd), parallel with main road. Where this ends, turn sharply L through bollards and cross service road beside bus stop. Turn R and after 70 metres, turn L across main road using staggered crossing. Turn R alongside main road (Watling St, A296), then continue past next roundabout. Dogleg R and L across slip road and cycle past huge **Bluewater** shopping mall in quarry below L (32km, 45m).

Bluewater, the sixth largest shopping mall in Europe, is built to a triangular floor plan inside a former cement quarry. It opened in 1999 with 330 stores and 40 restaurants employing 7000 staff. Accessible only by road, it has parking for 13,000 vehicles.

Follow cycle track beside main road then fork L through gate. Pass under road bridge then bear L to cross slip road beside roundabout. Turn R to continue beside main road, ascending to pass junction with A2 dual carriageway then descending into Ebbsfleet valley. Bear then zigzag down R to cross slip road for Ebbsfleet a staggered light controlled crossing (35.5km, 19m).

Turn L and follow road curving R past roundabout then cross second slip road at more traffic lights and continue on other side of road. Pass second roundabout R and follow slip road beside A2 as it ascends towards next junction. At top of hill turn immediately R across four staggered crossings over dual carriageway B262. Continue parallel with A2, soon bearing L through scrubland past Gravesend **Cyclopark** R (38.5km, 43m) (refreshments).

Dogleg R and L across entry road to Cyclopark then continue ascending past petrol station L and fork L or cycle track winding through scrubland along route of old motorway. Cross slip road and emerge on main road with car park R. Turn R and immediately cross road at light controlled crossing then follow cycle track bearing L pas

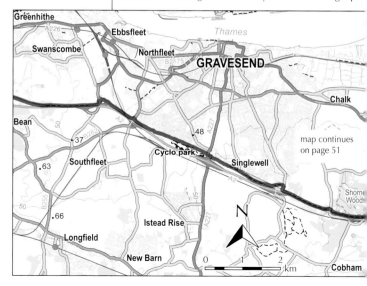

map continues on page 51

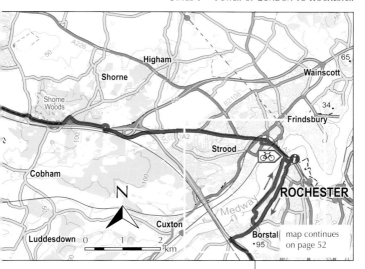

map continues
on page 52

oundabout to run parallel with motorway. Follow track
way from motorway to cross side road and pass Inn on
he Lake hotel L. At top of hill, bear L beside Brewers
Rd and turn R (Park Pale) just before entrance to **Shorne
Woods** country park L (43.5km, 111m).

Follow Park Pale descending to run beside motorway, then turn L (sp golf club) at first junction and fol-
ow road curving R over motorway bridge. Where road
ears L under railway, fork R on cycle track and turn
ack under bridge. Continue beside slip road and fol-
ow this over motorway to reach roundabout. Continue
eside Watling St on cycle track R, then after first turning
R, cross road at reservation. Keep R at fork beside petrol
tation and continue downhill on tree-lined cycle track
, then pass under railway and follow High St through
ne-way system in centre of **Strood** (refreshments, sta-
ion). Continue under second railway bridge and cross
Rochester bridge over river Medway to reach **Rochester**
50km, 4m) (accommodation, refreshments, youth hostel
in Gillingham), tourist office, cycle shop, station).

Gravesend Cyclopark has road and off-road cycle race tracks

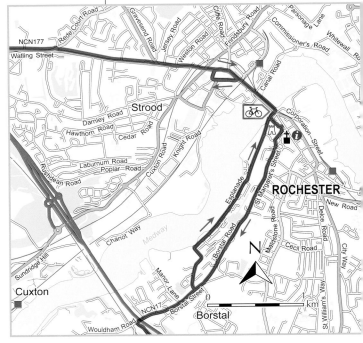

ROCHESTER

Rochester (pop 27,000) is, with Chatham and Gillingham, part of the Medway conurbation (pop 250,000). Founded by the Romans to control the place where Watling St crossed the Medway, it was further developed by the Normans who built a castle, the well-preserved main keep of which still stands, on a ridge overlooking the river crossing. The cathedral, built between 1080–1130 with later additions, is one of the oldest in Britain. High St, between the castle ridge and the river, has many old buildings including the Guildhall and Corn Exchange. One of Rochester's eminent Victorian residents was the author Charles Dickens who used it as a setting in *Pickwick Papers* and *Great Expectations*. Inspired by the works of Dickens, an annual Sweeps Festival is held every May, a revival of a longstanding tradition described in *Sketches by Boz* (a Dickens's nom de plume) that had died out in the early 1900s. One odd aspect of Rochester is that despite having a cathedral and being recognised as a city since 1211 it is now forbidden from using its city title. When the old city merged with Gillingham to form Medway in 1998, the new council failed to apply for the 'city' title to be transferred. Later in 2010 when the council started referring to the 'City of Medway' it was rebuked by the Advertising Standards Authority and told to desist.

REVERSE ROUTE: ROCHESTER TO TOWER OF LONDON

Cross Medway over **Rochester bridge** and pass under railway. Fork L (Commercial Rd, A2, sp London) and bear R around one-way system in **Strood** (refreshments, station). Turn L (High St) passing under railway, then continue uphill (London Rd, becoming Watling St) out of town. Go ahead at roundabout and cross motorway. Follow cycle track beside slip road and pass under bridge. Turn sharply back L then bear L to cross motorway. Follow road bearing L and turn R beside motorway to reach entrance to **Shorne Woods** country park R (6.5km, 111m).

Turn L, using cycle track R, then bear R to continue beside motorway, now descending. Go ahead over side road and continue to roundabout. Bear R beside first exit then turn L across road at traffic lights and follow cycle track away from road beside truck park L. Cross next road then continue ahead parallel with motorway past Gravesend **Cyclopark** L (11.5km, 43m) (refreshments).

Continue to road junction and use four-part staggered crossing to cross B262 and its slip roads. Turn immediately L beside motorway and follow cycle track past roundabout by slip road for Ebbsfleet (14.5km, 19m). After roundabout, turn L across road then bear L past second roundabout. Turn R across dual-carriageway using staggered crossing and continue ahead zig-zagging up embankment. At this point route joins NCN1. Bear R on cycle track beside motorway ascending then descending to reach roundabout by slip road for **Bluewater** shopping mall L (18km, 48m).

Pass roundabout and turn L across road. Bear R on cycle track under road bridge and continue through gate to run parallel with Watling St (A296). Continue ahead past next roundabout to reach complicated road junction. Turn L across middle of figure of eight roundabout using staggered crossing then turn R beside road for 75 metres. Turn L across service road beside bus stop then bear L on concrete ramp and turn sharply R (Princes Rd). Turn L beside house 604 then R into Fleet Rd. At end continue ahead on cycle track beside carpark of Dartford Bridge pub R. Turn R and spiral down R to pass under roundabout. Turn L over M25 motorway then R under other side of roundabout. Bear L then R beside A296. At next roundabout, bear R ahead on cycle track beside Park Rd and cross to L of road at next central reservation. Turn L (Downs Ave) and R downhill (Brent Lane). At end turn R (Darenth Rd) and bear L on cycle track beside road reserved for buses. Go ahead over crossroads and fork immediately R (Overy St). Pass under railway and turn R (Mill Pond Rd) past back of **Dartford station** L (23km, 8m) (accommodation, refreshments, cycle shop, station). *To avoid cycling in London, frequent trains run from Dartford to London Bridge and Charing Cross stations.*Continue past roundabout and fork L (Victoria Rd, A2026). Continue into Burnham Rd and fork R (Priory Rd North). Follow this bearing L (Lawson Rd) and turn R at end beside Burnham Rd. Follow cycle track across road to L and continue past next roundabout onto Thames Rd (A2026). Pass under railway to reach roundabout at Barnes Cray (25km, 8m).

Continue on cycle track beside A206, going ahead over first roundabout, bearing L at second and R at third (sp Erith), where cycle track ends. Pass under railway and continue over small roundabout to reach five-way roundabout in **Erith** (28.5km, 10m) (refreshments, station). *The roundabout has a fish statue in the centre.*

Go ahead R (third exit, Walnut Tree Rd, sp town centre) and bear L at roundabout (West St). Follow this round bends R and L into Lower Rd and go ahead over two small roundabouts onto B213 (still Lower Rd). Cross road and railway bridges and follow road through **Belvedere** (station). Go ahead over small roundabout and continue on Picardy St, Gilbert St and Abbey Rd. Pass

Lesnes abbey ruins L and go under road bridge. After bridge, turn R (Wilton Rd) to reach **Abbey Wood station** (33.5km, 2m) (refreshments, station).

Before station, turn L on cycle track L of Abbey Arms pub and pass between houses. Emerge onto road and go ahead (Abbey Grove, becoming Bracondale Rd). Pass under road bridge and continue into Marmadon Rd. At end, bear L (Barth Rd) and turn R (Hartville Rd). Turn R again at second cross-roads (Reidhaven Rd) and follow this bearing L. Turn L (Heverham Rd) and R into Plumstead High St (A206), passing **Plumstead station** L (36km, 6m) (refreshments, station).

Continue ahead between former **Woolwich Arsenal** R and Woolwich town centre L (accommodation, refreshments, cycle shop, station) and go ahead at large grassy roundabout by ramp for **Woolwich ferry** R (37.5km, 6m). Follow main road bearing L at next roundabout (A206, sp Greenwich) then ahead over two small roundabouts into **Charlton** (40km, 4m) (refreshments, station). Continue under motorway and pass between **National Maritime Museum** L and former **Royal Naval College** R to reach **Greenwich** (43km, 6m) (accommodation, refreshments, tourist office, cycle shop, station).

Follow one-way system bearing R (Church St) then turn L (Creek Rd, A200). Cross Deptford Creek then bear R at major road junction (Evelyn St). At one-way system, bear L (Bestwood St), then turn R (Bush Rd). Follow one-way street bearing L (Rotherhithe New Rd) and fork R (Rotherhithe Old Rd). Bear L into Lower Rd, past Surrey Quays station R (46.5km, 3m) to reach **Rotherhithe** roundabout. Bear L (first exit, Jamaica Rd, sp Bermondsey) and follow this to point where road bears L. Turn R across road between old brick warehouses (Shad Thames) and L (Queen Elizabeth St). Turn R at major crossroads (Tower

Bridge Rd) and follow this crossing Thames on **Tower bridge** to reach end of ride at Tower Hill beside **Tower of London** (50km, 18m).

The tea clipper Cutty Sark is preserved at Greenwich

STAGE 2
Rochester to Ashford

Start	Rochester bridge (4m)
Finish	Ashford, Henwood roundabout (37m)
Distance	47.5km (29.5 miles)
Ascent	400m
Waymarking	NCN17

After leaving Rochester the route climbs steeply up and over the chalk ridge of the North Downs at Blue Bell Hill. For the next 28km the medieval Pilgrims' Way is followed undulating gently along the southern slopes of the downs and passing above a series of spring-line villages before descending to the growth town of Ashford. The stage uses a mixture of quiet country roads and off-road tracks, some of which can become muddy when wet.

At SE end of **Rochester** bridge, turn R across road into Esplanade and follow this alongside Rive

The building of Rochester's Norman cathedral began in 1080

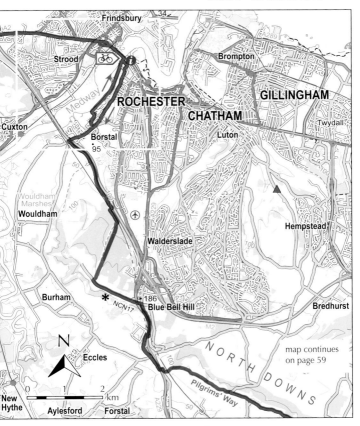

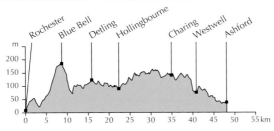

map continues
on page 59

Medway R. After 75m, turn L before entrance to Rochester castle following one-way street uphill into Castle Hill. Turn L at T-junction (Epaul Lane) then bear R (Boley Hill, cobbled) passing between cathedral L and castle keep R. At end of castle walls, fork L (St Margaret's St) and continue uphill passing St Peter with St Margaret church R. After old gun tower L, road becomes Borstal Rd with views of Medway below R. Bear R at angled crossroads (Borstal St) and descend through **Borstal** village (refreshments) continuing ahead on Wouldham Rd.

> In 1902, a large prison near **Borstal** was converted into an experimental reformatory for juvenile prisoners. Being the first of its kind, the name 'borstal' became synonymous with other juvenile reformatories established throughout Britain and the British Empire. In 1983, the name changed to Rochester youth custody centre, nowadays housing 700 young offenders.

Pass under motorway and turn immediately L (Nashenden Farm Lane) parallel with motorway. Pass Nashenden farm R then continue ahead through barriers with water works R. After 200m, fork L onto gravel track. Emerge onto quiet road (Stoney Lane) and turn R over railway. Where road ends, turn R away from railway on gravel track that climbs steadily through woods onto North Downs. Pass Robin Hood pub L (refreshments) and turn L on Common Rd. Cross bridge over dual carriageway (A229) to reach crossroads in **Blue Bell** village (9km, 183m).

Turn R through barriers on cycle track along old route of A229 (Chatham Rd). Continue downhill beside main road then follow rough track bearing L away from road and turn R on bridge across dual carriageway. At end of bridge turn R (Chatham Rd again) downhill on cycle lane L to reach crossroads beside Lower Bell pub (accommodation, refreshments). Continue ahead, using cycle track R, and follow this bearing R away from road. After 100m turn L under main road and emerge behind petrol station R. By entrance to motorhome sales centre, fork L onto gravel

...urfaced Pilgrims' Way then continue over railway and climb steeply on rough track for short distance.

THE PILGRIMS' WAY

Although the Pilgrims' Way follows the route of an ancient trackway that connects the Channel coast with the rest of England, its name is a Victorian invention. In 1871, Edward James, chief surveyor of the Ordnance Survey, published a pamphlet describing a route he believed medieval pilgrims followed from Winchester to Canterbury and subsequently the name 'Pilgrims' Way' was added to ordnance maps of Surrey and Kent. The idea received greater credence when the writer Hilaire Belloc romanticised the route. There is, however, little evidence to support James's conjecture and it is likely that most pilgrims, such as those described in Chaucer's *Canterbury Tales*, used Watling Street, the old Roman road north of the downs.

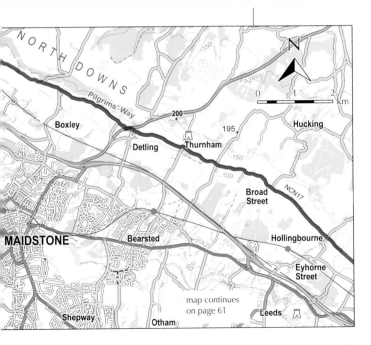

map continues on page 61

Track soon levels off and continues as sunken lane between hedges with **North Downs** escarpment rising L. Surface eventually becomes asphalt and emerges onto road. Turn R and where this road curves R downhill into **Boxley**, fork L beside timber yard to rejoin Pilgrims' Way. Just before reaching dual-carriageway Detling Hill (A249) turn sharply L under footbridge then use this to cross main road. At end of bridge bear L onto road then immediately R beside Cock Horse pub in **Detling** (16km, 119m) (accommodation, refreshments).

Turn L opposite pub and continue on Pilgrims' Way to reach Black Horse pub in **Thurnham** (17.5km, 119m) (accommodation, refreshments).

Thurnham Keep manor house is nowadays a luxury B&B

On the downs above **Thurnham** (pop 1100) are the ruins of a Norman motte and bailey castle, although only the earth mound of the motte and part of the bailey walls remain. Much of the stonework was reused for other buildings in the village including Thurnham Keep, an Edwardian manor house that nowadays provides up-market B&B accommodation.

Cycle ahead over crossroads in village and ahead again at next crossroads, passing Chobham Manor equestrian centre behind trees R. Continue through hamlet of Broad Street to reach Dirty Habits pub in **Hollingbourne** (2.5km, 91m) (refreshments, station).

Take no-through-road to L of pub heading out of village between fields. Where asphalt ends go straight ahead on gravel track which is badly eroded in places. Eventually asphalt resumes then cross sideroad, continuing past statue of '**Brother Percival**' L and industrial area behind trees R at **Lenham** (station).

Where asphalt road turns R, continue ahead on gravel track between fields. After 700m emerge on road and bear R following this for 150m then bear L onto another stretch of gravel track. Go ahead through barrier then pass **White Cross** cut into chalk hillside L and continue to reach another road. ▸ Turn L, following road uphill and where road bears L, fork R on gravel track

White Cross is a memorial for victims of the First and Second World Wars. Its memorial stone has been moved to Lenham churchyard.

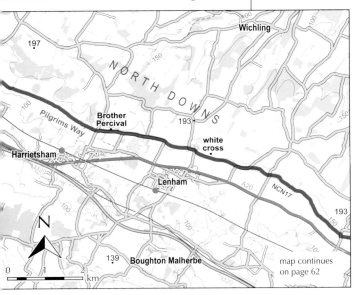

map continues on page 62

NCN17 turns right before the A252 to visit Charing (750 metres away), following the main road downhill and after 125 metres forking left into the village.

beside layby. Pass row of houses L and dogleg L and across next road onto gravel track below development executive houses on hillside L, on site of former TB isolation hospital in Highbourne Park. Pass barns at Cobham farm R and fork L on gravel track opposite farmhouse. Hart Hill farm, turn R onto minor road and L into trees on another gravel track. Continue to reach A252 at Charing Hill above village of **Charing** (35km, 142m) (accommodation, refreshments, station). ◄

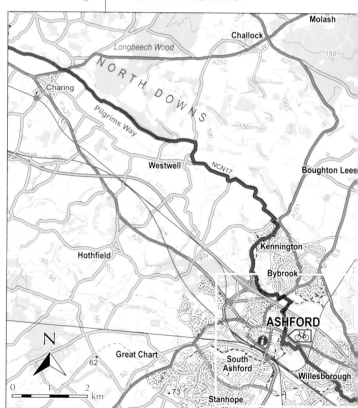

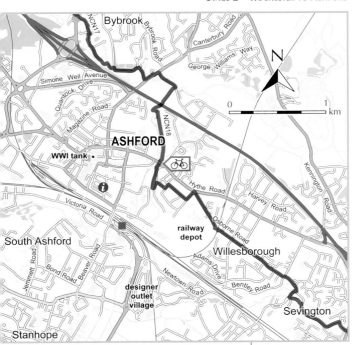

Turn L uphill and after 50m bear R on asphalt road
between houses. Continue through fields and follow road
round series of bends. By weighbridge at entrance to
Charing quarry, fork R onto gravel track through woods.
Continue with wooded hillside rising steeply L to emerge
on asphalt road and bear L. At T-junction turn R downhill
to leave Pilgrims' Way and reach beginning of **Westwell**
(9.5km, 89m) (accommodation, refreshments, camping).

Fork L avoiding village, then turn L at T-junction
(Tenacre St). Follow this winding between fields and
wooded copses to reach T-junction at beginning of
Kennington Lees, a residential district of Ashford. Turn R
(Sandyhurst Lane, sp Hothfield) and after 75 metres turn L
through barriers onto cycle track between houses. Emerge

This crossing of cycle tracks is the end of NCN17.

To reach the centre of Ashford, turn right (Mace Lane) then immediately left (East Hill) and cross Station Road into High Street.

onto Freathy Lane and turn L to reach T-junction. Turn on cycle track beside main road (Trinity Road) then pass roundabout and at next central reservation cross to L of road. Go ahead past two more roundabouts, both with trees in middle, and at third roundabout turn L (Rutherford Rd, second exit, first exit is entrance to Coty-Rimmel factory). Pass between Dobbies garden centre L and Beefeater restaurant R, then at next central reservation cross over to R of road. Pass Travelodge hotel R and follow cycle track climbing small bank beside car park. Pass attractive cable stay bridge R following cycle track winding past carpark then turn R on quiet road to reach T-junction. Turn R and continue to reach main road (Canterbury Rd, A28) then turn L using cycle lane L. Pass Holiday Inn hotel R then cross road at next central reservation to join cycle track of road. Turn R (Kinney's Lane) and at crossroads turn R c cycle track beside stream. ◀ Pass under motorway bridge and turn L at T-junction. Continue across stream, then turn R and fork immediately L on cycle track through Queen Mother's park. At end of park, reach Mace Lane (A292) beside Henwood roundabout in **Ashford** (47.5km, 37m) (accommodation, refreshments, tourist office, cycle shop, station). ◀

ASHFORD

Ashford (pop 75,000) is an ancient market town which became an industrial centre with the coming of the railways and is now a major growth town with a wide variety of trades and light industry. The market gained its first charter in 1243 (the

The designer outlet shopping village in Ashford was designed by Richard Rogers

market company claims to be the oldest surviving registered company in

England) and by the 19th century had grown to become a major livestock sales centre. Since 2000 it has occupied a new site on the edge of town.

The South Eastern Railway established its workshops in the town in 1847 and, by the time they closed in 1982, 797 locomotives had been built here. The railways still have a presence with a maintenance depot for high-speed trains and an international station with services to Paris and Brussels.

In the 1960s the government identified Ashford as a growth centre and since then several large housing developments have increased the population from 25,000 to 75,000. Part of the old town centre has been demolished and replaced with modern shopping malls, including the award-winning Designer Outlet Village, and an inner ring road. Several industrial estates provide employment for the increased population.

REVERSE ROUTE: ASHFORD TO ROCHESTER

From Henwood roundabout in **Ashford** follow cycle track N through parkland. Turn L over river Stour and R under motorway to crossing of tracks. Turn L (Kinney's Lane, NCN17) to reach T-junction. Turn L (Canterbury Rd, A28) and R (Cemetery Lane). Pass car park L and turn L (sp Leisure Park). After 300m, turn L on cycle track and follow this winding through Eureka Leisure Park beside Rutherford Rd. Follow cycle track across road and pass roundabout L then continue on cycle track beside Trinity Rd (A251) through **Kennington Lees**.

Go ahead past two roundabouts then cross road and continue past third roundabout. Turn L (Freathy Lane) and where this turns L, continue ahead on cycle track between houses. Turn R at T-junction (Sandyhurst Lane) and L (Lenacre St) winding through open country. Fork R at triangular junction (sp Westwell) and continue downhill to beginning of **Westwell** (8km, 89m) (accommodation, refreshments).

Turn R uphill, passing village L, then turn L before Dunn St farm (camping) onto Pilgrims' Way. *Pilgrims' Way, which is followed for 28km, is an ancient trackway from Winchester to Canterbury with a mixture of asphalt and gravel surfaces.* Follow this, forking L and later R through woodland. Pass Charing quarry R and emerge on asphalt road. Bear R to pass above **Charing** (12.5km, 142m) (accommodation, refreshments, station). Ignore NCN17 sign pointing L at triangular junction which indicates a detour through Charing.

The Pilgrims' Way is a cycle track and footpath along the North Downs

Continue to reach A252 then dogleg L and R onto narrow track beside Reeves Cottage. Follow track, doglegging R and L across Hart Hill and further on L and R across Rayners Hill. Emerge on Hubbards Hill and follow this for 350 metres before bearing R back onto Pilgrims' Way passing above **Lenham** (**station**). Turn R and briefly join Faversham Rd, then fork L on track, passing **Brother Percival** statue R to reach **Hollingbourne** (25km, 91m) (refreshments, station).

Continue through **Broad Street** and **Thurnham** (30km, 119m) (accommodation, refreshments) to reach **Detling** (31.5km, 119m) (accommodation, refreshments). Turn R and L beside Cock Horse pub, then bear R on cycle track leading to bridge over A249 dual carriageway. After bridge turn R and fork L following Pilgrims' Way to **Boxley**. Join road (sp Bredhurst) and where this turns sharply R uphill, continue ahead on track. Follow this downhill over railway and past motor caravan sales centre L. Route leaves Pilgrims' Way here. Bear R downhill behind petrol station then pass under main road. Turn R uphill on Old Chatham Rd then continue over crossroads beside Lower Bell pub R (accommodation, refreshments) and fork L uphill. Just before road joins A229, turn sharply back L onto bridge over main road then continue uphill on other side of road to **Blue Bell** village (38.5km, 183m).

Turn L at crossroads then pass over A229 and follow Common Rd along ridgetop. Turn R on gravel track past Robin Hood pub R (refreshments) and continue downhill through woodland. Turn L beside railway then R over bridge. Fork L through barrier on track between railway L and motorway R to emerge on road and continue downhill to T-junction. Turn R under motorway and follow road ascending through **Borstal** village (refreshments).

Pass church L and turn L beside house 14 (Shorts Way) downhill to reach Medway. Bear R on Esplanade beside river and continue past castle R to **Rochester** bridge (47.5km, 4m) (accommodation, refreshments, youth hostel (in Gillingham), tourist office, cycle shop, station).

STAGE 3

Ashford to Dover

Start	Ashford, Henwood roundabout (37m)
Finish	Dover Eastern docks (10m); or Cheriton Channel Tunnel terminal (65m)
Distance	49.5km (31 miles); or 31.5km (19.5 miles) to Channel Tunnel terminal
Ascent	206m
Waymarking	None to Romney marsh, then NCN2 to Dover

After Ashford, the gently undulating route heads south to cross the edge of Romney marsh. The going becomes completely level as the Royal Military canal is followed to Hythe and the coastal promenade to Folkestone. Here the route climbs steeply to run above the white cliffs before descending to reach Dover and the ferry terminal in the Eastern docks. An alternative route connects Hythe with the Channel Tunnel terminal at Cheriton.

From Henwood roundabout in **Ashford**, follow cycle track SW into woodland. Emerge beside road and bear to continue behind houses. Turn L at crossing of tracks and immediately L (Mill Court). Turn first R (Miller Close) and continue through barriers to reach T-junction. Turn L (Birling Rd) and R (Linden Rd). At end turn L (Mabledon Ave) then just before reaching main road turn sharply (Essella Rd) passing petrol station L. Where this road bears L, continue ahead over railway footbridge then turn L and bear R (Osborne Rd). ▶ At end of road, turn R (Sevington Lane), passing between William Harvey pub L and St Mary's church R. Follow road bearing R into Boys Hall Rd (cycle track L) then cross stream and turn L on cycle track through parkland. At end turn R through bollards into Church Rd and follow this bearing L through **Sevington**.

The footbridge has ramps that enable cycles to be pushed over it.

67

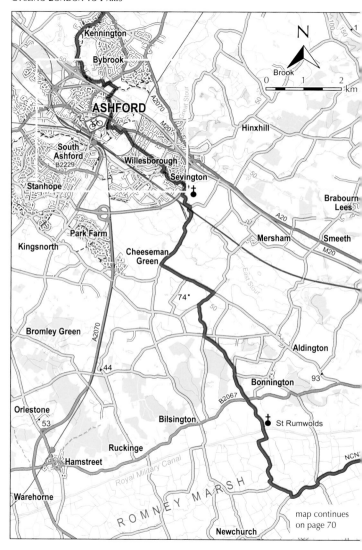

map continues on page 70

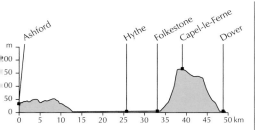

At end, turn R through barrier (sp Sevington church) and cross cycle bridge over Ashford ring road (A2070). Turn R into quiet country lane, passing Sevington church ‹‹. ▶ Turn L at T-junction, away from main road and follow road winding between fields and farms. Turn R (Cheesemans Green Lane, sp Bilsington) and cross railway. Follow road through open country to reach hamlet of **Cheeseman Green** (6km, 45m).

Turn L (sp Aldington) and continue through open country to crossroads. Turn R (sp Bilsington) then continue through fields and turn L at next road junction (Coopers Lane, sp Bilsington). At crossroads, go ahead into Priory Road then fork immediately L (Bourne Road). Bear R at road junction then keep R at next road junction (sp Bilsington) to reach crossroads. Go ahead over B2067 (sp St Rumwold's church) and descend to reach bridge over Royal Military Canal (12km, 2m).

The **Royal Military Canal** is a 45km waterway constructed between 1804–1809 as a defensive barrier against invasion during the Napoleonic Wars. Running from the sea near Winchelsea in the west to Sandgate near Folkestone in the east, it follows the northern boundary of Romney marsh. Originally there was a military road and a protective earth bank along the northern side of the canal, with artillery batteries every 500 metres. Attempts to use the canal commercially were unsuccessful and it was abandoned in 1877, after which it was maintained to control water levels. During the

Sevington church stands surrounded by fields, cut-off from Sevington by Ashford ring road.

69

Second World War, fear of German invasion led the canal to be refortified, this time with concrete pillboxes and barbed wire. After the war, German plans were discovered that did indeed earmark Romney marsh and the canal as targets for capture on the first day of invasion!

Continue over canal and follow road winding across **Romney marsh**. Fork L (sp Dymchurch) and turn L at T-junction to reach staggered crossroads. ◄ Go ahead (sp Hythe) and continue winding across marsh for 3.5km. Turn L (Aldergate Lane) to again reach Royal Military Canal. Cross bridge and turn R on gravel track parallel with canal. Pass **Port Lympne safari park**, with bison, antelope and giraffe grazing on hillside L, to reach car park beside bridge at **West Hythe** (22km, 7m).

Go straight ahead following canalside track to emerge onto asphalt road (Green Lane) at beginning of Hythe. Just before traffic lights turn R through gardens and continue over canal. ◄ Immediately after bridge

At the crossroads the route joins NCN2 South Coast cycleway.

The building on the right after the bridge is the terminus of Romney, Hythe and Dymchurch narrow gauge railway.

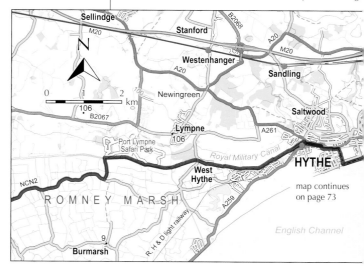

turn L across road to join asphalt cycle track along S bank of canal. This runs through gardens to emerge on Dymchurch Rd (A259). Bear L to reach canal bridge in **Hythe** (25.5km, 6m) (accommodation, refreshments, cycle shop, station). ▶

To visit the centre of Hythe, continue ahead over the canal.

Immediately before bridge cross road at light controlled crossing and turn R to continue on canalside cycle track. Go ahead over crossroads, passing Oaklands health

HYTHE

The ossuary at St Leonard's church; Romney, Hythe and Dymchurch railway uses scale models of main-line locomotives

Hythe (pop 14,500) was one of the ancient 'cinque ports', seven maritime towns that were grouped together for defensive purposes in 1155 (originally there were five, hence the name, but two were added later). In exchange for providing ships to defend the coast, these towns were granted special privileges over taxation and law enforcement, including the right to import goods without paying duty, an early version of a freeport. The towns became a haven for smugglers, an illicit trade that continued until the 19th century long after most of the ports had silted-up and ceased commercial operations.

Important sights in Hythe include St Leonard's church which has an ossuary displaying 2000 skulls and 8000 thigh bones and the Romney, Hythe and Dymchurch railway. This narrow-gauge line, which opened in 1927, runs for 22km parallel with the shoreline of Romney marsh to Romney and Dungeness. Originally operated as a local passenger and freight line, it now runs as a tourist service carrying over 100,000 passengers annually. Its main attraction is the use of steam engines built as scaled down versions (one-fifth size) of main line express locomotives from the 1920s and 1930s.

centre R, still following canal. Pass boat hire depot L and turn R opposite next small bridge (Ladies Walk) passing between bowls club R and cricket ground L. Dogleg R and L across South Rd, into Moyle Tower Rd. Pass sailing club R to reach Marine Parade promenade and turn L along seashore. The coastal promenade is followed for the next 3.5km, passing Hythe golf course and continuing along Princes Parade promenade.

CROSSING THE CHANNEL

There are two options to cross the Channel: the Channel Tunnel or the ferry. The Channel Tunnel cycle shuttle is slightly cheaper and slightly faster than the ferries and saves 17km of cycling from Folkestone to Dover. However, as this must be booked in advance with only two services per day it is considerably less flexible than the Dover ferries which run frequently throughout the day and night, providing a turn-up-and-go service.

The terminal is 3km from Princes Parade.

For Cheriton Channel Tunnel terminal

◄ Pass golf course then turn L away from promenade beside white beach shelter on cycle track through dunes and over canal. At end, turn R (Seabrook Rd) and L (Horn St) in front of Fountain pub. Pass under old railway bridge and follow road ascending steadily for 2km. Bear L at T-junction then cross railway bridge and turn L at traffic lights (Cheriton High St). Pick-up point for Channel Tunnel cycle transfer is in carpark of Holiday Inn Express Cheriton L (31.5km, 65m).

For Dover Eastern docks ferry port

Continue to Sandgate Esplanade (A259, cycle track R). Where A259 bears L away from seashore, cross to R and continue on road (Sandgate High St), into **Sandgate** (30.5km, 11m) (accommodation, refreshments).

Turn R beside Royal Norfolk hotel (Lachlan Way) to reach T-junction, with Sandgate castle ahead. Turn R (Castle Rd) and continue uphill into Radnor Cliff parallel with seashore below R. Where road ends, continue through gate on cycle track winding through

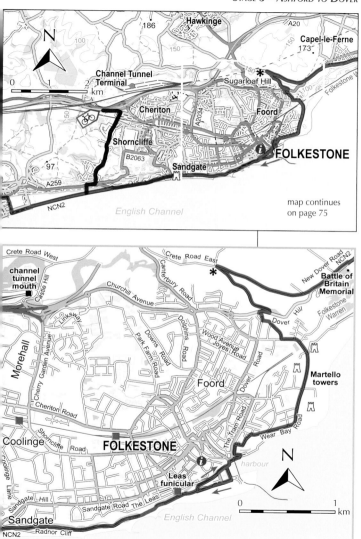

map continues
on page 75

73

The cycle track follows the promenade past Sandgate castle

cliffside gardens before descending to emerge on road beside carpark. In front of first large white house, fork L (Lower Sandgate Rd) then pass through barrier and continue ahead to reach **Folkestone** harbour (33.5km, 8m) (accommodation, refreshments, camping, cycle shop, tourist office, station).

FOLKESTONE

Folkestone (pop 47,000) developed around the mouth of a stream that ran into the English Channel between cliffs. Although a small fishing trade developed, shifting shingle and frequent cliff falls made maritime activity difficult. A harbour was built during the Napoleonic Wars but activity was still hampered by sand and silt. The harbour was bought by the South Eastern Railway in 1842 who built a new pier, dredged the harbour and made Folkestone their principal ferry port for passenger services to Boulogne. Large numbers of servicemen travelled through the harbour during both world wars but decline set in during the 1970s when cross-channel ferries became concentrated at Dover. Even before the Channel Tunnel opened (1994), services from Folkestone ended after nearly 150 years. The abandoned docks and adjacent amusement park are now subject to a development plan, but little has been done to resurrect the area. Away from the old harbour, however, the Channel Tunnel terminal at Cheriton has brought employment and prosperity to the town.

Bear L beside harbour then turn first R opposite True Briton pub on cobbled Beach St. Pass under railway into Fish Market. At end, dogleg L and R, then turn sharply L in front of Captains Table restaurant into The Stade, where cobbles end. Turn R (North St) steeply uphill then L again by Lifeboat pub into The Durlocks. Follow road continuing uphill and bear L to reach crossroads. Turn R (Wear Bay Rd, cycle lane L) with white bulk of Shakespeare cliffs visible in the distance and follow road along top of East Cliff. Road now climbs steadily past two **Martello towers** R and then bears L away from cliffs. ▶ Turn R (Stanbury Cres) beside house 130, continuing uphill. At end bear L on cycle track between houses 21–23 to reach Dover Rd. Turn R onto short dead-end road (cycle lane L) then R again beside Dover Hill (B2011). After 100m turn L across road at central reservation and follow narrow lane steeply uphill through woodland away from main road. At top of hill, with extensive views over Folkestone and the English Channel, turn sharply R (Crete Rd E) and continue along hilltop road to reach main road (B2011) opposite Valiant Sailor pub at top of Dover Hill (38km, 166m) (refreshments).

Bear L beside New Dover Rd (cycle track L). After 500 metres, just past entrance to **Battle of Britain memorial** R, cross road at central reservation and continue R of road. Fork R (Old Dover Rd), descending to pass between **Capel-le-Ferne** L and **Folkestone Warren** cliffs R. After village re-emerge onto main road (cycle track R). After 500 metres, fork R uphill on narrow road and where this ends continue through barriers onto gravel cycle track at first following cliff edge then bearing L away from cliffs to run parallel with dual carriageway A20 main road. ▶ Continue parallel with road, descending steadily with Dover visible ahead, to cross side road serving tunnel that gives access to **Samphire Hoe** nature reserve.

The first attempt at digging a **tunnel** from England to France occurred in 1881 when a railway tunnel that branched off the main line beneath

These small defensive forts were constructed 1804–1812 along the south-eastern coast to protect against invasion during the Napoleonic Wars: of 103 built, 47 remain.

Below Shakespeare cliffs to the right are an abandoned coal mine and the drilling sites and ventilation shafts of the Channel Tunnel.

Shakespeare cliffs reached 1.5km under the Channel before being abandoned. The current Channel Tunnel is the result of an agreement between British and French governments in 1984. Construction began in 1987 and first trains ran in 1994. Main services are frequent car, truck and coach shuttles between Folkestone and Calais. In addition, Eurostar high-speed trains run from London to Paris or Brussels and freight trains travel through to European destinations. A large amount of spoil was excavated during tunnelling and much of this was dumped off the coast below Shakespeare cliffs to create an area now known as Samphire Hoe nature reserve.

After 300m turn L on cycle bridge over A20 to reach Old Folkestone Rd and turn R descending into **Aycliff** (45km, 59m). Follow road curving R and L then continue round hairpin bend. Just before roundabout join cycle track L and bear L to follow Archcliffe Rd (A20). Descend

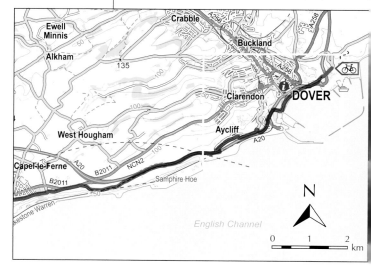

under road bridge to reach Limekiln roundabout at beginning of **Dover** (accommodation, refreshments, tourist office, cycle shop, station).

Continue straight ahead (Limekiln St, second exit) and after 75 metres cross to R of road using central reservation. Turn R (Union St, sp Dover Marina) and cross swing bridge over channel between yacht basins. Turn L and go ahead over small roundabout into Marine Parade (intermittent cycle track R), then follow this looping round Dover harbour R with **Dover Castle** on top of the 'white cliffs' L. Emerge on Townwall St and cross road at central reservation. Turn R (cycle track L) to reach roundabout and bear L on cycle track beside second exit. Follow this R across road and follow red line through carpark and under bridge to passport control in **Dover Eastern docks** (49.5km, 10m). Keep following red line past customs then bear R and continue through barrier to reach cycle check-in R. ▸

Frequent ferries connect Dover with Calais in northern France. The crossing takes 90 minutes.

DOVER

White cliffs of Dover

Standing below iconic 'white cliffs' at the narrowest part of the English Channel, Dover (pop 31,000) has a history and economy inextricably linked to maritime communication with continental Europe. Evidence of settlement goes back to palæolithic times, when it was still possible to walk to continental Europe. Dover was an important link in the Roman communication network with a road (Watling Street) linking it to London and the rest of England and a harbour linking it with Gaul (modern day France). Roman relics include the 'painted house' with the best-preserved murals north of the Alps and the eastern Pharos (lighthouse) in the grounds of Dover castle. The Romans built the first harbour which in medieval times became one of the 'cinque ports' (see under Hythe above). The coming of the railway (1844) brought trains to the quayside to connect with railway company packet boats sailing to France. The opening of the Channel Tunnel has reduced sea trade across the Channel from other ports and a concentration of remaining services in Dover, with around 50 sailings daily.

In contrast to its role in expediting cross-channel communication, Dover has played a key role in deterring invaders. The Romans built a 'Saxon Shore fort' of which little remains. Construction of Dover castle, on the eastern cliffs above the ferry port, started under the Normans and expansion continued for many centuries. Major rebuilding and additions during the Napoleonic Wars, including underground barracks tunnelled into the chalk cliffs, made it the largest castle in England. These fortifications were reused during the Second World War when Dover was subject to bombardment by German guns based in France and attack by enemy aircraft. The castle is now owned by English Heritage who have renovated part of the building and opened it for tourists.

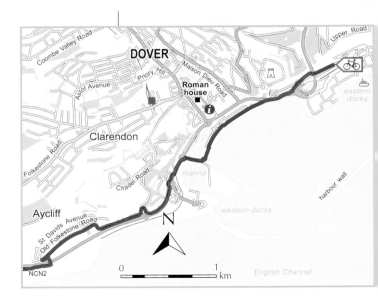

REVERSE ROUTE: DOVER TO ASHFORD

NCN2 cycle track along the top of Shakespeare cliffs

Follow red line out of **Dover Eastern docks** to join Marine Parade cycle track (NCN2) heading W along harbour side in Dover (accommodation, refreshments, tourist office, cycle shop, station). At end turn R (Union St) over swing bridge at entrance to inner harbour and L beside A20 at traffic lights. Follow cycle track across road and turn L (Archcliffe Rd) to continue past next roundabout. At third roundabout, turn R (Old Folkestone Rd) and fork L into **Aycliff** (4km, 59m).

Continue uphill round bends R and L, then where road turns R, turn sharply L opposite house 108 onto cycle bridge over A20. Follow cycle track uphill parallel with main road, past tunnel L leading to **Samphire Hoe** nature reserve L. Continue uphill, eventually forking L along crest of white cliffs. Emerge on New Dover Rd (B2011) then pass Royal Oak pub R and fork L (Old Dover Rd) passing between **Capel-le-Ferne** R and **Folkestone Warren** cliffs L (refreshments).

Bear L beside B2011 and by entrance to **Battle of Britain memorial** L, turn R across road. Opposite Valiant Sailor pub at top of Dover Hill (11km, 166m), fork R (Crete Rd E) along ridge top. Just before communications tower, turn sharply L downhill then cross main road and turn R. After 100 metres fork L (Dover Rd) downhill and turn L after 70 metres on track beside house 310. Emerge on Stanbury Cres and fork L. At end, turn L (Wear Bay Rd), continuing downhill with clifftop L. Turn L (East Cliff Gdns) and continue into The Durlocks. Bear R then turn L (North St) to reach T-junction. Turn L (The Stade) and R (cobbles) beside **Folkestone harbour** L (15.5km, 8m) (accommodation, refreshments, camping, tourist office, cycle shop, station).Pass under railway bridge then turn L (A260) to follow one-way system past marina. Bear R (Marine Parade) and continue on cycle track winding through cliffside gardens. Emerge on road and follow this downhill into **Sandgate** (18.5km, 7m) (accommodation, refreshments).

Bear L (Sandgate High St, A259) then where this reaches seashore join promenade cycle track and follow this ahead when road turns away from sea.

Route from Cheriton Channel Tunnel terminal
From Holiday Inn Express Cheriton, follow Cheriton High St E. Turn R at traffic lights into Horn Lane and follow this over railway and turn R downhill to T-junction. Turn R (Seabrook Rd, A259) then turn L opposite post box on track beside house 158 leading across canal to promenade cycle track (3km from Cheriton). Turn R to join main route.

Combined route continues
Follow cycle track, past golf course R, then turn R through easily missed small gate beside Saltwood sailing club. Dogleg R and L over main road and go ahead on cycle track (Ladies Walk) with sports fields R. Turn L on gravel track beside Royal Military canal and follow this closely past **Hythe** (24km, 6m) (accommodation, refreshments, cycle shop, station).

Turn R on third bridge across canal (A259) beside light-railway station, then turn L (Green Lane) parallel with canal and continue on gravel track past **West Hythe** (27.5km, 7m).

Follow canal past **Port Lympne safari park** R and where track ends turn L across canal. Continue to T-junction and turn R, winding across **Romney marsh**. Go L and R over staggered crossroads (sp Newchurch) where route leaves NCN2. Pass Bellfield farm R then turn R (unsigned) at next junction and continue winding across marsh. Recross canal and cycle uphill past **St Rumwold's church** R (37.5km, 3m).

Cross main road and continue to T-junction, then bear L (Cherry Orchard Lane). Fork L (Bourne Rd, sp Mersham) then at end turn R and continue over main road. Turn R at T-junction (Coopers Lane) and L at crossroads (sp Sevington) to reach T-junction in **Cheeseman Green** (43.5km, 45m). Turn R (sp Sevington) then follow road winding over railway and turn L (sp Sevington). Turn R just before dual carriageway then at apex of bend opposite Sevington church turn L through barriers onto cycle bridge over A2070. Turn is easy to miss. Turn L (Church Rd) then bear R through **Sevington**.

Pass through bollards and turn immediately L on track through parkland then bear R beside Boys Hall Rd. Continue into Sevington Lane past William Harvey pub R and bear L ahead (Osborne Rd). At end follow footbridge over railway and continue ahead on Essella Rd. *Footbridge has ramps that enable cycles to be pushed over bridge.* Turn L at end (Mabledon Ave) and R

The Grand Military Canal was built to protect against Napoleonic invasion

(Linden Rd). Turn second L between houses 1–1A (Birling Rd) and R between houses 5–6 through barriers into Miller Close. At end turn L (Mill Court) then R through bollards and immediately R again onto cycle track behind houses. Follow this turning L away from road to reach crossing beside Henwood roundabout in **Ashford** (49.5km, 37m) (accommodation, refreshments, tourist office, cycle shop, station).

STAGE 4

Calais to Desvres

Start	Calais Gare Maritime (8m); or Coquelles Channel Tunnel terminal (20m)
Finish	Desvres, Pl Léon Blum (92m)
Distance	41km (25.5 miles)
Ascent	394m
Waymarking	Vèloroute des Marais from Coulogne to Guînes then D127

If you cross the Channel by boat you arrive at Gare Maritime ferry terminal in Calais, if you use the Channel Tunnel you arrive opposite CIFFCO building near Channel Tunnel terminal in Coquelles. After a level ride from Calais to Guînes along a canal towpath and a disused railway, the stage uses minor roads that undulate over chalk downland before ending in Desvres, famous for ceramics and tiles.

Route from Coquelles Channel Tunnel terminal
From car park where Channel Tunnel cycle transport vehicle unloads, cycle SE past **CIFFCO building** L. Dogleg R and L across dual carriageway through walkway gap in central reservation and turn L to reach roundabout. Turn R (Bvd du Kent, sp Cité

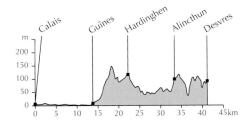

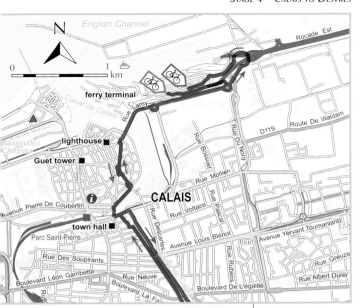

urope parking), passing between shopping centre L
nd Eurotunnel security fence R. Where road bears L,
ork R on minor road following security fence. Bear R
nto dual carriageway (Bvd de l'Europe) then continue
head over three roundabouts, and cross bridge over
ailway yards. At fourth roundabout, turn L (D246E1,
hird exit, sp Coulogne). Just before bridge over drain-
ge canal, turn R on side road (sp Rue du Pont Trois
lanches). At first junction, turn L over bridge and fork R
sp Coulogne, D247). Continue to T-junction then turn R
nd L (sp Ardres) across railway. Just before canal bridge
n **Coulogne** (7.5km 2m) (refreshments), turn R beside
anal to join route from Gare Maritime.

Route from Calais Gare Maritime ferry terminal
rom exit of Calais ferry terminal follow road E, pass-
ng terminal building L. Pass first turn R for *centre ville*

83

(town centre), then fork R at second turn. (First turn lead to locked security gates.) Turn R at roundabout (Ave d Commandant Cousteau, first exit, sp centre ville) repass ing terminal building behind fence R. Continue ahea over second roundabout (Rue Lamy, second exit) an follow road bearing L over lock at entrance to inner ha bour. At Pl de Suède take third exit from square (Rue d Londres). At next square (Pl d'Angleterre) follow one-wa circulation and leave by SE corner (third exit) turning into Rue de Hollande. At Pl Norvège take third exit (Qua de la Meuse, sp centre ville). Cross canal bridge and tur immediately L on narrow track over two railway crossing to reach road junction beside belfry near centre of **Calai** (3.5km, 5m) (accommodation, refreshments, youth hos tel, camping, tourist office, cycle shop, station).

CALAIS

Calais town hall is the iconic symbol of the town; Rodin's bronze 'The burghers of Calais' commemorates events in 1347

For over 200 years from 1347, Calais (pop 75,000) was held and governed by the English, sending a representative to the English parliament. As the major trading point between England and continental Europe, its custom revenue provided up to a third of English government income, with wool being the most important commodity traded. When it was lost to the French in 1558, Queen Mary of England was reported as saying 'when I am dead and opened you shall find Calais lying in my heart'. Textile production remained important and by 1830 there were 113 manufacturers producing wool, cloth and lace. The latter has maintained its importance and there are still two major lace manufacturers employing 3000 people. During the Second World War,

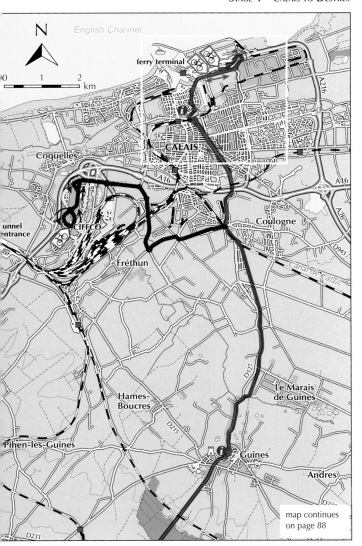

N

English Channel

0   1   2 km

ferry terminal

CALAIS

Coquelles

A16

tunnel entrance

CIFFCO

Fréthun

Coulogne

A16

A216

A26

Canal de Calais

D943

D127

Le Marais de Guines

Hames-Boucres

D215

Pihen-lès-Guînes

Guînes

Andres

D231

map continues on page 88

85

Calais was captured by the Germans (May 1940) when six days of shelling and bombing left the city in ruins. Post-war rebuilding was with new structures and very few old buildings were restored.

The skyline is punctuated by three towers. The Tour de Guet watchtower on Pl d'Armes (1229) has suffered damage by earthquake and fire, use as stables and from German shells; it has been restored many times. The 55m lighthouse (1848) replaced a light on the watchtower; its light can be seen from across the Channel. The belfry of the neo-Renaissance town hall (built 1911–1925) is even taller (74m) and is the emblem of the city. In front of the town hall is a bronze group by Rodin depicting the 'Burghers of Calais', six men sentenced to execution by the English in 1347 but who were reprieved after intercession by the Queen. The military importance of Calais over the centuries is reflected by a series of forts. Fort Risban was built by the English during the invasion of 1346, the Citadel after the French reconquest in 1560 and fort Nieulay by the great French military architect Vauban in 1679. Further extensive fortifications were built by the occupying Germans between 1940–1944.

Turn L (Rue Paul Bert) then cross bridge over **Canal d** **Calais** and turn R beside canal (Quai de la Gendarmeri sp Université) on cycle lane R. At roundabout continu ahead beside canal (Quai de l'Yser). Bear R to pass und next bridge and continue along Quai Lucien Lheureu Pass pedestrian bridge then turn immediately R acros canal on lifting bridge (Pont Curie) and L along opp site bank (Quai Gustave Lamarle). Pass under rail an road bridges and continue on Quai d'Amérique to liftin bridge in **Coulogne** (7km, 2m) (refreshments).

Combined route continues

Cycle ahead along towpath, between canal L and railwa R, then cross bridge over Guînes canal. ◄ Immediatel after bridge, turn sharply L back beside canal and bear under bridge beside Guînes canal. Follow asphalt trac turning L away from canal. Cross side road and drain age ditch then turn immediately L and bear R along trac of disued railway. Go ahead over next crossroads an over drainage canal, then ahead over second crossroad and continue beside Guînes canal. Follow track bearin

From Coulogne to Guînes the route follows voie verte along Vèloroute des Marais.

away from canal and go ahead over crossroads in **Le Marais de Guînes**. Where asphalt surface ends, turn R and rk R in front of gates across track to reach canal bank. rn L along towpath and where canal ends, emerge into rpark of Dynamite store. Turn R across main road and to follow road (D127). Where road turns L, continue ead (Rue du Maréchal Joffre, sp mairie) then bear L to ach crossroads. Turn R (Rue Massenet) to reach Pl Foch **Guînes** (14km, 10m) (accommodation, refreshments, mping, tourist office).

Guînes (pop 6000) stands on the edge of now-drained marshes that once extended to Calais. The Tour d'Horloge and some fragments of stonework are all that remain of a castle and walls that surrounded the town. Built in the 11th century, they failed to prevent it being captured (1351) by the English forces of Edward III during the first phase of the Hundred Years' War. In 1520 a diplomatic gathering took place near Guînes at the 'Field of the Cloth of Gold', so named because of the sumptuous golden cloth that decorated the royal

Mural in Guînes depicting the 'Field of the Cloth of Gold'

87

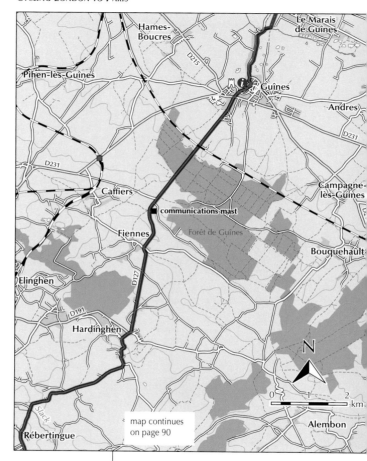

tents, where François I of France and Henry VIII of England signed a treaty guaranteeing peace. This treaty was soon broken, and in 1558 the town fell to the French a few days after they had captured Calais, making Guînes the last English possession in France.

map continues on page 90

Cross Pl Foch into Rue Clemenceau and continue past Tour d'Horloge R into Rue de Guizelin. ▶ Go ahead over crossroads (Ave de Verdun, D127, sp Fiennes) out of town into open country. Road ascends steadily, crossing TGV high-speed railway line and climbing through Guînes forest to reach summit of ridge (Le Mont de Fiennes, 145m) beside concrete **communications mast** L. Descend past **Fiennes** R (19.5km, 105m) (accommodation, refreshments). Continue on Rue du Vert Genêt (D127) then ascend gently through open country past Œœucres to reach **Hardinghen** (22.5km, 115m) (accommodation, refreshments, camping).

Follow road winding though village (Rue de l'Église) passing church L and continue downhill crossing river back to reach **Rébertingue** hamlet. Turn L (D127) and follow road ahead over roundabout into **Le Wast** (31km, 43m) (accommodation, refreshments).

Follow Rue Principale through village and into open country. Go ahead over roundabout then cross motorway. Go ahead again at next roundabout (Rue des Lichottes, D127) and bear R. After 350m turn L (Rue du Mont Éventé, D127) and follow this winding steeply uphill through **Alincthun** (33.5km, 99m).

Continue ascending, now less steeply, for short distance then descend steeply to cross river Liane. Follow road steeply uphill into Desvres forest, then continue on undulating road to emerge from forest at roundabout on edge of Desvres. Continue ahead (Rue Jean Jaurès, sp centre) uphill to reach crossroads and turn L (Rue Dupontchel) steeply uphill into Pl Léon Blum in centre of **Desvres** (41km, 92m) (accommodation, refreshments, tourist office).

The road through Guînes is one-way with a contra-flow cycle lane.

Desvres (pop 5000) has been a production centre for *faïence* (ceramics and porcelain) since 1764. A century later they began producing tiles to match the plates, dishes and vases for which they were already famous. Local craft workshops and factories can be visited. The Maison de la Faïence is a modernist building decorated in giant iconic blue and

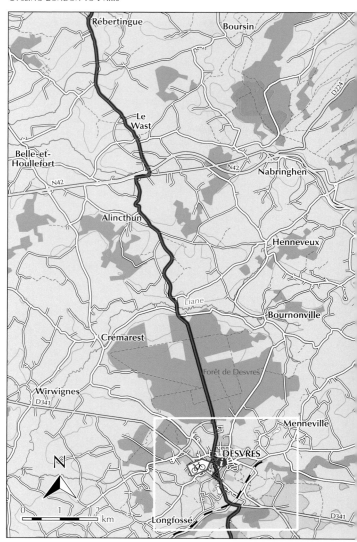

Desvres millennium clock reflects the local ceramic industry

white tiles that houses a museum tracing the history of the industry and an exhibition of designs by local craftsmen. The modern millennium clock in Place Léon Blum also features local tiles.

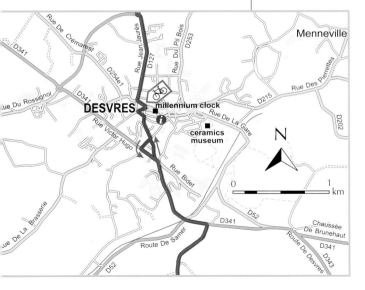

REVERSE ROUTE: DESVRES TO CALAIS

From Pl Léon Blum in **Desvres** follow Rue Dupontchel NW downhill and turn R (Rue Jean Jaurès). Go ahead over roundabout (D127) through Desvres forest. Descend to cross river Liane and ascend to **Alincthun** (7.5km, 99m). Descend again to T-junction and turn R to reach roundabout. Go ahead over motorway and continue through **Le Wast** (10km, 53m) (accommodation, refreshments).

Continue to **Rébertingue** (14.5km, 48m) and follow D127 forking R. Cross river Slack, then cycle uphill to **Hardinghen** (18.5km, 115m) (accommodation, refreshments, camping). Fork R in village then fork L (D127). Continue past **Fiennes** L (21.5km, 105m) (accommodation, refreshments) then climb to summit (145m) and descend through Guînes forest. Go ahead at crossroads (Rue de Guizelin, D127) and continue on Rue Clemenceau to reach Pl Foch in **Guînes** (27km, 10m) (accommodation, refreshments, camping, tourist office).

Continue across square into Rue Massenet and turn L (Rue du Maréchal Joffre). Follow road bearing R and continue into Rue Baudoin (D127, sp Coulogne). Dogleg R and L into service road in front of Dynamite superstore R and pass through carpark to reach beginning of asphalt Vèloroute des Marais cycle track across Marais de Guînes marshland. *Vèloroute runs for 7km partly along the towpath of Guînes canal and partly on an old railway trackbed.*

Follow cycle track beside canal then where asphalt towpath ends, turn R and L along route of old railway. This returns briefly to canalbank then continues through fields crossing series of minor roads and drainage canals. After 4.5km, turn R beside canal under railway bridge then R and R again, sharply up onto bridge you have just passed under. Continue along towpath, now following **Canal de Calais** with railway L, to reach lifting bridge in **Coulogne** (34km, 2m) (refreshments). From Coulogne separate routes lead to Coquelles Channel Tunnel terminal or Calais Gare Maritime ferry port.

Route to Coquelles Channel Tunnel terminal

Turn L opposite bridge, cross railway, then turn R and L into Rue Charles de Gaulle. L turn is difficult due to raised central kerb that prevents cars entering Rue Charles de Gaulle which is one-way with contra-flow cycling permitted. At end bear L across drainage canal and turn R beside canal. Turn L at crossroads then R at roundabout (D304, first exit). Cross railway bridge and go ahead over first roundabout. Fork L at second roundabout (second exit) then go ahead over third. At fourth roundabout turn L (Bvd du Kent, sp Cité Europe est) past shopping centre R. Go ahead over next roundabout (Bvd du Parc) and pass Channel Outlet shopping mall L to reach point opposite **CIFFCO** building where cycle transport through Channel Tunnel loads (41.5km, 20m). *Pick-up point is behind bus stop in carpark on opposite side of road to CIFFCO.*

Route to Calais Gare Maritime ferry terminal

Continue ahead on towpath, passing under motorway and railway bridges. Where road ahead becomes one-way, fork L (Rue de la Vendée). Go ahead at traffic light (Quai du Commerce), rejoining towpath. Where this turns away from canal, dogleg L and R to reach T-junction. Turn L (Rue Paul Bert) near centre of **Calais** (37.5km, 5m) (accommodation, refreshments, youth hostel, tourist office, camping, cycle shop, station).

After 75m, turn R through gate over two railway crossings then R again (Quai de la Meuse) beside canal to roundabout in Pl de Norvège. Turn L (Rue de Hollande, fourth exit) then continue ahead through Pl d'Angleterre into Rue de Londres to reach Pl de Suède. Continue ahead (Rue Lamy) over lock at entrance to inner harbour and follow road past terminal buildings L over two roundabouts. At third larger roundabout, follow signs L into **Gare Maritime ferry port** (41km, 8m).

STAGE 5

Desvres to Hesdin

Start	Desvres, Pl Léon Blum (92m)
Finish	Hesdin, Pl d'Armes (29m)
Distance	49.5km (31 miles)
Ascent	190m
Waymarking	None, but follows D127 to Montreuil then D113

After a short steep climb out of Desvres, there is a long steady descent on a minor road down the very pretty valley of the river Course passing a series of small villages and farms to reach Neuville-sous-Montreuil, across the river Canche from the historic town of Montreuil. From here the route turns east to follow the Canche valley on a gently undulating minor road to Hesdin.

Leave Pl Léon Blum in **Desvres** by SW corner on Ru des Écoles. Turn first L (Rue Emile Gugelot) and fork (Rue Victor Hugo), soon starting to ascend. Where roa becomes one-way street, turn R (Rue Pasteur) to reac T-junction. Turn L (Chausée Brunehaut, D341) to reac roundabout with two tile clad stelae in middle. Turn (D341, sp Montreuil) then continue across railway an

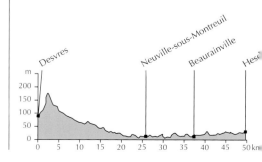

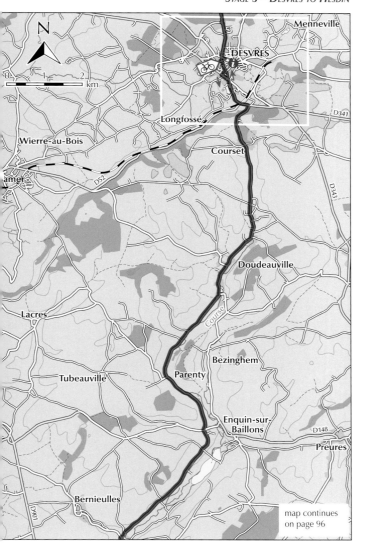

map continues
on page 96

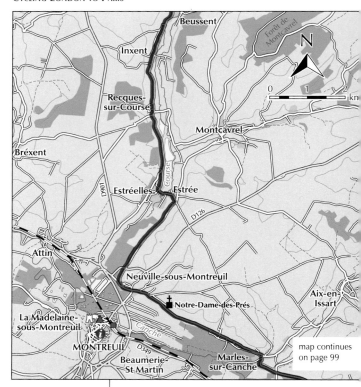

go ahead uphill (D341, sp Hesdin). After 250m, turn (D127, sp Courset) climbing steeply then descendir through **Courset** hamlet (3km, 156m) (accommodation)

Continue downhill following D127 into valley of riv Course, passing through Course to reach **Doudeauvill** (7.5km, 87m) (accommodation). Pass through **Paren** (10.5km, 67m), Zérables (15km, 45m) (refreshment camping), **Beussent** (16.5km, 32m) (accommodatio refreshments), **Inxent** (18km, 29m) (accommodatio refreshments), **Recques-sur-Course** (19.5km, 25m (accommodation) and La Ballastière (accommodation stréelles (accommodation), road bears L to cross river ...urse into sister village of **Estrée** (22km, 10m) (accom-...dation, refreshments).

Turn R at T-junction (D150, sp Neuville) and con-...e on tree-lined road into open country. Go ahead at ...ssroads then bear L at T-junction to reach staggered ...ssroads in centre of **Neuville-sous-Montreuil** (26km, ...n) (accommodation, refreshments). ▶

To visit Montreuil (accommodation, refreshments, youth hostel, camping, tourist office, station) turn right on Rue de Montreuil and continue for 1.5km.

MONTREUIL

Montreuil (pop 2500) is a walled town some distance from the sea. But this was not always so; from Roman times until the 13th century it was an important port at the head of the Canche estuary with a royal castle (two towers of which remain), a cloth industry and an abbey and churches with relics that attracted many pilgrims. This prosperity ended when the estuary silted-up and the town was destroyed by the English during the Hundred Years' War. The town was later rebuilt and surrounded by 17th-century fortifications designed by Vauban. During the First World War the military academy became headquarters for the British army in France and its commander, General Haig, was accommodated in a nearby château. After the war, a bronze equestrian statue of Haig was erected in what is now Place Charles de Gaulle. This was melted down by occupying German forces during the Second World War then reconstructed in the 1950s using the original mould. Victor Hugo used the town as the setting for some of the initial scenes in *Les Misérables*; where Jean Valjean is a local factory owner and Fantine lives and works, then dies in a local hospital.

Cycle ahead over crossroads (Rue de la Chartreuse, ...13, sp Marles), then pass calvary cross L where road ...ads to former *chartreuse* (abbey) of **Notre-Dame-des-**...s R.

The former Carthusian chartreuse of **Notre-Dame-des-Prés** was founded in 1325. During the French Revolution it was closed and partly dismantled. After being rebuilt (1872–1875) to the original plans, the abbey had a brief period of prosperity with a successful print works publishing religious tracts. The monks were expelled again in 1901, this time emigrating to Sussex in England, after which the building was used as a hospital. Since this closed in 1997 it has been empty, despite several plans to develop the site.

Continue through hamlet of Le Petit Marles to rea **Marles-sur-Canche** (30km, 17m) (accommodatic refreshments). Pass church R then continue over cro roads and through Le But de Marles to **Marenla** (33.5k 18m) (camping). Pass first turn-off R to Beaurainville a cycle ahead to T-junction. Turn R towards **Beaurainvi** (37.5km, 16m) (accommodation, refreshments, campi station).

Go ahead at mini-roundabout (D113, sp Cont and continue through fields to **Contes**. Turn R in v lage (D113, sp Aubin-St Vaast) to reach T-junction. Tu R downhill into **Aubin-St Vaast** (43.5km, 23m) (s tion). Turn L in village (D113, sp Guisy) and follow rc through **Guisy** (46km, 26m) (accommodation, cam ing) into **Huby-St Leu** (48.5km, 28m) (accommodatic refreshments).

Beaurainville mill is on the Créquoise, a small tributary of the Canche

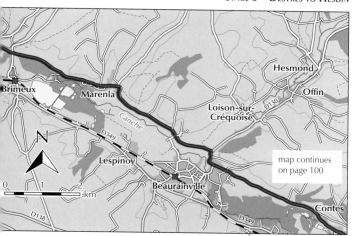

map continues on page 100

Follow road bearing R at T-junction (Rue du Huit [M]ai 1945, D113, sp Hesdin) and after 125 metres turn [R] at second T-junction (D928, sp Hesdin). Cross river [Tu]rnoise and railway level crossing then bear L at com[pli]cated road junction (Ave de la République, D340, sp [ce]ntre ville). Follow road bearing L and immediately fork [R] (Rue du Pavillon Doré). Go ahead over two crossroads [an]d cross river Canche on narrow brick bridge between [ho]uses into Rue de l'Ancienne Poissonnerie. Continue [int]o Rue Prévost, passing abbey R, and turn second L [op]posite green balcony (Rue Hennebert) to reach Pl [d']Armes in centre of **Hesdin** (49.5km, 29m) (accommo[da]tion, refreshments, tourist office, cycle shop, station).

Hesdin (pop 4000 in urban area) was a 'new' city built from 1554 astride the Canche after Vieil-Hesdin (old Hesdin, 6km upstream) was destroyed on the orders of Emperor Charles V. Most of the principal buildings date from the mid-16th century and include elements of both late Gothic and Renaissance styles. The main material for domestic buildings is brick, although stone is used for some

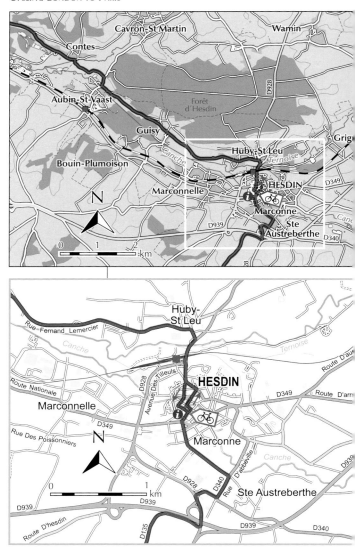

of the ecclesiastical structures. The most notable is the brick town hall overlooking Place d'Armes although the stone Renaissance portal and belfry were added later. Other significant buildings include Notre Dame Church, Hospice of St John, Jesuit college and houses in the Rue des Nobles.

REVERSE ROUTE: HESDIN TO DESVRES

From north corner of Place d'Armes in centre of **Hesdin**, cycle NE (Rue de la Paroisse). At end turn L (Rue de St Omer) and fork R (Rue de la République) on tree-lined road. Go ahead (D928) across railway and river Ternoise then turn L (D113) and L again into **Huby-St Leu** (accommodation, refreshments). Continue through **Guisy** (3.5km, 26m) (accommodation, camping) to **Aubin-St Vaast** (6km, 23m) (station).

Bear R then turn L through open country. Turn L into **Contes** and continue past **Beaurainville** (12km, 16m) (accommodation, refreshments, camping, station). After village, turn L (D113) and continue through **Marenla** (16.5km, 18m) (camping), **Marles-sur-Canche** (19.5km, 17m) (accommodation, refreshments) and Le Petit Marles. Pass former chartreuse (abbey) of Notre-Dame-des-Prés R to reach **Neuville-sous-Montreuil** (23.5km, 15m) (accommodation, refreshments). To visit **Montreuil** (accommodation, refreshments, youth hostel, camping, tourist office, station) turn L (Rue de Montreuil) and continue for 1.5km.

Pass through village on D901 then fork R (D150). Go ahead over crossroads to **Estrée** (27.5km, 10m) (accommodation, refreshments). Turn L (D127) through village over river Course into **Estréelles** (accommoda-

tion) and start climbing gently up Course valley through La Ballastière (accommodation), **Recques-sur-Course** (30km, 25m) (accommodation), **Inxent** (31.5km, 29m)

Estrée is one of many pretty villages in the Course valley (accommodation, refreshments), **Beussent** (33km, 32m) (accommodation, refreshments), Zérables (34.5km, 45m) (refreshments, camping), **Parenty** (39km, 67m), **Doudeauville** (42km, 87m) (accommodation), Course and **Courset** hamlet (46.5km, 156m) (accommodation) to reach summit (179m). Descend to crossroads and turn L (D341) across railway to reach roundabout. Turn L and fork immediately R (Rue Victor Hugo). At end, turn L (Rue Emile Gugelot) then R at crossroads (Rue des Écoles) to Pl Léon Blum in **Desvres** (49.5km, 91m) (accommodation, refreshments, tourist office).

Brick-built Hesdin town hall has a carved stone portico and tower

STAGE 6
Hesdin to Abbeville

Start	Hesdin, Pl d'Armes (29m)
Finish	Abbeville fairgrounds (15m)
Distance	40km (25 miles)
Ascent	316m
Waymarking	None

After climbing out of Hesdin, this stage undulates on minor roads across wide open chalk downland of the Ponthieu with large fields, few trees and only occasional villages. Descent is made into three small valleys, one of which holds the only town en route, Crécy-en-Ponthieu where an English army defeated the French in 1346. Towards the end, the route descends into the Scardon valley to follow a voie verte into Abbeville.

From SW corner of Pl d'Armes in **Hesdin**, follow Rue André Fréville then go ahead L at mini-roundabout (D113, Ave de Ste Austreberthe, third exit) and continue through **Marconne**. Turn R at crossroads (Rue de Abbeville, D340). Where this road bears L at next crossroads, turn R (Rue de Brévillers, D135) and continue to T-junction. Turn L on main road (D928, sp Brévillers)

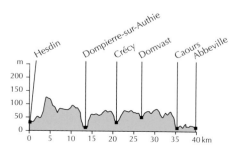

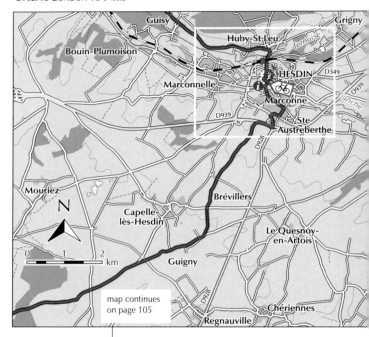

and follow this over motorway then turn immediately
R (D135, sp Brévillers) beside motorway. Follow road
bearing away from motorway and ascend to **Brévillers**
(4.5km, 121m).

Pass through village then go ahead over crossroads
and descend across open downland. Bear R at T-junction
and continue descending to **Guigny** (7km, 85m). Follow
road across level plateau, then descend steeply into
Rapéchy (13km, 16m). Where road turns L in village,
continue ahead (D111, sp Dompierre) across floor of
Authie valley. Cross river Authie and follow road winding
through **Dompierre-sur-Authie** (14km, 15m).

At end of village, keep ahead L (D111, sp Wadicourt)
then climb steeply out of valley and continue across downland plateau to **Wadicourt** (18km, 77m). Turn R opposite

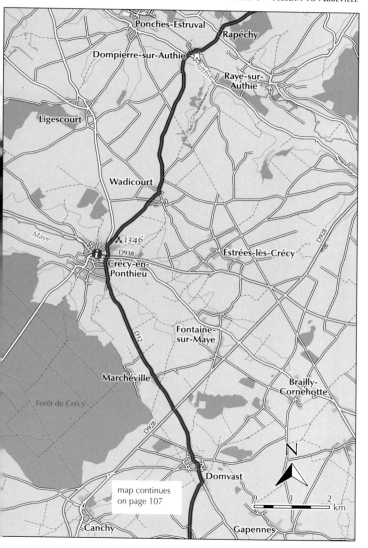

map continues
on page 107

church (still D111) and continue across plateau to reach watchtower L overlooking site of Battle of Crécy. Cycle downhill then bear L at T-junction (D12) and fork L (D12 sp toutes directions) into **Crécy-en-Ponthieu** (20.5km 40m) (accommodation, refreshments, tourist office).

THE BATTLE OF CRÉCY

The Battle of Crécy (1346) was a decisive English victory during the first phase of the Hundred Years' War. Historians regard Crécy as a significant technological advance over previous battles with the rise of the English long-bow as the dominant weapon and an early use of cannon. Approximately 10,000 English, Welsh and German soldiers led by King Edward III faced 30,000 French, Genoese and Majorcan troops commanded by the French king, Phillip VI. Tactics and terrain played a major part. The English army was composed mostly of bowmen and infantry, drawn from the common people. The French relied more upon the use of heavily armoured mounted knights of aristocratic birth and pikemen. Arriving at Crécy before the French, the English established hillside defensive positions overlooking the village. When the French attacked, their knights and pikemen were at a disadvantage, charging uphill under a hail of arrows from 5000 bowmen and fire from English cannons. In comparison with modern warfare, casualties were light; less than 300 English soldiers and an estimated 2000 French knights being killed. The outcome was disastrous for France, with the English going on to capture Calais and establish a firm footing in northern France.

Turn R (D938) and immediately L (Rue de St Riquier D12, sp Marchéville). Cross river Maye and continue out of town climbing back onto chalk downland. Pass through **Marchéville** (24km, 77m) and continue through open fields to cross main road (D12, sp Domvast) and descend into **Domvast** (27km, 59m) (accommodation) Pass church R and towards end of village turn R (D82, sp Agenvillers). Continue through **Agenvillers** (29km, 68m) and through open country. Descend to go ahead at cross-roads and climb again to pass through **Millencourt-en-Ponthieu** (33km, 70m).

After gentle ascent, road now descends into valley of river Scardon and winds past **Caours** L (35.5km,

The route crosses the open fields of the Ponthieu chalk downland

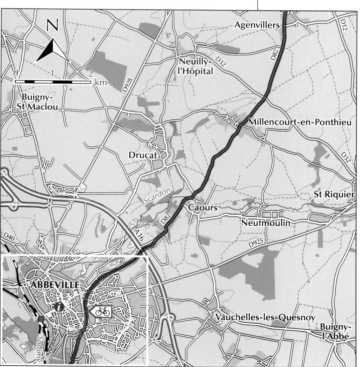

16m) (accommodation, refreshments). Continue through l'Heure on Rue des Pres, passing church R. Fork R beside house 144 on gravel cycle track along old railway trackbed. Follow this under motorway and into suburbs of Abbeville. Go ahead across road junction and pass gendarmerie barracks behind high wall L. Cross another main road to reach Champ de Foire fairgrounds beside Bvd Vauban in **Abbeville** (40km, 15m) (accommodation, refreshments, camping, tourist office, cycle shop, station).

ABBEVILLE

Place Max Lejeune and St Wulfran's church in Abbeville

Abbeville (pop 24,000) sits beside the river Somme, surrounded by marshland. It was originally a small settlement on an island in the river, which was developed by the monks of Riquier abbey (Abbeville means town of the abbots). By the 12th century it had grown into a port city at the head of the Somme estuary, however, subsequent silting-up has left it 25km inland. Trade in wool led to the development of a textile industry, mostly based around home-working. The most important textile company, Manufacture de Rames, was established in 1665 to produce tapestries and high-quality linens which were exported to all the major European courts.

Its closeness to the English Channel and the northern border of France has led to the town being frequently overrun by foreign armies from the Hundred Years' War until the Second World War. This last was particularly destructive, with streets of medieval houses destroyed and much of the town left in ruins. Post-war rebuilding has seen important buildings restored, including the 13th-century belfry (one of the oldest in France) and St Vulfran's church, a masterpiece of Gothic art.

An infamous event occurred in 1765 when the Chevalier de Barre, a young nobleman aged 20, was tortured, beheaded and his body burnt for blasphemy and sacrilege, with a copy of Voltaire's *Philosophical Dictionary* burnt alongside the body. Fearing his own safety, Voltaire fled from Paris to Switzerland from where he continued writing passionately, condemning the verdict. Subsequently the Chevalier was pardoned posthumously and became a hero among anti-clerical factions. A statue was erected in Abbeville (1907), close to the execution site.

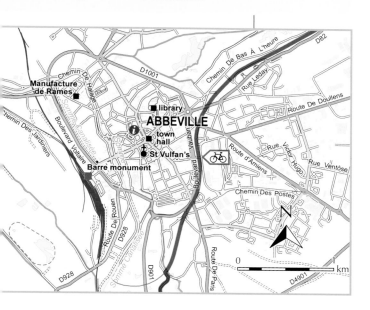

REVERSE ROUTE: ABBEVILLE TO HESDIN

From Champ de Foire in **Abbeville** follow cycle track N along former railway trackbed. Pass under motorway and turn L at first crossroads (D82) past **Caours** R (4.5km, 16m) (accommodation, refreshments). Follow road uphill onto downland and pass through **Millencourt-en-Ponthieu** (7km, 70m) and **Agenvillers** (11km, 68m). At beginning of **Domvast** (13km, 59m) (accommodation) turn L (D12) and continue across plateau through **Marchéville** (16km, 77m) then descend to **Crécy-en-Ponthieu** (19.5km, 40m) (accommodation, refreshments, tourist office).

Turn R (D938) and immediately L (D12) then fork R at end of village (D111) uphill past watchtower R overlooking site of Battle of Crécy. Continue winding through **Wadicourt** (22km, 77m) then descend to **Dompierre-sur-Authie** (26km, 15m).

Wind through village then cross river Authie into **Rapéchy** (27km, 16m). Fork R (still D111) and climb back onto plateau. At top of hill enter Pas-de-Calais département, where road becomes D135. Fork R (D134) uphill through **Guigny** (33km, 85m) then after village, fork L (un-marked apart from 'trucks prohibited' symbol). Cross main road into **Brévillers** (35.5km, 121m) and continue climbing to summit (126m) at end of village. Descend steeply and turn L (D928) over motorway. Turn R (D135) then L at crossroads (D340) into **Marconne**. Turn L at next crossroads (D113) and continue to mini-roundabout. Go ahead R (Rue André Fréville) to Pl d'Armes in **Hesdin** (40km, 29m) (accommodation, refreshments, tourist office, cycle shop, station).

STAGE 7
Abbeville to Amiens

Start	Abbeville fairgrounds (15m)
Finish	Amiens, Maison de la Culture (32m)
Distance	46.5km (29 miles)
Ascent	39m
Waymarking	Vèloroute Vallée de Somme (V30)

This is a completely level stage that follows the towpath of the canalised river Somme, all the way from the outskirts of Abbeville to the centre of Amiens. A few riverside villages are passed, but no major towns. Rough track is followed at first but then good surface takes over after Pont Remy.

From Champ de Foire in **Abbeville**, follow gravel cycle track S, parallel with Bvd Vauban R. Go ahead over road junction and follow cycle track bearing L away from main road and into woods. Where track crosses asphalt side road, turn L and after 50m, fork R (Rue du Grand Marais). Follow causeway across marshland to emerge on main road. Turn L (D901) and follow road ascending through woodland to reach roundabout. Continue ahead (first exit) into **Épagnette** (refreshments) and turn second R downhill (Rue du Pont, sp Vèloroute Vallée de Somme). Cross river Somme and turn L on gravel towpath beside river (4km, 7m).

Cycle past first bridge (leading to Épagne on opposite side of river) to reach blue girder bridge leading to Laucourt-sur-Somme. Continue ahead for short distance on road beside canal, then fork L to continue on towpath, passing overgrown ruins of **Eaucourt château** on opposite bank. Pass Pont-Remy lock to reach bridge in **Pont-Remy** (9km, 11m) (accommodation, refreshments).

CYCLING LONDON TO PARIS

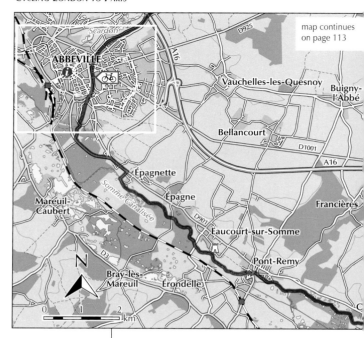

map continues
on page 113

Turn L over river and R past church L onto riverside
road (Rue Roger Salengro). Fork R along towpath the
after end of village recross river and continue on tow
path. Pass under bridge that leads to **Cocquerel** (12.5km
8m) and continue past lock at Long. Pass under bridge
leading to **Long** (15.5km, 12m) (accommodation, refresh
ments, camping).

> The 18th-century **Château de Long** is perched on a
> hillside beside the Somme. Built by Honoré-Charles
> de Buissy, it replaced a medieval fortress on the
> same site. Subsequently abandoned, it fell into dis-
> repair and parts were dismantled and sold in the
> USA. The château was purchased in 1964 by a local
> industrialist who reinstated it to its former glory.

A legend of Long concerns de Buissy's son Pierre who was rumoured to have had a relationship with Princess Adélaïde, daughter of Louis XV, a tryst that was undertaken in the château.

Long château has spectacular riverside gardens

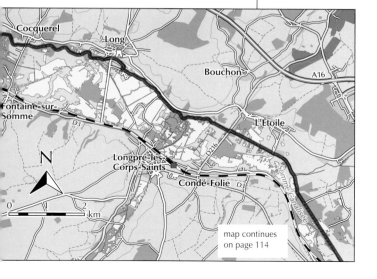

map continues on page 114

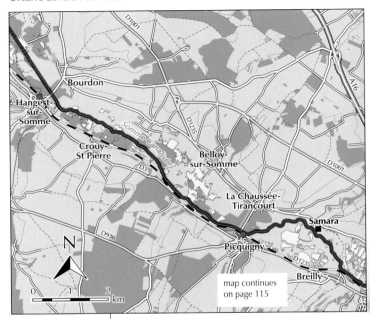

map continues
on page 115

Continue past Long château rising above opposite bank L then dogleg over weir and turn L past old red-brick hydro-electric station R. Pass campsite R and follow towpath to emerge on road. Turn L (D216) over bridge and R along opposite bank, passing **L'Étoile** L (19.5km, 11m).

Pass under two old railway bridges and La Breilloire lock then follow straight section of canalised river to pass under bridge that leads across canal to **Hangest-sur-Somme** R (25km, 12m) (accommodation, refreshments, station).

Continue beside canal, with railway on opposite bank, to reach road bridge and lock at **Picquigny** (32km, 13m) (refreshments, camping, station). Continue past **Samara** archaeological park L (refreshments) to reach road bridge and lock at **Ailly-sur-Somme** (37.5km, 14m) (accommodation, refreshments, tourist office, station).

During the Roman conquest of Gaul in 54BC, Julius Caesar ordered the construction of winter quarters for his army on a bluff overlooking the Somme valley. An encampment covering 20ha was built, surrounded by a ditch and earth bank up to 11m high. Modern day excavations have discovered much older remains below this site, suggesting that both Stone Age and Bronze Age settlements had existed here. Nowadays the site is part of **Samara archaeological park**, with reconstructed dwellings from the Stone Age and Bronze Age surrounded by a nature reserve in the riverside marshes. Other parts of the park include an arboretum and botanical gardens.

Continue along towpath to emerge on road and pass bridge that leads over canal to **Dreuil-lès-Amiens** (40km,

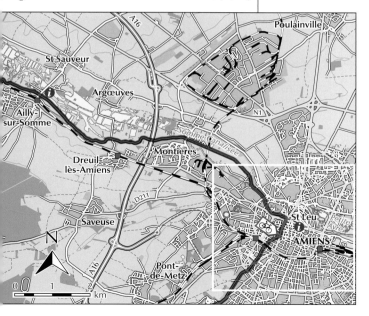

16m) (refreshments, station). Continue under motorway and across next road beside lock at **Montières** (refreshments, camping). Dogleg under railway then emerge on road (Quai de la Somme) and follow this beside river to reach a huge concrete bowl that looks like a flying saucer has landed in front of **ESIEE** graduate school of engineering. Immediately after ESIEE, turn R on pedestrian bridge over canal and R beside river after bridge (Quai de la Passerelle). Bear R on next bridge and R again over Somme. Go ahead over wide main road into Rue du Général Leclerc. Follow this to Pl Léon Gontier where stage ends in front of modernist Maison de la Culture R in centre of **Amiens** (46.5km, 32m) (accommodation, refreshments, youth hostel, tourist office, cycle shop, station).

AMIENS

Maison de la Culture is a modern multi-art centre in Amiens

Amiens (pop 133,000) has a long history going back to Roman times. During the medieval period the city developed as a textile and dyeing centre based around the production of *waide* (woad), a blue dye, and velvet material. The prosperity brought by these industries is reflected in Notre Dame cathedral, which dominates the city centre and is the largest in France. Built in 50 years (1220–1270) it has a nave three times higher than its width and was described by Ruskin as the Parthenon of Gothic architecture. The richly decorated west front is illuminated by a son-et-lumière light show every summer.

Another landmark is the old belfry. Built in the 13th century it had many uses including a meeting place for civic leaders, prison and watchtower. The bell and copper roof were destroyed during the Second World War and not reinstated until 1990, since when the bell has chimed hourly.

The St Leu district was the old industrial heart of the city with a maze of narrow streets, canals and dilapidated houses. Since 1990 a major renovation programme has breathed new life into this area with restaurants, entertainment venues and food shops. Many of the previous working-class residents have left and been replaced with a younger more affluent population. Nearby, in an area of reclaimed marshland, the Hortillonnages is a huge area of irrigated water gardens close to the centre, which are both a green lung for the city and a producer of fruit and vegetables. They can be visited by shallow bottomed electric boats.

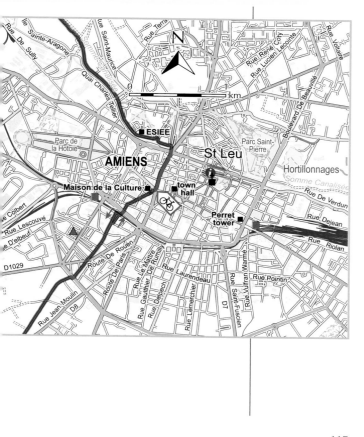

REVERSE ROUTE: AMIENS TO ABBEVILLE

From Maison de la Culture in **Amiens** follow Rue du Général Leclerc N. Fork L over Somme and turn L alongside canalised river (Somme Canalisée). Cross bridge over side canal and pass **ESIEE** graduate school of engineering R. Continue out of Amiens under railway and past lock at **Montières** (refreshments, camping). Follow canal under motorway then past **Dreuil-lès-Amiens** L (6.5km, 16m) (refreshments, station) and **Ailly-sur-Somme** L (9km, 14m) (accommodation, refreshments, tourist office, station).

Follow canal through area of marshland passing **Samara** park R (refreshments), **Picquigny** (14.5km, 13m) (refreshments, camping, station) and **Hangest-sur-Somme** L (21.5km, 12m) (accommodation, refreshments, station).

A long straight reach past La Breilloire lock leads on to **L'Étoile** R (27km, 11m), where route crosses canal to continue on L bank. Pass caravan site L and turn R over weir beside disused hydro-electric power station. Pass château on opposite bank in **Long** (31km, 12m) (accommodation, refreshments, camping) and continue on towpath past lock through more marshland. Pass **Cocquerel** R (34km, 8m) and just before Pont-Remy cross to R bank for short distance, crossing back at next bridge in **Pont-Remy** (37.5km, 11m) (accommodation, refreshments). *After Pont-Remy, track surface deteriorates.*

Pass blue girder bridge (leading to Eaucourt-sur-Somme) and concrete arch bridge (leading to Épagne), then at second concrete arch bridge, turn R over canal on road ascending to **Épagnette** (43km, 16m) (refreshments). Turn L (D901) then fork L (second exit) at roundabout. After 1km, turn R (unmarked) and immediately L on Rue du Grand Marais winding through marshland. Turn L at T-junction (Rue du Petit Marais) and immediately R onto voie verte along former railway trackbed. Follow this to Champ de Foire in **Abbeville** (46.5km, 15m) (accommodation, refreshments, campimg, tourist office, cycle shop, station).

STAGE 8
Amiens to Beauvais

Start	Amiens, Maison de la Culture (32m)
Finish	Beauvais, cathedral (69m)
Distance	65km (40.5 miles) (road route); 64.5km (40 miles) (Coulée Verte)
Ascent	317m
Waymarking	Coulée Verte, Bacouel-sur-Selle–Crèvecœur-le-Grand; otherwise none

This stage leaves Amiens by crossing a low ridge before following the Selle valley on a gently rising grade, using minor roads and the Coulée Verte (green corridor) along an old railway, past the head of the valley and across chalk downland to the hilltop town of Crèvecœur-le-Grand. Minor roads are then used to descend into the Thérain valley and reach Beauvais.

om cobbled pedestrian area in front of Maison de la ulture in **Amiens**, follow Rue Marc Sagnier SW and con- ue into Rue Robert Pierre. Where this bears R, fork L ue Lhomond), then continue ahead over dual-carriage- ay and railway. Turn R (Bvd Guyencourt) and first L (Rue éranger) soon starting to ascend. Where this ends, dog- g R and L across main road into Rue Alfred Lemaire. At d, cross next main road then turn R and L into Rue des uatre Lemaire (one-way street). Pass mini-roundabout

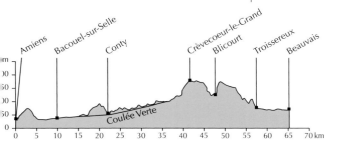

and continue ahead now on contra-flow cycle lane
Where this ends, bear R on cycle track beside Rue Je
Moulin then follow cycle track as it forks R beside Ch c
Thil, passing Jules-Verne campus of **university of Picard**
R. At end, bear R on cycle track beside Ave de la Cro
Jourdain. At top of ascent, go ahead over roundabo
(second exit), where cycle lane ends and route star
descending. Go ahead again at second roundabout (R
de Conty, D8, second exit) passing **university hospital**
in Salouël (4km, 64m).

Go ahead at traffic lights then fork R downhill (R
Ernest Cauvin) and follow this bearing R over river Sell
Turn L at T-junction (Rue Jean Catelas) and cycle throug
Saleux (6km, 34m) into open country. Follow road bea
ing L and R under motorway then continue on Ch c
Bacouel to T-junction in **Bacouel-sur-Selle** (10km, 38m)

THE COULÉE VERTE

The Coulée Verte (green corridor) is a waymarked footpath/off-road cycle
trail along the track-bed of part of the Amiens–Beauvais railway which
closed in 1972. Much of the going is rough earth or grass with no surfacing
which can become muddy when wet. The 30km section from Bacouel-sur-
Selle to Crèvecœur-le-Grand can be cycled throughout by mountain bike
and, except after a lengthy period of wet weather, is easily cycleable on a
hybrid. During a dry spell, much of it can be ridden using a tourer. The track
is not suitable for racing bikes. There is a proposal to surface the whole path
to voie verte standards (3m wide, asphalt surface) and it appears on French
cycling maps as a proposed part of national cycle trail V32 (Véloroute de
la Mémoire) from Paris to Lille. Both the Coulée Verte and an alternative
road route are described here. They intersect frequently and if you start on
one route and change your mind it is easy to access the alternative. The
sections of Coulée Verte between Lœuilly–Conty and Fontaine-Bonneleau–
Crèvecœur are the most suitable if you wish to cycle just a part.

Coulée Verte route
The Coulée Verte is shown in blue on the route maps.

Turn R at T-junction (Grande Rue, sp Coulée Vert
and where road curves L, bear R ahead out of village. Ju

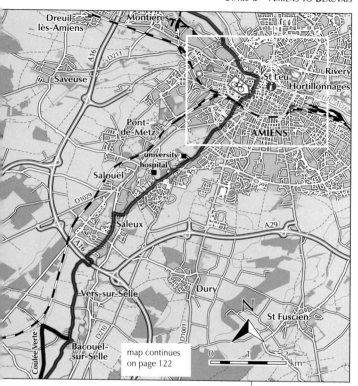

map continues
on page 122

efore carpark L, turn L between trees onto Coulée Verte.
ss site of Bacouel station and continue past **Prouzel**
3km, 44m), **Fossemanant** (14.5km, 53m), **Neuville-lès-
euilly** (16km, 45m) (refreshments) and **Lœuilly** (18km,
8m) (accommodation, refreshments, camping).

Continue ahead through woodland, passing between
·veral water-filled aggregate quarries now used as
·mmercial angling lakes. Cross river Selle, continuing
·rough woods. At carpark for anglers, dogleg R and L
·to parallel gravel vehicular track to reach road. Dogleg
· and L onto parallel minor road (Rue du Marais) and

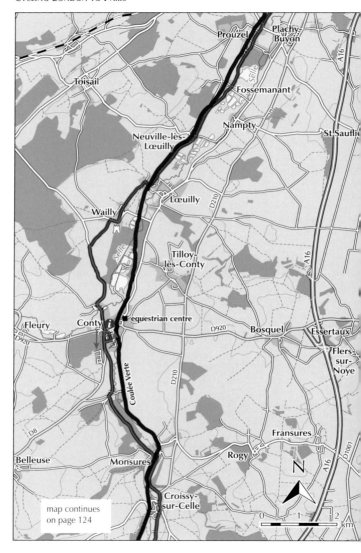

Prouzel
Plachy-
Buyon

Toisail

Fossemanant

Nampty

St Saulflie

Neuville-lès-
Lœuilly

Lœuilly

Wailly

Tilloy-
les-Conty

Fleury

Conty

equestrian centre

Bosquel

Essertaux

Flers-
sur-
Noye

Coulée Verte

Fransures

Belleuse

Monsures

Rogy

N

Croissy-
sur-Celle

map continues
on page 124

0   1   2
km

122

low this past equestrian centre into **Conty** (22km, 56m)
commodation, refreshments, tourist office).

Continue ahead over roundabout (Rue du Hamel)
d follow this turning R over river Selle. Turn immedi-
ly L on cycle track beside river then dogleg L and R
er Selle to regain route of old railway and continue
ead through woods. Emerge on farm road and dogleg L
d R onto asphalt road for 150 metres then bear R oppo-
e barns back onto Coulée Verte. Surface eventually
comes asphalt and reaches crossroads. Turn R and bear
n grassy track past houses to follow Coulée Verte into
nsures (26km, 68m). Go ahead over crossroads and
ntinue on Coulée Verte to reach old station in **Croissy-
-Celle** (27.5km, 72m) (accommodation). ▶

Follow cycle track ahead past **Bonneleau** R (30km,
m) and **Fontaine-Bonneleau** L (32km, 95m) (camping)
reach Fontaine-Bonneleau station. Turn L beside goods
ed and sharply R on gravel track parallel to old railway.
join Coulée Verte then cross main road (D106) and
ntinue in trees past **Catheux** (34km, 107m). Dogleg
ross sideroad and follow tree-lined track as it climbs
adily across downland to reach T-junction. Turn R (Rue

The river Selle's name
changes to Celle
where it crosses from
Somme département
into Oise.

*The two wings
of Crèvecœur-le-
Grand château
hold the town hall
and hospital*

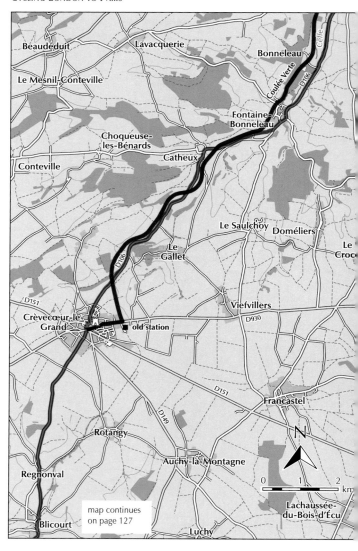

map continues
on page 127

du Breteuil, D930) past entrance to Crèvecœur station L and cemetery R, then fork L (Ave du Château, D930). Pass château R to reach roundabout in **Crèvecœur-le-Grand** (41km, 178m) (refreshments), and turn L (Rue Victor Hugo, D615, third exit, sp Blicourt).

Road route

The road route is shown in red on the route maps.

Turn L at T-junction and R (Rue de Plachy) to reach **Plachy-Buyon** (11.5km, 41m). Go ahead over angled crossroads (Pl du Petit Plachy) and continue on Rue de la Gare into **Prouzel** (12km, 43m). Continue over off-set crossroads into Rue du Stade then cycle through **Fossemanant** (13.5km, 43m) and **Neuville-lès-Lœuilly** (15.5km, 45m) (refreshments) to **Lœuilly** (17.5km, 48m) (accommodation, refreshments, camping).

Turn R (Rue d'Outre l'Eau), then cross Coulée Verte and turn L uphill (Ch de Wailly) to reach T-junction in **Wailly** (19km, 81m). Turn R (Rue du Petit Rond) and at end of village turn L at crossroads (Rue du Fleury). Bear L onto main road (D38) and follow this downhill into **Conty** (22.5km, 60m) (accommodation, refreshments, tourist office).

Turn R and immediately L (Rue du Général Debeney, D8) at mini-roundabout. At end of town, fork L (D109, sp Monsures) and continue to Luzières (24.5km, 67m). Bear L at end of hamlet through woodland to reach **Monsures** (26.5km, 65m). Cross Selle and turn R in front of church (Rue du Croissy, D4109). Bear R on main road (D11) into **Croissy-sur-Celle** (28.5km, 79m) (accommodation).

Fork R in village (D106, sp Fontaine-Bonneleau) and follow road through **Fontaine-Bonneleau** (32.5km, 88m) (camping). Continue past mineral water factory R by turn-off for Fontaine-Bonneleau station, then cross Coulée Verte again and pass through **Catheux** (35.5km, 105m). Ascend steadily across open downland to reach T-junction. Turn R (Rue du Général Moret, D621, sp centre ville) then bear L following Rue Gambetta past church and château (both L) to reach roundabout in **Crèvecœur-le-Grand** (41.5m, 178m) (refreshments).

Go ahead into Rue Victor Hugo (D615, second exit, sp Blicourt).

> **Crèvecœur-le-Grand** (pop 3500) sits on top of the Picardy plateau, surrounded by chalk downland. Until the 19th century this was sheep country and the main occupation was wool production. During the revolution, the 16th-century château was split and sold as separate lots. Nowadays part of the building houses the town hall and another part the local hospital. South of Crèvecœur, the trackbed of the old Beauvais–Amiens railway has been purchased by a railway preservation society who plan to run narrow-gauge steam trains on the 10km of line to St Omer-en-Chaussée. The first trains ran on a 1km reinstated section in 2015, but it will be many years of hard work before the whole line is reopened.

Combined route continues

Follow Rue Victor Hugo out of town across chalk plateau past windfarm R, then descend to T-junction in **Regnonval** (46km, 127m) (accommodation). Turn L (Rue du Mont Pommeret, D615, sp Blicourt) and continue across open downland. Turn L at crossroads, crossing former railway trackbed beside Blicourt station and bear R on winding road past church L into **Blicourt** (47.5km, 123m) (accommodation).

Turn L at triangular junction and immediately fork R (Rue du Pisseleu, sp Pisseleu) ascending onto plateau. Turn L at T-junction, then fork R (Rue de Juvignies, D52, sp Juvignies) past church in **Pisseleu-aux-Bois** (49.5km, 158m). Continue across downland and fork R (sp Sauqueuse) on quiet road to reach five-way crossroads in **Sauqueuse-St Lucien** (52km, 149m).

Go ahead R (Rue de Péronne, sp Troissereux) then descend through open country and pass over road bridge. Bear R (Rue du Puits) at T-junction and continue to crossroads in centre of **Troissereux** (57km, 80m) (accommodation, refreshments).

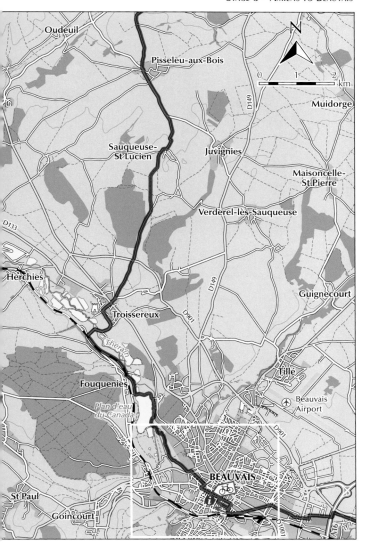

127

Blicourt has many half-timbered buildings

Go ahead (Rue du 16 Août 1944) and just before entrance to château turn L into Rue de la Gare (D616),

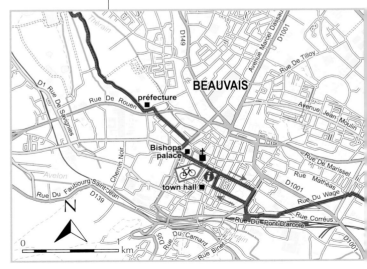

nding out of town. Cross river Thérain and just before
ilway crossing, turn L beside railway. Pass through bar-
er to reach carpark in **Fouquenies**, then continue ahead
rough second barrier on gravel track to reach gate at
ttrance to Beauvais *plage* (beach). Turn L between high
edges and follow track along shore of **Plan d'eau du
anada** reservoir (61.5km, 68m).

Fork L immediately before watersports centre then
ear R on tree-lined track between centre R and carpark
Follow concrete track winding through woodland
en continue beside reservoir. At end of reservoir fork
through gate and cross bridge, then continue on gravel
cle track winding through woods. Emerge on road (Rue
u Marais St Quentin) and continue ahead with **préfec-
re** behind high wall L. Do not follow cycle route road
arkings L over bridge into préfecture gardens. Bear L (Pl
la Préfecture) and turn second R (Ave Victor Hugo).
o ahead over first crossroads then turn R at traffic lights
vd Amyot d'Inville) to reach complicated road junc-
on. Turn L over Thérain and fork L (Rue St Pierre, sp
ntre-ville) past **Bishop's palace** L to reach cathedral in
eauvais (65km, 69m) (accommodation, refreshments,
urist office, cycle shop, station).

BEAUVAIS

*The highly ambitious
Beauvais cathedral*

Beauvais (pop 55,000)
grew as a prosperous
medieval woollen tex-
tile town. This wealth
was reflected in St Pierre
cathedral upon which
work started in 1225. In
high Gothic style it was
intended to be the tallest European cathedral both inside the nave and to
the top of the tower. However, the full plan was never realised as first a

funding crisis, then the Hundred Years' War and then the plague led to work ceasing (1573) after almost 250 years. In an attempt to surpass the cathedrals in Amiens and Rouen, technology was pushed beyond known limits, with disastrous results. While the choir, transept and apse were completed both the nave and tower collapsed during construction. Even unfinished, the cathedral represents the zenith of Gothic architecture.

A few other medieval buildings survived German bombing (1940), when 80 per cent of the town was destroyed. These include the Bishops' Palace with pepper pot towers, which incorporates part of an old Roman fortress and nowadays houses the regional museum. Just outside town, the small regional airport has become the ninth busiest in France, since the arrival of Ryanair in 1997.

REVERSE ROUTE: BEAUVAIS TO AMIENS

Beauvais town hall in Place Jean Hachette

From cathedral in **Beauvais** cycle NW on Rue St Pierre. Cross river Thérain and turn R (Bvd Amyot d'Inville). Turn second L (Ave Victor Hugo) then go ahead over main road and turn L (Pl de la Préfecture). Pass **préfecture** and turn R (Rue du Marais St Quentin).

Where this ends continue on gravel track winding through woods then bear R beside reservoir passing watersports centre at **Plan d'eau du Canada** L (3.5km, 68m).

Bear L continuing beside reservoir, and opposite Beauvais plage (beach) turn R through gate and bear R on rough track between fields. Emerge into carpark and continue ahead beside railway L. Turn R at crossroads (Rue de la Gare) and follow this winding into **Troissereux** (8km, 80m) (accommodation, refreshments).

Turn R at T-junction (Rue du 16 Août 1944) then go ahead over crossroads onto Rue du Puits (C2) and soon fork L (sp Sauqueuse) ascending through fields. Go over road bridge and fork L continuing uphill to **Sauqueuse-St Lucien** (13km, 149m). Fork half-L (sp Pisseleu) out of village, then fork L at unmarked junction to join D52 and reach **Pisseleu-aux-Bois** (15.5km, 158m). Bear R and L in village then fork R (sp Blicourt) through fields and descend to **Blicourt** (17.5km, 123m) (accommodation). Bear R (D615) and follow this through village passing church R and over old railway crossing. Continue to **Regnonval** (19km, 132m) (accommodation) and follow D615 turning R to reach roundabout in **Crèvecœur-le-Grand** (23.5m, 178m) (refreshments). *From Crèvecœur-le-Grand there is a choice of routes: the unsurfaced Coulée Verte or a route following minor roads.*

Coulée Verte route

Turn R at roundabout (D930) and cycle past chateau L to reach site of old station at end of town. Turn L on Coulée Verte and follow this descending steadily across downland past **Catheux** L (30.5km, 103m). Dogleg L and R across D106 then continue on Coulée Verte and dogleg L and R past former Fontaine Bonneleau station. Follow track past **Fontaine Bonneleau** (32.5km, 85m) (camping), **Bonneleau** (34.5km, 81m) and **Croissy-sur-Celle** (37km, 75m) (accommodation) to reach **Monsures** (38.5km, 66m) where Coulée Verte intersects road route. At end of village dogleg R and L to continue on Coulée Verte. Turn L across river Selle to emerge on road. Turn R over Selle and immediately L beside river (Rue du Hamel) to reach mini-roundabout in **Conty** (42.5km, 59m) (refreshments, accommodation, tourist office).

Go ahead (Rue du Marais) past tourist office L and where road ends, dogleg R and L onto Coulée Verte. Continue past several angling lakes in old aggregates quarries to reach **Lœuilly** (48km, 47m) (accommodation, refreshments, camping). Coulée Verte continues past **Neuville-lès-Lœuilly** (50m, 45m) (refreshments), **Fossemanant** (51.5km, 43m) and **Prouzel** (53km, 42m). Pass site of Bacouel station and turn R at next crossroads, leaving Coulée Verte. Bear L at T-junction (Grande Rue) into **Bacouel-sur-Selle** (54.5km, 38m) then turn L (C9, Rue du Vers) out of village.

Road route

Go ahead over roundabout (Rue Gambetta, D151, sp Conty) past château R and bear R past church. Turn L (Rue d'Amiens, D106 sp Conty) and follow road out of town descending across open downland. Cycle through **Catheux**

(29.5km, 105m) and **Fontaine-Bonneleau** (32km, 88mm) (camping) then bear L (D11) to reach **Croissy-sur-Celle** (36.5km, 79m) (accommodation).

At end of village, fork L (D106, sp Monsures). Road number changes to D4109 before reaching **Monsures** (38km, 65m). Turn L (Rue du Pont, D109, sp Conty) and continue through Luzières (40.5km, 67m). Bear R (D8) and where this becomes one-way, turn R (Rue Henri Dunant) and second L (Rue des Écoles, sp Bibliothéque) to reach T-junction in **Conty** (42.5km, 60m) (accommodation, refreshments, tourist office).

Turn L past town hall, then R before mini-roundabout (Rue Caroline Follet, D38, sp Wailly). Follow this uphill for 2.5km then fork R at triangular junction on unmarked road downhill to crossroads at edge of **Wailly** (46.5km, 81m). Turn R (Rue du Petit Rond) then L (Rue du Boissy) and continue downhill. Turn R at crossroads (Rue d'Outre l'Eau) into **Lœuilly** (48km, 48m) (accommodation, refreshments, camping).

Turn L (Rue Didier Lucet) on quiet road past **Neuville-lès-Lœuilly** (50km, 45m) (refreshments) and through **Fossemanant** (51.5km, 43m) to **Prouzel** (53km, 43m). Go ahead over staggered crossroads (Rue de la Gare) to reach **Plachy-Buyon.** Turn L at mini-roundabout (D162, sp Creuse), then fork R (sp Bacouel) through open country to **Bacouel-sur-Selle** (55km, 38m). Turn L past town hall then fork R (C9, Rue de Vers) out of village.

Combined route continues
Pass through **Vers-sur-Selle** then follow road doglegging R and L under motorway and continue through **Saleux** (59km, 34m) on Rue Jean Catelas. Turn R beside house number 2 (Rue Ernest Cauvin) and cross river Selle. Emerge on main road (D8) and bear L. Pass Amiens University **hospital** L in Salouël (61km, 64m) and go ahead over two roundabouts. Fork L (Ch du Thil, sp Présidence de l'Université), passing **University of Picardy** L, then continue on cycle track beside D8. Fork L (Rue des Quatre Lemaire, one-way) then dogleg R and L across main road (Rue Alfred Lemaire) and go ahead over next main road into Rue Béranger. Where this becomes one-way, bear R then turn L (Rue François Meusnier). Go ahead over railway (Rue Lhomond) then ahead R over complicated junction (Rue Robert Pierre). Follow this to Pl Léon Gontier in front of Maison de la Culture in **Amiens** (65km, 32m) (accommodation, refreshments, youth hostel, tourist office, cycle shop, station).

STAGE 9

Beauvais to Chantilly

Start	Beauvais, cathedral (69m)
Finish	Chantilly, Pl Omer Vallon (52m)
Distance	46km (28.5 miles)
Ascent	196m
Waymarking	None

South of Beauvais the direct route to Paris crosses a limestone plateau known as the Vexin. To avoid the high ground, this stage follows the attractive Thérain valley south-east from Beauvais to its junction with the Oise, leaving only a low ridge to be crossed to reach the racehorse training town of Chantilly. This is a very gently undulating stage with a short climb and descent near the end.

From cathedral in **Beauvais**, cycle SE (Rue St Pierre) and continue through pedestrian zone into Rue des Jacobins. At end, cross main road and turn R on cycle track through gardens. Cross road at traffic lights and fork L, on cycle track R, to reach station. Turn L in front of station (Pl de la Gare) and continue through carpark. Dogleg L and R out of carpark, then bear R beside Rue Corréus and fork L beside Rue du Wage (sp Marissel), passing under road bridge. Where road curves L, turn R into narrow side road

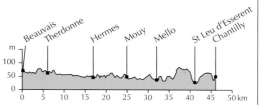

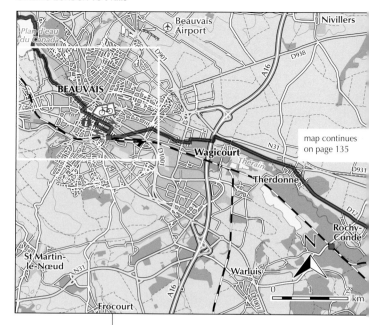

map continues
on page 135

(Rue Mathéas) and follow this winding L and R. Continue
into Rue des Aulnaies and at end cycle ahead through
barrier onto gravel track through woods. Emerge on Rue
Lesteur and continue ahead. Keep L at first junction and
fork R at second (Rue Arthur Magot) beside house 24 then
fork L under road bridge. Turn L (Ch de Sans Terre) uphill
and R at crossroads (Rue de Wagicourt). Pass industrial
estate L and cross motorway, then follow road zigzagging
L and R to reach roundabout. Cross road onto cycle lane
L and cycle through **Wagicourt**. Where cycle lane ends,
cross road to cycle through **Therdonne** (6.5km, 68m).

Near end of village, fork R (Rue du Maréchal Leclerc,
sp Ballieul-sur-Thérain) to reach main road (D12) and
continue on cycle track beside road R. Pass **Rochy-Condé**
(accommodation) R and continue across railway. Follow
road bypassing centre of **Ballieul-sur-Thérain** L (12.5km,

52m). Go ahead over roundabout in L'Alouette to reach road junction at beginning of Hermes and fork R (D125, sp Hermes centre). Follow Rue de Marguerie into centre of **Hermes** (16.5km, 51m) (accommodation, refreshments, station).

Cross bridge over Thérain, then immediately after railway crossing turn L (Rue de Friancourt, D512, sp Heilles). Follow road through Friancourt and bear L out of village into open country. Continue through woods and fields to reach **Heilles** (20km, 54m) (refreshments, station).

Turn L at T-junction and immediately fork R (Rue de l'Église, D512, sp Mouy). Pass successively church L and

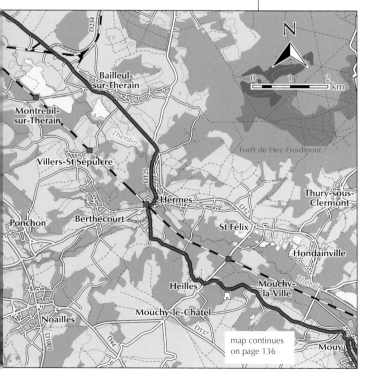

map continues on page 136

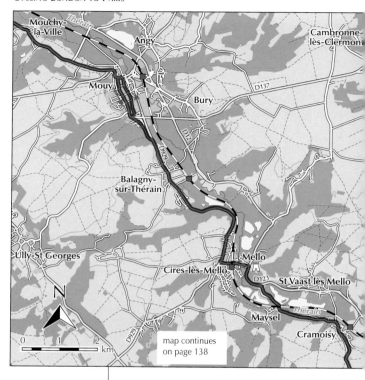

map continues
on page 138

The restored château is above the road on the right, while what remains of its parkland and formal lake are to the left.

château R. ◄ Pass above **Mouchy-la-ville** L and continue through Coincourt. At crossroads, bear L (D137, sp centre ville) then go ahead over roundabout (Rue Robert Belleil, second exit). Where this becomes one-way, turn R (Rue des Caves), passing above centre of **Mouy** (24.5km, 50m) (accommodation, refreshments, station).

Mouy (pop 5250) grew rapidly during the early 19th century when water from the Thérain was used to power textile and carpet mills, tanneries and brush factories using local wool, leather and broom. Decline started after the First World War

Most of the buildings in Mouy are made from local limestone

and nowadays few of these buildings remain. In the attractive town centre, buildings are built from local limestone, including the 12th-century St Leger church.

Continue on Rue du Général Leclerc (D929) and here road bears L on tree-lined avenue, fork R (still ue Général Leclerc). Cycle through Fourneau into open ountry and turn R to follow main road (D929) through **alagny-sur-Thérain** (28km, 42m) (refreshments, camp-g, station). Pass town square and church L and continue road winding through woods into **Cires-lès-Mello** freshments, camping, station). Turn L in middle of town ue de la Ville, D123, sp Mello) then go ahead across ilway and cross river Thérain into **Mello** (32.5km, 45m) ccommodation, refreshments). ▶

Turn R at T-junction by war memorial (D123, sp St aast) with chateau on hillside ahead, and follow road rough woods into Messie. Fork R (Rue de St Leu, D12, Maysel) and follow road back over river and rail-ay. Fork L in **Maysel** and continue through woods to amoisy (36km, 57m) (station).

Two châteaux sit on a bluff overlooking Mello, the 16th-century fortress castle and 19th-century Princess castle, which together form a conference centre.

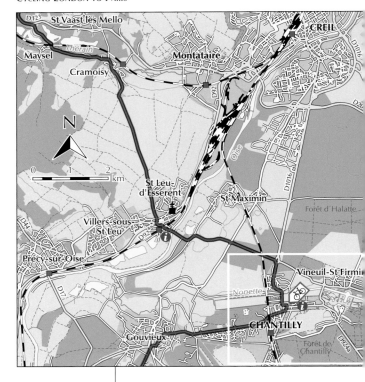

Fork R by mini-roundabout (D12, sp St Leu-d'Esserent) and follow road ascending through villa past church R into open country to reach summit (85m) on top of broad limestone plateau. Cross plateau a descend into **St Leu-d'Esserent** (40.5km, 31m) (accor modation, refreshments, camping, tourist office, station

Go ahead over mini-roundabout (Rue du Pilori) ar then ahead over angled crossroads (Rue Jean Jaurè D44, sp Chantilly) and bear R at mini-roundabout (Ru Pasteur) across railway. Road becomes Rue de l'Hôte Dieu and crosses suspension bridge over river Ois Continue through woods, going ahead at first roundabo and turning R (D1016, sp Chantilly) at second (larger) roundabout. Go ahead at third roundabout, immediately crossing road to reach cycle track L. Just before arched gateway L, follow cycle track back to R and cross river Nonette. Continue round bends L and R to reach Pl Omer Vallon in **Chantilly** (46km, 52m) (accommodation, refreshments, tourist office, station).

CHANTILLY

Chantilly's grandes écuries *(great stables) stand between the* château *and the racecourse*

The prosperous town of Chantilly (pop 11,000) is the main centre for horseracing in France. Trainers operate from 84 stables around the town, training over 2500 thoroughbred racehorses on over 150km of training gallops and trails in the surrounding forests. The racecourse is the venue for two of France's most prestigious races: the Prix du Jockey Club and Prix de Diane held in early June.

The old town centre grew up to service a great 16th-century château, most of which was destroyed during the revolution, although the stables and park survived. After the revolution, the town became a small manufacturing centre for lace, pottery, textiles and photographic plates. All this industry has gone and the half of the population not employed in equine activities nowadays commutes to work in Paris.

The principal tourist attractions are the new château (built in 1876 to replace the original castle), the *grandes écuries* (great stables) and the gardens and parks that surround them. The Condé museum in the château holds the second oldest collection of paintings in France (after the Louvre), while the vast stables host a museum dedicated to the living horse with a collection of different worldwide breeds and displays of horsemanship. In the park, the river Nonette was diverted and transformed into a grand canal to provide water for the moat and numerous fountains and water features.

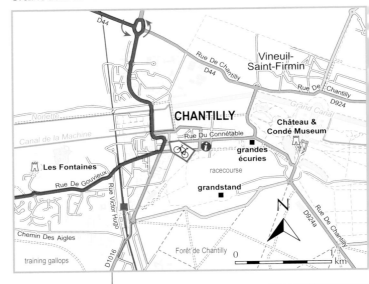

REVERSE ROUTE: CHANTILLY TO BEAUVAIS

From Pl Omer Vallon in **Chantilly** follow D1016 N winding out of town into open country. Turn L at second roundabout (D44) and continue over Oise into **St Leu d'Esserent** (5.5km, 31m) (accommodation, refreshments, camping, tourist office, station).

Go ahead across railway and turn R (Rue Pasteur) at mini-roundabout. At end turn L (Rue de la République) then R at crossroads (D12). Follow road ascending over limestone ridge then descend through **Cramoisy** (10km, 57m) (station). Continue on D12 past **Maysel** L and over river Thérain to Messie. Bear L (D123) and continue to **Mello** (13.5km, 45m) (accommodation, refreshments).

Turn L following D123 back over river into **Cires-lès-Mello** (refreshments, camping, station). Turn R at T-junction (D929) and continue through **Balagny-sur-Thérain** (18km, 42m) (refreshments, camping, station). Pass village-end sign and after 100 metres turn L and follow minor road through Fourneau. Go ahead R over angled crossroads (Rue du Marais, sp Souville) and turn first L (Rue du Abattoir). Continue into Rue Cayeux, becoming Rue

Gambetta, to reach Pl Cantrel in **Mouy** (21.5km, 50m) (accommodation, refreshments, station).

Turn L (Rue Auguste Baudon, D137) and continue to roundabout. Go ahead, then fork R (D512) through Coincourt and on past **Mouchy-la-ville** R. Turn R (still D512) in **Heilles** (26km, 54m) (refreshments, station) and continue through Friancourt to reach T-junction in **Hermes** (29.5km, 51m) (accommodation, refreshments, station).

Turn R (D125) across railway and cycle through town to T-junction. Turn L on cycle track beside D12, and continue past **Ballieul-sur-Thérain** R (33.5km, 52m) and **Rochy-Condé** L (accommodation) to reach roundabout. Turn L (Rue du Général de Gaulle) through **Therdonne** (39.5km, 68m).

Continue past **Wagicourt** L and bear L at roundabout. Zigzag L and R to cross motorway and reach crossroads. Turn L (Ch de Sans Terre) and R (Rue Arthur Magot) then pass under bridge and continue into Rue Lesieur. Where this bears L, continue ahead on cycle track. Emerge on Rue des Aulnaies and continue ahead (Rue Mathéas) to T-junction. Turn L, then bear R to reach main road. Turn L and fork immediately R (Rue du Wage). Pass under bridge and follow cycle track bearing L through carpark and past station. Turn R opposite station then bear half-L (Rue de la Madeleine, sp centre ville). Cycle ahead across Pl des Halles and turn R through Pl Jeanne Hachette. Turn L into pedestrianised Rue St Pierre and continue to cathedral in **Beauvais** (46km, 69m) (accommodation, refreshments, tourist office, cycle shop, station).

CYCLING LONDON TO PARIS

STAGE 10
Chantilly to St Denis market

Start	Chantilly, Pl Omer Vallon (52m)
Finish	St Denis market (30m)
Distance	38.5km (24 miles)
Ascent	184m
Waymarking	None

This stage starts by traversing forests and fields, climbing gently to the edge of the Paris basin, before descending into the *banlieue* (suburbs) of Greater Paris. This latter stretch uses mostly roadside cycle tracks but there are a few stretches on busy roads.

The stone wall on the right is the boundary of Domaine des Fontaines park which surrounds Château Rothschild.

From Pl Omer Vallon in **Chantilly** follow Rue de Paris SW. Turn R (Rue de Gouvieux, D909, sp Gouvieux) and pass under railway out of town. Pass gatehouse of Domaine des Fontaines park R and continue ahead (Rue de Chantilly) using cycle lane R, over three roundabouts. ◄ At fourth roundabout bear L (second exit) downhill into **Gouvieux** (3.5km, 35m) (accommodation, refreshments).

Follow road bearing L (Rue Colliau, sp autres directions) to wind through town. Turn L at T-junction and

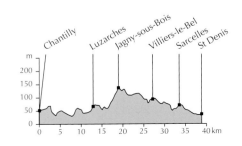

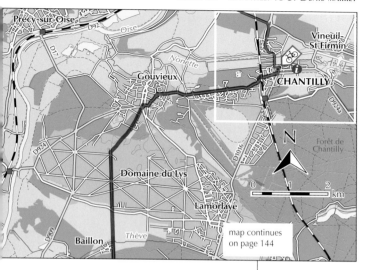

fork L (Place du Général de Gaulle, D162, sp Lamorlaye) beside war memorial. Where road bears L, continue ahead into Ave de la République gently ascending on road with series of traffic calming chicanes. Where this ends, continue ahead on cycle track through trees (Allée Roger Duchêne). Emerge on roundabout and bear ahead L (9ème Ave, fourth exit of six) through **Domaine du Lys** private housing development (accommodation, refreshments). Go ahead over next roundabout, then cross road and go through barriers on cycle track into forest to reach road head in **Baillon** (8.5km, 34m).

Pass village on Rue Santiago Soulas and cycle uphill through forest. Follow road bearing L to reach roundabout in **Chaumontel** (accommodation, refreshments, cycle shop). Turn R (Rue de Paris, first exit) and then go ahead over second roundabout. Continue over third roundabout (Ave du Maréchal Joffre, second exit, sp centre ville) and continue uphill on Rue du Pontcel to centre of **Luzarches** (13.5km, 69m) (refreshments, tourist office, station).

143

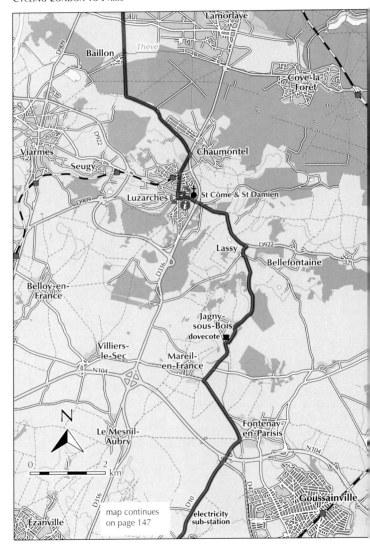

map continues
on page 147

144

Luzarches (pop 4500) was a prosperous medieval walled town astride the old Roman road from Paris to Amiens and Dunkerque with a 13th-century castle and collegiate church. After the town was bypassed by the railways it became a forgotten backwater whose only claim to fame was as the furthest point the German army reached when advancing towards Paris during the battle of the Marne (1914). The population did not regain medieval levels until the 1960s and most modern residents commute to work in the capital. Important buildings include the old castle gateway, church and market hall.

Pass old covered market hall L, and turn L (Rue St Damien, sp Office du Tourisme). Pass 12th-century church L and cross road bridge into open country on D922 (sp Bellefontaine). Turn R at roundabout (D47, sp Lassy) into **Lassy** (16.5km, 60m).

Turn L at T-junction in front of church (Rte du Plessier, D47, sp Jagny-sous-Bois) then fork R and ascend through open country into **Jagny-sous-Bois** (18.5km, 130m). Continue climbing through village on Rue Chef

The lookout tower at Jagny-sous-Bois summit was previously a dovecote

145

The tower that looks like a lighthouse, on the right of the road before the summit, is actually a dovecote that is now a viewing platform.

Villiers-le-Bel is the start of Greater Paris and from here the urban landscape is unbroken.

These are two difficult junctions and D125 is a busy road with no cycle lane.

The tracks of a guided busway are followed to St Denis.

de Ville, passing ruined church L and tree in middle of road, to reach summit (141m). ◄ Follow road downhill through fields and keep ahead at road junction (D9, sp Fontenay-en-Parisis). Turn L at T-junction, using cycle track R, to reach roundabout on edge of **Fontenay-en Parisis** (24.5km, 112m).

Turn R (D10, second exit, sp Villiers-le Bel) and follow road over motorway and straight ahead at roundabout. Join cycle track R then pass enormous **electricity substation** which feeds 17 transmission lines L, and continue downhill through fields past **Bouqueval** L. Go ahead over next roundabout, where cycle track ends, then at third roundabout rejoin cycle track and take first exit past construction depot R. Where road ends continue on cycle track, emerging beside main road and follow this to reach beginning of **Villiers-le-Bel** (27.5km, 97m). ◄

Continue ahead on Ave du 8 May 1945 and go ahead over roundabout onto Ave des Érables, using cycle track R. At next roundabout turn R (D10, sp Sarcelles, first exit) to reach crossroads at second traffic lights (29.5km, 82m) (accommodation, refreshments). Turn L (Ave de Tisson-villiers, D209, sp Sarcelles) and follow this or cycle track R winding through industrial area to reach T-junction (accommodation). Turn R (D125, sp Sous Préfecture) and after 400m, turn L (Ave Paul Langevin, sp Sarcelles-Flanades). ◄ Continue to roundabout and turn R (Ave Charles Péguy) beside North Paris private hospital. Turn L at mini-roundabout (still Ave Charles Péguy) to reach T-junction. Turn R (Ave Paul Valéry) on cycle track R and follow this bearing L beside Bvd Albert Camus in **Sarcelles** (33.5km, 70m) (refreshments).

At crossroads with tracks of guided busway in centre of road, turn R (Ave du 8 Mai 1945, sp St Denis) on cycle track R. ◄ At next crossroads, turn L across road and busway then continue on cycle track beside bus track parallel with dual-carriageway (D316) R. Follow cycle track bearing L beside Bvd Jean Mermoz following busway. After 100 metres, follow cycle track R and L across road and continue on opposite side, following busway through **Pierrefitte-sur-Seine** (refreshments). Bear L following

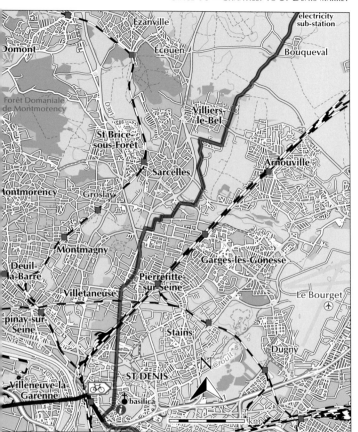

usway into Ave Lénine and pass under railway. Where
ycle track bears R beside cemetery, keep L to follow
ain road over railway. Where main road turns L across
usway, continue ahead on cycle track beside busway
to reach busway terminus at **St Denis** market (38.5m,
0m) (accommodation, refreshments, tourist office, cycle
hop, station).

Louis XII is one of many kings buried in St Denis basilica

ST DENIS

St Denis (pop 110,000) gets its name from Christian martyr Denis who was buried here after bringing Christianity to Gaul in the third century AD. The site of his burial became a church which grew over the centuries into a great basilica, the site of some coronations and the burial place of most French kings from Clovis (AD511) to Louis XVIII (1824).

In contrast to its royal connections, 19th- and early 20th-century industrialisation saw St Denis become one of the largest industrial cities in France. A period of industrial decline since 1970 made it a depressed area with crumbling factories, poor quality social housing, high levels of unemployment and local government controlled by the communist party. A major regeneration plan resulted in construction of many new buildings including the Stade de France.

REVERSE ROUTE: ST DENIS MARKET TO CHANTILLY

From **St Denis** market, cycle N, following road with busway in centre for 5km through **Pierrefitte**. Continue following busway bearing R beside D316 then where busway turns R, cross road and continue on cycle track on other side, still following busway, turning R (sp Sarcelles) into **Sarcelles** (5km, 65m). Turn first L (Bvd Albert Camus) and follow this R beside Ave Paul Valery. Turn first L (Ave Charles Péguy), then turn R at mini-roundabout. At next roundabout turn L (Ave Paul Langevin) to reach T-junction. Turn R (Rte des Refuzniks, D125) then L beside D209, on cycle track L, climbing steadily and winding

The route follows the track of a guided busway between St Denis and Sarcelles

through industrial area. At junction with major dual-carriageway (accommodation, refreshments), turn R (D10, sp Villiers-le-Bel) then L at roundabout (still D10) through **Villiers-le-Bel** L (10km, 84m).

Continue into open country, finally leaving Greater Paris, passing **Bouqueval** R. Go ahead over motorway junction then turn L (D47, sp Jagny-sous-Bois) at roundabout on edge of **Fontenay-en-Parisis** (16.5km, 112m). Continue climbing and at top of hill turn R (D47, sp Jagny-sous-Bois) undulating across plateau (summit 141m) and descend through **Jagny-sous-Bois** (20km, 130m) and **Lassy** (23.5km, 60m). Turn L at roundabout (D922) then cross road bridge and pass church R. Fork R (Rue Abbé Soret) then bear L following one-way system around grassy Pl de la République. Continue on Rue Bonnet to centre of **Luzarches** (25.5km, 69m) (refreshments, tourist office, station).

Turn R by market hall (Rue du Pontcel) then go ahead descending over two roundabouts into **Chaumontel** (accommodation, refreshments, cycle shop). At third roundabout, turn L beside Aldi (Rte du Baillon, fourth exit) and follow road eventually bearing R through forest to **Baillon** (30.5km, 34m). Go ahead (Rue Santiago Soulas) and where this ends, continue on cycle track through forest. Rue Santiago Soulas is one-way with contra-flow cycling permitted. Go over crossroads onto 9ème Ave private road through **Domaine du Lys** private housing development (accommodation, refreshments). Continue over roundabout and at second roundabout bear R ahead on forest track. Emerge on Ave de la République and continue to Pl Général de Gaulle in **Gouvieux** (34.5km, 35m) (refreshments).

Bear R (Rue Colliau, D909, sp Chantilly) and follow this winding through town. Continue past Domaine des Fontaines and Château Rotschild L then pass under railway. Bear L (D1016) to reach Pl Omer Vallon in centre of **Chantilly** (38.5km, 52m).

STAGE 11
St Denis market to Eiffel Tower

Start	St Denis market (30m)
Finish	Eiffel Tower (36m)
Distance	16.5km (10.5 miles)
Ascent	16m
Waymarking	Avenue Verte (occasional), N-S Véloroute

From St Denis the route follows urban canal towpaths, city sidestreets through the Marais and cycle tracks beside grand boulevards to end at the Eiffel Tower on the left bank of the river Seine. It is level and busy, with Parisien cyclists everywhere. An alternative end at Notre Dame cathedral is described in Stage 9 of Avenue Verte.

To visit St Denis basilica, burial mausoleum of French kings, turn left on Rue de la République.

Cycle S across Bvd Carnot into Rue Gabriel Péri, one-way street with contra-flow cycling permitted. Pass covered market hall L and cross Rue de la République. ◀ Continue ahead to reach Pl de la Résistance and turn R beside square. Continue into Rue Désiré Lelay and go ahead across tram tracks (Sq Pierre de Geyter) beside park R. At end turn L parallel with Canal St Denis and bear R to join towpath. Continue along towpath, passing under series of bridges and curve L round huge bulk of **Stade de France** stadium on opposite side of canal R.

> **Stade de France** (capacity 81,000) was built on the site of a former gasworks for the 1998 FIFA World Cup finals. As the French national stadium, it stages international football and rugby matches and finals of national competitions. It also hosts major music concerts. The most noticeable features are the roof which although it weighs 13,000 tonnes appears to float above the stadium and the lower tier of seats which retract to reveal an athletics track.

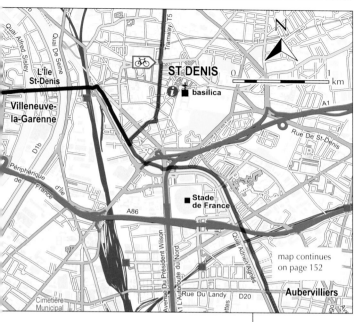

Follow towpath past more locks and bridges. Pass ~~ck 2, where cycle track becomes Quai de l'Allier, and ~o under two road bridges. ▸ Bear L up cobbled ramp ~assing under railway bridge to reach major road junc-~on above Pont de Flandre bridge. Go ahead across ~oad and turn R on cycle track on opposite side. Cross ~ridge and turn L to continue on Quai de la Gironde ~eside canal now on opposite bank, with futuristic build-~gs of **Museum of Science and Industry** in Parc de la ~illette L across canal. Follow cycle track bearing R and ~ontinue on Quai de l'Oise beside Villette canal basin L. ~Vhere this ends, turn R beside Rue de Crimée (cobbled) ~nd immediately L (Quai de la Seine) on cycle track L. ~ontinue parallel with canal basin L to reach T-junction ~nd follow cycle track L to reach square with fountains in ~ont of **Rotonde de la Villette** (8km, 53m).

The first bridge carries the Bvd Périphérique motorway ring road that surrounds central Paris.

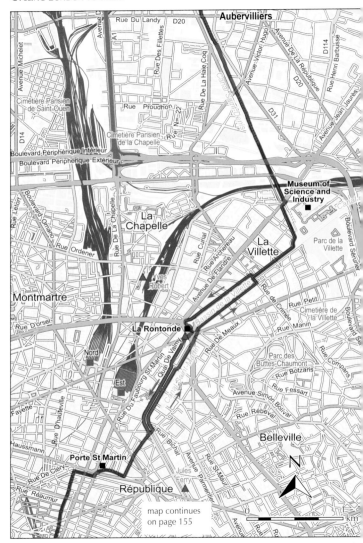

map continues
on page 155

Cycle past La Rotonde R and follow cycle track ~aring R under railway. Cross side road and continue ~ead for short distance on cycle track down middle of ~ue Lafayette. Follow cycle track forking L beside Quai ~ Valmy and continue over crossroads following canal ~ Martin L. Pass two locks and immediately after second ~ck turn R beside number 85 (Rue de Lancry) away from ~nal. ▸ Cross dual-carriageway Bvd Magenta and con-~ue to T-junction in front of bust of Johann Strauss. Turn ~ (Rue René Boulanger) on cobbles and follow street to ~uare with **Porte-St Martin** archway in centre.

Porte-St Martin is a triumphal arch standing on the line of the medieval city walls which was commissioned by Louis XIV in 1674 to commemorate French victories on the Rhine. It is heavily ornamented with three of the four reliefs featuring Louis as Mars, Hercules and Fame.

Bateaux Mouches river cruises are a popular way of seeing Paris from the Seine

Rue de Lancry is a one-way street with contra-flow cycling permitted.

153

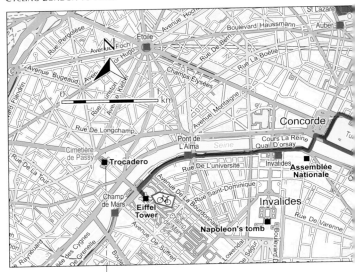

Turn R and L opposite arch into Rue St Martin th
first R (Rue Ste Apolline). At end, turn L (Rue St Den
and follow this ahead across series of crossroads. Pa
square R with Fontaine des Innocents fountain in cen
and continue for 100 metres, turning third R into narrc
alleyway (Rue Courtalon) between buildings 23 and 2
Emerge into Pl Ste Opportune and bear L across Rue c
Halles into Rue des Lavandières Ste Opportune.

Turn R (Rue de Rivoli) and continue past **Louv**
museum L, Palais Royal R and **Tuileries** gardens L
reach Pl de la Concorde. Turn L on contra-flow cy
lane L of square, passing golden gates of Tuileries g
dens L, then bear L to cross river Seine on Pont de
Concorde. ◄ On opposite bank (Rive Gauche) turr
(Quai d'Orsay) and continue past Les Invalides L i
Quai Branly. Where this drops down to pass unc
Pont d'Iéna, turn L across road to reach **Eiffel Tov**
(16.5km, 36m).

The building ahead
is Assemblée
Nationale, the French
parliament building.

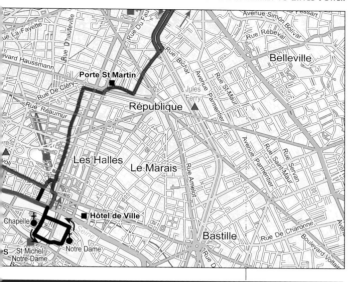

THE EIFFEL TOWER

In 1889, when Paris hosted a world fair to commemorate 100 years since the French Revolution, a competition was held to find a centrepiece for the exhibition. A lattice iron tower designed by the Gustaf Eiffel company was selected, which subsequently became known as the Eiffel Tower. With a height of 324m it became the world's tallest man-made structure, a distinction it held until surpassed in 1930 by New York's Chrysler building. The tower has become a much-loved iconic symbol of Paris with nearly seven million visitors paying to ascend it in 2015. Most ascend by high-speed lifts, but some choose to climb the 1710 steps to the top gallery.

At the time it was built, the tower was not universally popular. A petition by writers, painters and sculptors claimed it would dominate and humiliate the many other prominent buildings in Paris. One of the signatories, the writer Guy de Maupassant, was said to have eaten in the tower's restaurant every day as he claimed it was the only place in the city where he could not see the hideous structure. The tower was intended to last for 20 years, after which time it was to be dismantled. However, subsequent use for radio and television broadcasting has extended its life and it is now a permanent part of the Paris scene.

REVERSE ROUTE: EIFFEL TOWER TO ST DENIS MARKET

From Champs de Mars below **Eiffel Tower** (36m), follow Quai Branly NW par
allel with Seine. Continue into Quai d'Orsay and turn L opposite **Assemblé
Nationale** building R across river on Pont de la Concorde. Turn R along riv
erside boulevard and follow this past **Tuileries** gardens and **Louvre** (both
L). Opposite sixth bridge (Pont au Change) turn L into Pl de la Châtelet (s
République, Stalingrad). Turn is between Fontaine du Palmier column toppe
by golden angel L and Théâtre de la Ville R.

Continue into Bvd de Sébastopol past Tour St Jacques R, then turn L (Ru
de Rivoli). Turn first R into pedestrianised Rue St Denis and follow this throug
square past Fontaine des Innocents L and continue across series of streets an
boulevards. With Porte-St Denis gateway just ahead, turn R beside no246 int
Rue Ste Apolline. Turn second L beside Rue St Martin then follow cycle trac
winding R and L past **Porte-St Martin** gateway into Rue René Boulanger. Ru
René Boulanger can be found behind Théâtre de la Renaissance. Emerge int
Pl Johann Strauss and turn L (Rue de Lancry). After this crosses canal turn
beside Canal St Martin (Quai de Jemmapes). Pass two locks and where roa
ends continue under railway and turn L (Bvd de la Villette). Cycle ahead ove
road junction and bear half-R beside canal L (Quai de la Loire) with **Rotonde
de la Villette** (8.5km, 53m) visible across canal L.

Continue beside canal basin and turn L (Rue de Crimée) over secon
bridge then R (Quai de l'Oise) along opposite bank. Follow cycle track bearin
L beside Canal St Denis, with **Museum of Science and Industry** behind lock R
to reach complicated road junction on next bridge. Turn R then L across tra
tracks to join cycle track along opposite bank. Follow this along towpath pa
three locks and under 10 bridges to pass **Stade de France** L.

Pass lock 5 (with three bridges above) then cycle under next bridge. Jus
after house 3 bear R off towpath onto parallel road. *Avenue Verte continue
along towpath.* Bear R (Sq Pierre de Geyter) beside park L, then go ahea
over tram tracks (Rue Désiré Lelay) and turn L in Pl de la Résistance onto Ru
Gabriel Péri. Follow this to reach guided busway terminus at **St Denis** mar
ket (16.5km, 30m) (accommodation, refreshments, tourist office, cycle shop
station).

AVENUE VERTE
(via Newhaven–Dieppe)

The London Eye is the start of Avenue Verte

STAGE 1
London Eye to Redhill

Start	London Eye (10m)
Finish	Redhill station (78m)
Distance	40.5km (25 miles)
Ascent	320m
Waymarking	CS7 Kennington–Colliers Wood, NCN20 Colliers Wood–M25 motorway, NCN21 M25–Redhill

From London's South Bank this stage joins cycle superhighway CS7 in Kennington and follows this to Colliers Wood. The Wandle Trail is then followed through suburban south London on a mixture of off-road cycle tracks and quiet residential streets. Leaving the capital, the route climbs over the North Downs on minor roads and tracks before descending to the commuter town of Redhill. If you wish to avoid cycling in London, frequent trains from Victoria station run to Coulsdon South and Redhill.

THE LONDON EYE

The London Eye was one of two major attractions constructed in London to celebrate the new millennium in 2000 (the other was the Millennium Dome). The Eye was an immediate success, instantly becoming a much visited landmark that is now ridden by nearly four million people every year. When it opened it was the world's largest Ferris wheel at 135m tall, although it has since been overtaken by new wheels in China, Singapore and Las Vegas. Located on the south bank of the river Thames, close to Westminster, it provides spectacular views of central London. There are 32 pods mounted on the outside of the wheel, and it takes 30 minutes to complete one revolution. Pods are normally filled with fare paying tourists, although individual pods can be booked for special events with a bar and catering facilities. When it opened, the Eye was jointly owned by British Airways and Madame Tussauds with the cost of a ride (one rotation) being BA's most expensive flight on a cost/mile basis, even exceeding Concorde. It was anticipated that the structure would have a short life span and the land on which it was built was acquired on a short lease. When the landowners tried to end the lease after five years there was a public outcry and after a judicial review its life has now been extended by 25 years.

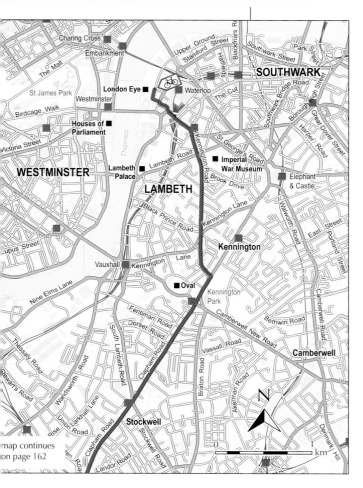

map continues
on page 162

The houses of Parliament in Westminster, across the Thames from the start point

County Hall was seat of London County Council and later Greater London Council until the latter was abolished in 1986. It now houses two hotels and an aquarium.

From Jubilee Gdns in front of **London Eye**, cycle through barriers on Belvedere Rd, passing old Lond County Hall R. ◄ Opposite County Hall, bear L acr Forum Magnum Sq and cross road at light control crossing. Turn R and follow road bearing L around cular Park Plaza Westminster Bridge hotel then bear se ond L (Westminster Bridge Rd) under Waterloo railw bridge. Fork R opposite Lambeth North tube station (A2 sp Kennington) past Christ Church L into Kennington F Continue ahead over Lambeth Rd passing Geraldine Ma

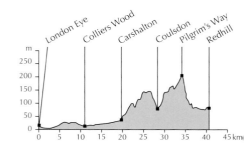

armsworth park L. ▶ Continue ahead over Kennington ane to T-junction then turn R (Kennington Park Rd) past **ennington Park** L to reach major road junction beside **val tube station** R (2.5km, 9m). ▶

Cycle ahead on Clapham Rd (A3) passing Stockwell nd Clapham North tube stations and go under railway ridge to reach **Clapham Common** (5.5km, 25m). Bear (Clapham Common South Side, A24) past clock-ower R and continue past Clapham South tube station. ycle ahead into Balham High St past **Balham station** Continue past Tooting Bec station and along Upper ooting Rd to **Tooting Broadway**. Road becomes Tooting igh St and continues to reach **Colliers Wood tube sta-on** L (11.5km, 15m) and end of CS7.

Continue ahead over road junction into **Merton** igh St (A238), then cross river Wandle and pass Merton us garage R to reach next light controlled crossing. eside entrance to Sainsbury's/M&S superstore, bear L cycle track beside river Wandle (do not cross pedes-an bridge over river). ▶ Emerge onto Station Rd then gleg R and L through small arch to cross Merantun ay. Continue on gravel track beside Wandle, past erton mills with old waterwheel L. Cross Windsor Ave, en pass entrance to Deen City farm R and continue ead on gravel track, eventually bearing R away from ver. Zigzag across Croydon–Wimbledon tram tracks d continue ahead winding through **Morden Hall** rk. Bear R at first junction of tracks and L at next junc-on. Follow track over two small bridges then turn L er main river and continue through park, bearing R tree-lined avenue to emerge on Morden Rd (A239) side Surrey Arms pub L. Turn R on multi-use pave-ent beside road, then cross road at traffic lights. Turn on service road then L to rejoin Wandle Way beside er. Follow cycle track, turning R over circular bridge d continue winding through woodland. Pass bridge then turn R on next bridge across sidestream. Turn again to emerge beside Bishopsford Rd (A217) and ntinue past **Tooting and Mitcham football ground** L 5.5km, 21m).

The domed classical style building in the park is the Imperial War museum.

From Kennington Park Rd, Cycle Superhighway 7 (CS7) which is marked in blue asphalt is followed for 9.5km to Colliers Wood.

Wandle Trail cycle track is followed for 7km.

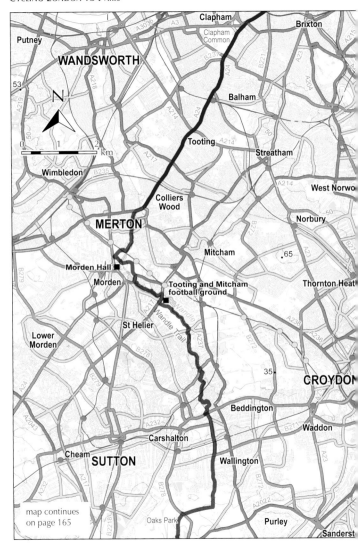

map continues on page 165

Turn L through gateway (sp Bishopsford House) and
here this road turns R, continue ahead on gravel track.
ear R beside Wandle, eventually forking L to emerge
 road (Watermead Lane). Dogleg R and L across
iddleton Rd and follow cycle track bearing L away
m road. Briefly ride beside Budge Rd, then bear L (sp
ckhurst Ave) into woods. Turn L over Wandle then
k R and continue on cycle track to reach Culvers Ave.
ogleg R and L across road and follow cycle track to
ackbridge Rd.

Turn R over river, then L between river and house
4. Emerge onto The Causeway, bearing R at rounda-
ut and turn second L (River Gdns). Follow road curving
then continue into Mill Lane and pass under railway
idge. Turn L on cycle track opposite house 63, then
again on small bridge over Wandle. ▸ Follow cycle
ack ahead with Papermill Cl R and continue between
uses. Turn L through barriers into Arcadia Cl and fol-
w this winding R and L on red brick block surface to
ach T-junction. Turn L (Devonshire Rd) following road
aring R and turn first R (Parkfields Cl). At end continue
ead into Westcroft leisure centre car park. Turn L oppo-
e main entrance of centre to emerge on Westcroft Rd
d follow this to T-junction with High St (A232) close to
x and Hounds pub in **Carshalton** (19.5km, 38m).

At this point the route
leaves Wandle Trail.

Cross road at controlled lights and turn L along
cle track on opposite side. Turn R (Park Lane) and start
cending. Continue over railway bridge into Boundary
l and go ahead at small roundabout, following cycle
ck wrong way round junction. Go ahead again at next
ini-roundabout. Where road turns R, continue ahead
elegraph Track) through bollards to reach top of climb
02m) at crossing of tracks between market gardens.
rn R (Oaks Track) along ridge, then descend through
rrier to reach Woodmansterne Rd. Dogleg R and L
ross road into **Oaks Park**. Follow tree-lined road uphill
st golf course L, then winding past café and craft cen-
 R. Continue ahead on gravel track, bearing L and R
 reach Croydon Lane (A2022). Cross road and turn L
side **Mayfield** lavender fields.

Mayfield lavender farm is a popular tourist attraction

Mayfield lavender farm is a small family business that has resurrected commercial growing of lavender on 25 acres in north Surrey, an area where it was once an important crop. The business was established in 2002 to supply organic lavender to Yardley, an English fragrance house. However, after Yardley changed ownership in 2005, Mayfield was left without a customer. They have subsequently developed their own range of lavender products and expanded by opening a nursey and shop in Ewell. The fields are a popular tourist attraction from late May–mid September, particularly in July and August when the lavender is flowering.

At end of lavender fields turn R (Carshalton Rd, B27 Follow this uphill past Old Walcountians sports club L, reach T-junction at top of hill by **Woodmansterne** chur (25km, 146m). Turn L (Rectory Lane, still B278) a after 250 metres turn L on unmade track through tree

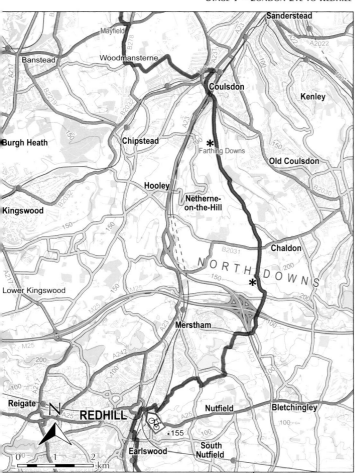

ollow this bearing R, then fork L on track beside woods
. Emerge through bollards into The Mount and continue
head through residential area to T-junction. Turn R (Grove
ane) downhill and bear L at T-junction (Woodmansterne

Rd). Go ahead over crossroads (The Avenue) to reac
T-junction. Turn R (Brighton Rd, A2032) under railw
bridge passing **Coulsdon Town station** L. Fork L at cobble
mini-roundabout and bear L (A237) at traffic lights to read
roundabout. Follow cycle track L around roundabout ar
take second exit (B276) under road and railway bridg
past **Coulsdon South station** R (29km, 88m) (accommod
tion, refreshments, cycle shop, station).

Follow road bearing R uphill and fork R (Dow
Rd). After 100 metres, fork L (Ditches Lane) and fo
low this climbing onto broad grass swathe of **Farthi**
Downs.

FARTHING DOWNS

The grassy ridge and ancient woods of Farthing Downs, which are owned
and managed by the city corporation and lie near the most southerly point of
London, are the largest area of semi-natural chalk downland in the capital.
The grassland holds several rare herbs and wild-flowers including the legally
protected greater yellow rattle. In the past, rabbits grazed the downs until
their numbers were greatly reduced by myxomatosis. Nowadays the corporation graze sheep and cattle to maintain the grassland.

This area, above the forests and marshes of lower ground, was inhabited
in ancient times and the remains of Iron Age cultivation can still be traced
on the ground, over 2000 years since the land was tilled. Later the Saxons
buried their leaders in 16 seventh-century barrows alongside the earlier
earthworks.

There are fine views over London and a toposcope identifies key landmarks. A solitary beech is all that remains of a grove of seven trees blown
down by a hurricane in 1987. Replacement trees have been planted.

Pass carpark and board marking corporation
London's ownership of the area and continue climbin
now alongside woodland to reach Chaldon church
(32.5km, 164m). Route now undulates past **Chaldon** vi
lage L with road becoming Hilltop Lane. One final asce
brings you to Hilltop farm R. Here at summit (204m
route crosses Pilgrims' Way and extensive views of Surre
Weald open out ahead. ◄ Road now winds steep

For details about the
Pilgrims' Way see
Stage 2, classic route.

ownhill, becoming Warwick Wold Rd and crossing
25 London orbital motorway. ▶ Continue to T-junction
nd turn R (Bletchingley Rd) under M23 motorway. Pass
oppice Lea care home R and turn L through gate on
ravel cycle track into Spynes Mere nature reserve, wind-
ng between worked out aggregate lakes to reach farm
oad at Mercers farm. Track can by muddy when wet.
ontinue ahead and dogleg L and R across Nutfield
Marsh Rd to reach Inn on the Pond pub L (37.5km, 85m)
efreshments).

After crossing the
motorway, the route
becomes NCN21.

Opposite pub, turn R on narrow track beside
Nutfield cricket ground, passing club house R. Continue
n Chilmead Lane to reach T-junction. Cross road and
urn R on unmade track behind hedge parallel with road.
fter 120 metres, turn L through gate, continuing par-
llel with road. Turn L away from road circling disused
ullers' earth quarry now being used for landfill. ▶ Fork
beside lake then turn R over railway and R again into
avendish Rd. Continue over bridge to reach road and
urn L (Noke Drive). Pass Royal Mail sorting office R to
each traffic lights. Turn R under railway bridge, using

The track can be
muddy when wet.

Avenue Verte passes beside Nutfield cricket ground

cycle track R, to reach roundabout in front of **Redhi** **station** (40.5km, 78m) (accommodation, refreshment cycle shop, station).

> **Redhill** (pop 18,000) is mainly a commuter town for London (to the north) and Gatwick/Crawley (south). It developed on the south side of the North Downs after a turnpike road opened through a gap in the downs in 1818. With the coming of the railways, and the digging of Merstham tunnel under the downs that emerged nearby, the town grew and assumed the name Redhill in 1856. A local industry used to be the quarrying and processing of fullers' earth, a product used in the textile industry for fulling (degreasing) wool. The last quarry closed in 2000.

REVERSE ROUTE: REDHILL TO LONDON EYE

From **Redhill station** cycle E under railway bridge and turn L (Noke Dr). Just before gates of Warwick school, turn R over bridge and continue on Cavendish Rd. Turn L on cycle track over railway and L again past old quarries. Just before reaching road, turn R over wooden bridge and continue parallel with Cormongers Lane, soon bearing R along road. Turn L (Chilmead Lane) and follow track past **Nutfield** cricket club L to Inn on the Pond pub R (3km, 85m) (refreshments).

Dogleg L and R across Nutfield Marsh Rd and continue past Mercers farm and through fields to reach Bletchingley Rd. Turn R under M23 motorway and L (Warwick Wold Rd) ascending to cross M25 motorway. Continue ascending over summit (204m) on Hilltop Lane and go ahead (Church Lane) past **Chaldon**. Continue (Ditches Lane) to reach large grassy expanse of **Farthing Downs**. Follow road descending to reach T-junction and bear L (Marlpit Lane) under rail and road bridges by **Coulsdon South station** L (11.5km, 88m). *To avoid cycling in London, frequent trains run from Coulsdon South to Victoria station in the city centre.*

Follow cycle track circling roundabout and take third exit (Brighton Rd). Fork R through Coulsdon town centre, passing under railway and turn L uphill (The Avenue). Continue over crossroads and fork third R (Woodmansterne Rd) continuing uphill on Grove Rd. At top of hill (144m)

Wandle Trail crosses the river Wandle in Morden Hall park

turn L (The Mount) and at end continue ahead on cycle track winding through trees. Turn R at T-junction (Rectory Lane) and R again (Carshalton Rd) opposite **Woodmansterne** church (15.5km, 146m).

Cycle downhill past **Mayfield** lavender fields L and turn L on gravel track just before mini-roundabout. Turn R across road into **Oaks Park** and follow cycle track bearing L. Pass café R, and follow tree-lined road downhill past golf course L. Dogleg R and L across main road onto track uphill through fields. At crossing of tracks turn L downhill then continue ahead on Boundary Rd passing through edge of **Wallington**. Go over railway and continue (Park Lane) to reach T-junction close to Fox and Hounds pub in **Carshalton** (21km, 38m).

Dogleg L and R across Acre Lane into Westcroft Rd and continue into leisure centre carpark. Bear R and emerge on Parkfields Cl. Turn L (Devonshire Rd) and second R (Arcadia Cl). At end turn R on cycle track between houses then continue over river Wandle and turn R to reach road. *Wandle Trail cycle route is followed for 7km.* Turn R (Mill Lane) and continue on River Gdns to T-junction. Turn R (The Causeway) and at end continue on cycle track. Turn R (Nightingale Rd) and use cycle lane L of road to cross Wandle. After bridge, turn immediately L through railings and continue on cycle track to Culvers Ave. Dogleg R and L across road continuing on cycle track beside Wandle. Fork L and after 120m L again, then cross river and bear R through woods.

Bear R beside Budge Lane to reach Middleton Rd then dogleg R and L into Watermead Lane. Where this ends continue ahead on gravel track beside Wandle, eventually turning L away from river. Pass **Tooting and Mitcham football ground** R then turn R beside Bishopsford Rd (25km, 21m).

Just before bridge over river Wandle, cross road onto cycle track L of road over parallel bridge, then turn L following Wandle Trail beside river. Cross bridge 70 and turn immediately L. At path junction, fork L, continuing with Wandle L to reach service road beside Morden Rd. Turn R, then cross road at traffic lights and just before Surrey Arms pub, turn L into **Morden Hall park**. Follow cycle track through park between avenue of trees, bearing L to cross Wandle. Turn R after bridge and follow track over two smaller bridges and continue winding through park. Cross tram tracks and follow Wandle Trail out of park. Turn R over small bridge then bear L beside river. Emerge onto road and go ahead beside pylons. Cross Windsor Ave and continue beside river to Merantun Way. Go across road and through small archway, following river past Sainsbury's/M&S superstore R to Merton High St in **Colliers Wood** (29km, 16m).

Turn R and continue past office tower R to join Cycle Superhighway 7 (CS7). *CS7, which is marked in blue asphalt, is followed for 9.5km to Kennington.* Continue ahead on Tooting High St (A24) (past **Tooting Broadway station**) and Upper Tooting Rd (past Tooting Bec station). Pass **Balham station** on Balham High St and continue past Clapham South station L. Pass **Clapham Common** L (35km, 25m) and continue on Clapham Rd (A3) past Clapham North and Stockwell stations to reach major road junction by **Oval tube station** (38km, 9m).

Continue ahead (Kennington Park Rd) and turn L (Kennington Rd, A23) at next traffic lights, leaving CS7. Go ahead over Kennington Lane and Lambeth Rd to reach T-junction by **Lambeth North station**. Turn L (Westminster Bridge Rd) passing under Waterloo railway bridge. Fork R before circular Park Plaza hotel then bear R (York Rd) and turn immediately L across Forum Magnum Sq. Turn R (Belvedere Rd) past County Hall L to reach Jubilee Gdns and **London Eye** L (40.5km, 10m).

STAGE 2
Redhill to Eridge

Start	Redhill station (78m)
Finish	Eridge station (59m)
Distance	49km (30.5 miles)
Ascent	193m
Waymarking	NCN21

This is a stage of two parts. The first heads south undulating gently over the Surrey greensand ridge then level across the Surrey Weald passing through extensive built-up areas of Horley, Gatwick and Crawley on a mixture of cycle tracks and minor roads. Leaving Crawley everything changes as the route turns east following a rural cycle track along a disused railway that connected Three Bridges with Tunbridge Wells. This climbs gently onto the mid-Wealden ridge, skirting the Worth forest, to reach a high point (134m) in East Grinstead, before descending through Ashdown forest into the Sussex Weald.

From roundabout beside **Redhill station**, cycle S along Marketfield Way (A23), passing Abbot pub R. At next roundabout continue ahead (Brighton Rd) under railway bridge, joining cycle track L. Pass red-brick Furness House R and turn L (Brook Rd). Follow this bearing R

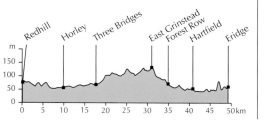

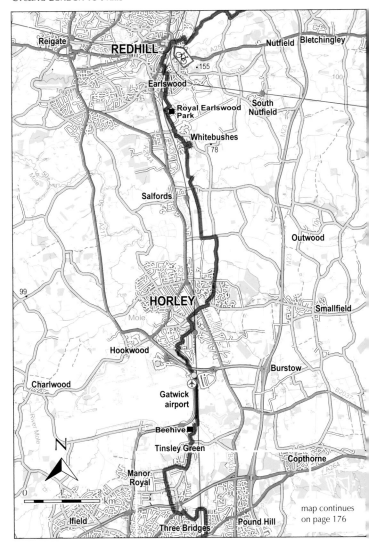

map continues
on page 176

reach T-junction. Turn L (Hooley Lane) under railway
ridge and first R (Earlsbrook Rd). Continue ahead over
aggered crossroads (still Earlsbrook Rd). Pass approach
ad to **Earlswood station** R and continue ahead into
rinces Rd to reach crossroads at entrance to **Royal
arlswood Park**, formerly Royal Earlswood asylum.

ROYAL EARLSWOOD ASYLUM

*The former Royal Earlswood asylum
is now private apartments*

Royal Earlswood asylum, which opened in 1855 as a hospital for people with
learning difficulties, was built using money raised by public subscription with
subscribers including Queen Victoria and the Prince of Wales. A royal charter was conferred in 1862. The first superintendent, John Down, was famous
for identifying 'Down's syndrome'. Patients were taught manual trades such
as carpentry, printing, brush making, gardening and farming. The asylum
remained a charitable trust until 1955, then was part of the NHS until closure
in 1997. The main building, workshops and gate lodges are preserved as listed
buildings; the rest has been redeveloped into residential apartments.

Turn R (Asylum Arch Rd) and just before railway
ridge turn L onto cycle track through trees. Emerge
eside Three Arch Rd bearing R to reach roundabout.

Go ahead (second exit) and fork immediately R on grave
cycle track into woodland. Follow this winding past hou
ing development at **Whitebushes** to reach T-junctio
Turn R (Bushfield Dr) and follow this road bearing
Turn R (Yeoman Way) and R again (Spencer Way). Afte
125 metres, turn L on gravel track (Green Lane) betwee
trees. Emerge on concrete road from Dean farm and tu
R. Go ahead over crossroads past Perrywood busine
park L and continue on cycle track (Gail Lane). Whe
this reaches T-junction, follow cycle track sharply L f
short distance then continue ahead on Cross Oak Lan
After 300 metres, turn R on gravel track (Lake Lane) an
follow this through new housing developments int
beginning of Horley. Go ahead over four crossroads an
continue on road (Langshott Lane). Fork R (still Langsho
Lane) passing through barriers to reach T-junction. Turn
(Smallfield Rd) and continue over crossroads into Static
Rd. Where this bears L, join cycle track R of road and fo
low this down ramp and under railway. Emerge on Hig
St and turn L. Continue ahead into pedestrianised cent
of **Horley** (9.5km, 57m) (pop 22,000) (accommodatio
refreshments, cycle shop, station).

At end of pedestrian area, turn L (Victoria Rd) the
R at second traffic lights and immediately L (The Drive
After 75 metres, fork R (Cheyne Walk) and continue t
roundabout. Turn L (Upfield, first exit) then R (Micha
Cres) to reach T-junction. Turn L (Crescent Way) and
into Riverside. Where this ends, go ahead over strea
and turn L on cycle track along riverbank. Turn L at junc
tion of tracks and follow cycle track bearing R und
motorway and Gatwick North terminal shuttle railwa
Continue under airport service road to emerge bedsid
main road. Fork L passing behind bus shelters and follo
cycle track bearing L away from road and R behind Sou
terminal building of **Gatwick airport** (11.5km, 60m
(accommodation, refreshments, cycle shop, station).

Gatwick, despite being London's second airport
(after Heathrow), is a major international airport
with 40 million passengers annually, making it the

A lily pond close to Gatwick airport terminal buildings

ninth busiest airport in Europe. Originally the site of Gatwick Park racecourse, it began use as an airfield in the late 1920s with the first terminal building, the 'Beehive', being built in 1935. Gatwick was designated as London's second airport in the 1950s and subsequent developments have included two major terminals. Further growth is restricted by runway capacity; it's one runway making it the world's busiest single runway airport, with up to 55 flights per hour. Plans to build a second runway have been proposed several times but have been blocked by local opposition.

Dogleg R and L around air conditioning plant and continue on cycle track between railway L and main road R. Cross bridge over stream and turn L through carpark. At end of carpark, bear R to reach roundabout in Gatwick City Place. Turn L on dual carriageway (Beehive Ring Rd, first exit), then continue ahead over second roundabout and curve R past **Beehive** building R. Turn L at T-junction (Gatwick Rd) joining cycle track L. Go ahead over roundabout, after which cycle track switches to R. At next roundabout turn R (Fleming Way, cycle track still R) and continue to traffic lights. Turn L (Newton Rd), passing

Vent-Axia factory R to reach T-junction. Turn R (Manc Royal) and immediately L at traffic lights onto cycle trac between bollards. Follow this winding between facto ries and emerge on road. Turn R (Woolborough Lane then continue ahead through bollards and under roa bridge to reach T-junction. Turn L and immediately R o cycle track into parkland. Fork L at junction of tracks then cross main road at traffic lights and turn L and onto cycle track beside North Rd. Go ahead over stag gered crossroads (Pond Wood Rd) and turn L on cycl track between houses 52–54 to reach main road. Cros road by underpass R, then turn sharply R on cycle trac beside road (Hazelwick Ave). Bear L at first roundabou (Bycroft Way) then go ahead at second roundabout cross ing entrance to Tesco. Follow road bearing R (St Mary Drive) under railway bridge and continue to T-junctio with dual carriageway close to **Three Bridges statio** (18km, 68m) (in Crawley, accommodation, refreshments cycle shop, station).

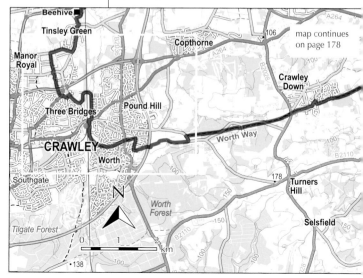

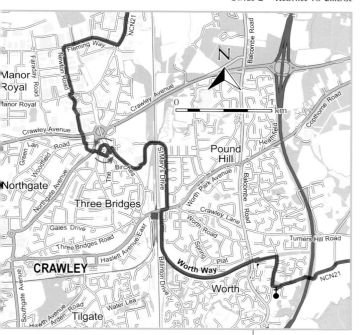

Three Bridges is a district of **Crawley** (pop 110,000), one of seven 'new towns' circling London built from the 1950s to absorb overflow population growth from the city. After a slow start, the town has grown into a successful and prosperous community with one of the lowest unemployment rates in Britain. Industrial development is concentrated in one area, Manor Royal, between Crawley and Gatwick.

Turn R and immediately L (Station Hill, cycle track R) parallel with railway (do not go under railway bridge) and continue into Billinton Dr. Where cycle track ends, cross road and soon turn L on gravel track through wooden barriers into trees. ▶ Follow railway embankment between Crawley districts of **Pound Hill** L and **Worth** R.

This is the beginning of the Worth Way cycle track along an old railway line that, with a few short deviations, runs to the end of the stage.

177

After 1km zigzag R and L above cutting and continue 1 reach road. Turn R (Church Rd) through leafy residenti area and then third L (also called Church Rd). After 7 metres, bear L on cycle way (Worth Way) into woodlan Cross motorway bridge and cycle through open countr Cross approach road to Worth Lodge farm and go ahea through gateway on gravel track to reach Turners Hill R Turn L (cycle track L), then where cycle track ends, tur R across road and through gateway to rejoin route of o railway. Just before site of Rowfant station, bear L awa from railway, cross road and continue past industri area in trees R. Climb R onto embankment to rejoin o railway and cross another quiet road. Emerge onto O Station Cl and continue to reach staggered crossroads **Crawley Down** (25km, 116m) (refreshments).

Continue ahead (Burleigh Way), with Royal Oak pi L, then turn second R (Woodland Drive) and L (Haz Way). Where road bears L, turn second R (Cob Cl) ar at end continue on cycle track into woodland. Emerg

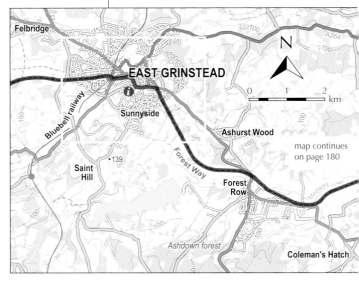

STAGE 2 – REDHILL TO ERIDGE

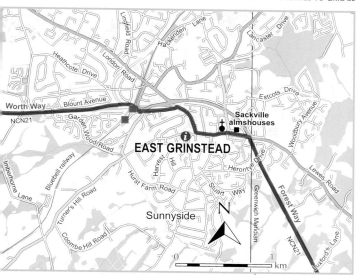

...eside carpark for East Grinstead station, cross approach ...oad and continue over narrow footbridge. Descend past ...tation entrance and turn L to reach roundabout. ▶ Go ...traight ahead (Railway Approach, second exit) and at ...nd turn R (London Rd). Follow this to mini-roundabout ...nd turn L (High St) in centre of **East Grinstead** (30.5km, ...32m) (accommodation, refreshments, tourist office, ...ycle shop, station).

Descent is down a series of widely spaced steps.

EAST GRINSTEAD

East Grinstead (pop 24,000) sits astride the mid-Wealden ridge in West Sussex near the borders of East Sussex, Surrey and Kent with extensive views over Ashdown forest. By the entrance to St Swithun's churchyard are memorials to three martyrs killed in 1556 for refusing to renounce Protestantism. The town's most notable building, Sackville college almshouse, stands nearby. This cloister-like sandstone building was built in 1609 and was later the place where the carol 'Good King Wenceslas' was written. Its composer,

Sackville college almshouse in East Grinstead

John Neale, is buried in the churchyard. High Street and Middle Row have some of the longest runs of timber-framed buildings in England.

At the railway station is the newest addition to the town's tourist attractions: the Bluebell railway, Britain's first and most popular preserved railway. It started operating trains in 1960 between Sheffield Park and Horsted Keynes along part of the previously closed East Grinstead–Lewes line, and in 2013 extended its services to East Grinstead. Services along the 18km line are run using preserved steam locomotives hauling vintage carriages.

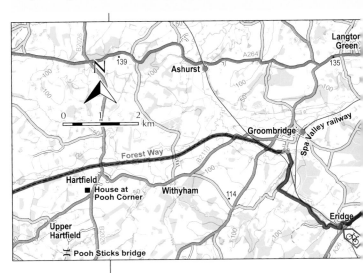

Cycle through town passing alleyway L leading to S Swithun's church and **Sackville almshouse**. Go ahead a

ini-roundabout (Lewes Rd, B2110) and at larger round-
out turn R across road through barrier onto cycle track
wnhill (**Forest Way**). ▶ Cross residential road and con-
ue on gravel track into open country. Cross main road
22) at traffic lights and soon reach site of old station in
rest Row** (35km, 64m) (accommodation, refreshments,
mping, cycle shop). ▶

After station, beside lattice mobile phone mast R, fork
onto narrow gravel track. Although waymarked, track is
sy to miss. Cross small bridge over river Medway (at
is point a narrow stream) and continue along old rail-
ay to **Hartfield** (41km, 47m) (accommodation, refresh-
ents) where cycle track doglegs L and R around house
d gardens built on old station site. ▶

Continue to cross quiet road and pass site of
ithyham station. Drop down R to cross Hambridge
(B2110), where old railway overbridge has been
moved, and up again to reach and ride parallel with
isting railway line. After 1km, drop down R a second
ne, to cross B2188, then continue on cycle track. Turn
under railway and pass sewerage works R to reach edge
Groombridge** (46km, 48m) (refreshments). ▶

Turn R (Corseley Rd), eventually ascending. At trian-
lar junction, turn L (Forge Rd, sp Eridge station) and
llow road undulating through woods and fields to
junction. Turn L to reach **Eridge station** L (49km, 59m)
freshments, station).

At this point the
route crosses the
Greenwich meridian
into the eastern
hemisphere.

To visit the village,
turn right at the traffic
lights and follow A22.

Near Hartfield, on
the edge of Ashdown
forest, is an area
made famous by
AA Milne as the
setting for his Winnie
the Pooh stories;
Pooh Sticks bridge
is 3km south.

To visit the village
turn left.

REVERSE ROUTE: ERIDGE TO REDHILL

From **Eridge station** follow road SW for short distance and turn R (Forge
Rd). Ascend to reach triangular junction and turn R (Corseley Rd, sp
Groombridge), descending over railway to reach sewerage works L at begin-
ning of **Groombridge** (3.5km, 48m) (refreshments).

Turn L on gravel cycle track passing under railway then dogleg across a
road and continue on **Forest Way** along old railway trackbed. Dogleg across
another road and pass Withyham station to reach **Hartfield** (8.5km, 47m)
(accommodation, refreshments). Pass new houses on old station site then
dogleg L and R under bridge and continue on Forest Way to **Forest Row**

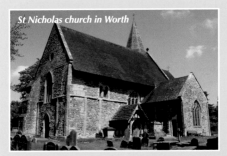
St Nicholas church in Worth

(14.5km, 64m) (accommodation, refreshments, camping, cycle shop). Fork R uphill and turn L onto quiet road. Cross main road and continue on cycle track. Cross side road and fork L uphill to reach roundabout. Turn L (Lewes Rd) then follow High St through **East Grinstead** (19km, 132m) (accommodation, refreshments, tourist office, cycle shop, station).

Bear R (London Rd) in town centre then L at mini-roundabout (Railway Approach). Go ahead over next roundabout then turn R into station carpark and follow cycle track over railway footbridge. Footbridge has steps, so you must carry your cycle onto bridge. Pass carpark L, and follow another old railway cycle track (**Worth Way**) to emerge on road (Cob Cl) in **Crawley Down** (24km, 116m) (refreshments).

Bear L (Hazel Way) then turn R at T-junction (Woodland Dr) and L into Burleigh Way. Dogleg across Station Rd into Old Station Cl and at end continue on cycle track through Worth Forest, passing site of Rowfant station to reach Turners Hill Rd. Turn L on cycle track R, then turn R and pass farm L. Cross motorway then pass **Worth** church L and bear R to reach road. Turn R (Church Rd) then just before narrow bridge turn L on cycle track beside old railway cutting. After 225 metres, turn R (easy to miss) zig-zagging down into cutting. Continue to Billinton Dr and turn R passing back of **Three Bridges station** L (31km, 68m) (in Crawley, accommodation, refreshments, cycle shop, station).

Turn R beside Haslett Ave then turn L across main road into St Mary's Dr. Follow this under railway and continue into Bycroft Way. Pass Tesco R and turn R (Hazelwick Ave) at roundabout. Bear L on slip road and turn L (North Rd). Turn second R then dogleg L and R over main road. Continue ahead and bear R onto cycle track. Dogleg L and R into Woolborough Lane and pass under road bridge. Where road turns R, bear L on cycle track through barriers. At end turn R and L (Newton Rd) then where this ends, turn R on cycle track beside Fleming Way. Bear L at roundabout beside Gatwick Rd and continue ahead over second roundabout. Turn R (Beehive Ring Rd) past

Beehive building L. Go ahead over first roundabout, then turn R at second into carpark. Bear L past warehouse over stream and turn R on cycle track beside railway. Follow this under south terminal building of **Gatwick airport** (38km, 60m) (accommodation, refreshments, cycle shop, station).

Before end of terminal, turn L and R parallel with main road. Fork R under motorway and through Riverside Park. Where cycle track ends, turn R over bridge and continue to T-junction. Turn L (Crescent Way) and R (Michael Cres). At end turn L (Upfield) and R at roundabout into Cheyne Walk. Follow this bearing L into The Drive. At end turn R and fork immediately L at traffic lights (Victoria Rd). Continue to second traffic lights and turn R into pedestrianised High St in **Horley** (40km, 57m) (accommodation, refreshments, cycle shop, station).

Go ahead over crossroads and fork immediately R on pedestrian underpass under railway. *The right fork into the underpass is easy to miss.* Turn L (Station Rd) and continue into Smallfield Rd. Turn second L (Langshott Lane) then go ahead through bollards and bear L at road junction to reach cycle track. Continue out of Horley and through fields to T-junction. Turn L (Cross Oak Lane) then fork R on cycle track and R again (Gail Lane) just before main road. Pass Perrywood business park R and continue ahead on Deans Farm Lane. Just before farm, turn L on cycle track to **Whitebushes**. At end turn R (Spencer Way) and L (Yeoman Way) to T-junction. Turn L (Bushfield Dr) and follow this bearing R. Just after Denton Cl, turn L on cycle track through trees to main road. Turn L and go ahead over roundabout. Where road bears R, continue ahead on cycle track past **Royal Earlswood Park** R.

Turn R (Asylum Arch Rd) and L at crossroads (Princes Rd). Continue past **Earlswood station** L into Earlsbrook Rd. Go ahead over staggered crossroads and turn L at T-junction (Hooley Lane) under railway. Immediately after bridge turn R on cycle track beside Brook Rd. At end turn R (Brighton Rd), then pass under bridge and fork R at roundabout (Marketfield Way) to reach second roundabout by **Redhill station** (49km, 78m) (accommodation, refreshments, cycle shop, station).

STAGE 3

Eridge to Newhaven

Start	Eridge station (59m)
Finish	Newhaven ferry terminal (2m)
Distance	62.5km (39 miles)
Ascent	573m
Waymarking	NCN21 (Eridge to Polegate), NCN2 (Polegate to Newhaven)

This stage starts by following NCN21 on minor country roads through the Sussex Weald, climbing over two ridges to reach Heathfield, from where the Cuckoo Trail is followed along a disused railway line on a long steady descent south to Polegate. At Polegate, the NCN2 (South Coast cycleway) is joined and followed on a winding but generally level route on minor roads, cutting through the South Downs by way of the Cuckmere gap, to reach Newhaven ferry terminal.

Easy to miss, the route follows the track marked 'Private'.

From front of **Eridge station**, follow road NE. Where roa turns sharply L beside Huntsman pub, continue ahead o side road and fork immediately R through gate. ◀ Pas under road bridge and fork L onto gravel track windin steeply uphill for short distance through woods. Continu parallel with main road then emerge onto layby besid road. Follow road for short distance then fork R to joi course of old road. Turn R at triangular junction ont

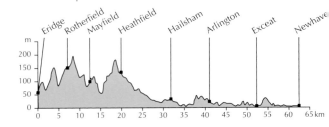

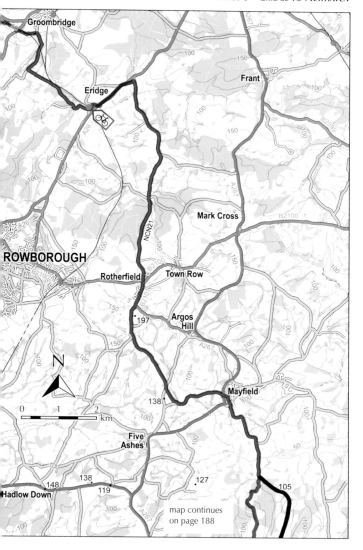

Groombridge

Frant

Eridge

ROWBOROUGH

Mark Cross

Rotherfield

Town Row

• 197

Argos
Hill

N

138

Mayfield

0   1   2
km

Five
Ashes

• 127

Hadlow Down

148   138

119

105

map continues
on page 188

undulating minor road (Sham Farm Rd) first descend
ing then ascending 100m over a ridge and descending
85m into a coombe. Ascend again (Eridge Lane), through
woodland, to reach Catts Inn pub by junction with B210
in **Rotherfield** (7.5km, 156m) (refreshments).

Go ahead through village (High St becoming South
St then Mayfield Rd) into open country and continue
ascending on Cottage Hill to reach summit (193m)
Gables End. Descend through woodland and fork L
(Five Ashes Rd, sp Five Ashes) continuing downhill
After 2km, fork L (Fir Toll Rd, sp Mayfield). Bear L at
T-junction and follow winding road to reach Mayfield
by-pass. Cross road using central reservation and follow
zigzag cycle track up embankment on opposite side
Emerge on Fir Toll Cl and continue to reach T-junction
on edge of **Mayfield** (12.5km, 109m) (accommodation
refreshments). ◄

To visit the village
turn left onto
Station Road uphill
and continue into
High Street.

Turn R (Stone Cross) and after 200 metres, turn L and
bear immediately R (Newick Lane) winding up and over
small hill. Cross bridge over river Rother and continue
ahead. Just after bend L, with row of half-tiled cottages
turn R through gate on grassy cycle track into field.

Alternative route to Heathfield avoiding rough track
To avoid rough track main route uses to reach Heathfield
continue on Newick Lane ascending steadily to reach
A265 main road. Turn R along A265 then turn L at traffic
lights into Tower St.

The alternative
route rejoins here.

Follow this as it becomes very rough track winding
steeply uphill through woods (ascending 125m)
emerge on Marklye Lane. Continue uphill to reach traffic
lights at top of hill and go ahead across A265 main road
into Tower St. ◄

To visit the town
centre, turn right
(Station Road) uphill
to reach High Street.

After 75 metres turn R (Downs View) and at end
turn L (Cuckmere Rise), then R (Marshlands Lane) and L
(Highcroft Cres). At end turn L (Gibraltar Rise) to reach
T-junction with Station Rd near centre of hilltop town
Heathfield (19.5km, 132m) (accommodation, refresh
ments, camping, cycle shop). ◄

Turn L then R (Newnham Way) and L again beside car park through barriers onto start of **Cuckoo Trail** cycle track along course of old railway which is followed for 16km, descending all the way. Dogleg across two roads as trail leaves Heathfield then continue through open country. Between two road crossings route passes 'Frenches Halt'

▶ Pass **Maynard's Green** (refreshments, camping) and continue to site of station in **Horam** (23.5km, 63m) (camping) where cycle track briefly diverts away from old railway. Bear L on Hillside Drive and where this ends, continue on track between houses. Cross Downline Cl and rejoin cycle track. Continue through open country, then cross side road which leads to **Hellingly** (29km, 23m) (camping).

Pass site of Hellingly station and continue across traffic lights at Horsebridge Rd (A271). At beginning of Hailsham, follow Cuckoo Trail forking L under bridge, then where trail ahead becomes pedestrians only, turn R (The Cedars) into residential estate and turn L beside house 38 to rejoin trail. Pass through barrier then fork R under road bridge and reach carpark on site of old station (32km, 23m) in **Hailsham** (accommodation, refreshments, camping). ▶

Frenches Halt, a garden on the Cuckoo Trail decorated to look like a level crossing

This house has been decorated to look like a railway level crossing complete with train sounds.

To visit the town centre, fork left before the road bridge.

187

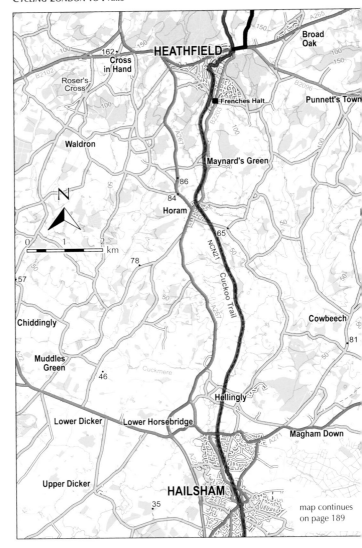

map continues
on page 189

Hailsham (pop 20,500) is a market town on a site inhabited since pre-Roman times. The site was captured by Saxon invaders in AD491 who built a settlement here (…ham suffix in Anglo-Saxon means 'forest clearing'). A market charter was granted in 1252 and a weekly livestock market has been held ever since, nowadays the last market remaining in Sussex. Its future was in doubt after 1997 when the market site was sold for redevelopment as a supermarket but it was reprieved in 2012 when it was shown that the nearest operating markets were in Ashford (Kent) or Salisbury (Wiltshire). The town's oldest industry is rope making and the town has a grisly past as the official producer of hangman's ropes for use throughout the British Empire. Ropes are still made, in a modern factory on the same site, but nowadays for yachtsmen not hangmen.

Turn L before car park and R beside Station Rd. continue past Common Lake L then turn R (Lindfield Dr) nd immediately L (Freshfield Cl). At end pass through

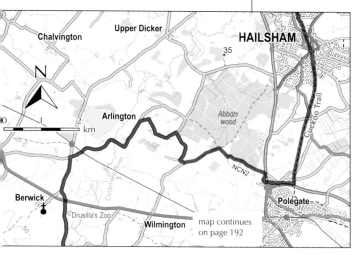

To reach Polegate (accommodation, refreshments, camping, cycle shop, station) continue ahead over bridge.

A mammoth car boot sale is held here every Sunday.

barrier to rejoin cycle route along old railway. Cycle through open country, crossing a series of minor road to reach cycle bridge over dual carriageway A27. A this point leave the NCN21 and join the NCN2. ◄ Turn immediately R before bridge, parallel with road. Pass turning circle R and continue on gravel track to emerge beside Bay Tree Lane. Follow this under A22 road bridge to reach entrance of Cophall Farm L (36.5km, 14m). ◄

Bear R, then continue parallel with A22 and after 100 metres turn L on gravel track through trees. Dogleg L and R past another entrance to Cophall farm and continue winding through **Abbots wood**. At next crossing of track turn L through barriers to emerge on farm road (Robin Post Lane) and continue past farm. At triangular junction turn R (Thornwell Rd, sp Arlington) then R again (Bayley Lane) at next triangular junction. Reach T-junction and turn L (Wilbees Rd) then follow road winding through fields to arrive at crossroads in **Arlington** (41.5km, 12m) (refreshments).

Turn L opposite Yew Tree inn then after 800 metres turn R at T-junction (Chilver Bridge Rd) and continue under railway bridge. Go ahead over crossroads near Berwick station (refreshments, station) and turn immediately L on cycle track beside Station Rd. Where cycle lane ends continue on road, passing turn R that leads after 600 metres to **Berwick village**.

This area of Sussex was closely associated with the **'Bloomsbury set'**, a group of English writers, artists and philosophers who met in the Bloomsbury district of London between 1907–1930 to discuss aesthetic and philosophical questions. The group included Virginia Woolf, her husband Leonard, Lytton Strachey and John Maynard Keynes. Three other members of the group (Vanessa Bell, Quentin Bell and Douglas Grant) decorated the village church in Berwick with four major murals and many smaller works painted in a flamboyant and colourful way known as the Bloomsbury style.

The interior of Berwick church was decorated by the Bloomsbury set

Continue to roundabout and cross A27 main road to reach **Drusillas zoo** and amusement park L (45.5km, 5m). Continue ahead on Alfriston Rd then turn L at triangular junction (Lullington Rd, sp Lullington). Cross river Cuckmere and turn R at next triangular junction. Pass turn-off R that leads over pedestrian bridge to **Alfriston** (accommodation, refreshments, camping) and continue to T-junction in Lullington.

Alfriston (pop 850) is a pretty village on the opposite bank of the Cuckmere with many historic buildings. St Andrew's Parish Church, nicknamed the cathedral of the South Downs due to its size, stands on a mound in the middle of the village green. Nearby, the 14th-century clergy house is a timber framed Wealden hall house with a thatched roof. It was the first property acquired for preservation by the National Trust (1896). The Star Inn was formerly a religious hostel, built (1345) to house monks on their way between Battle abbey and Chichester, before becoming an inn during the 16th century. During the 18th–19th centuries the village was the base for a smuggling gang whose leader was caught and transported to Australia in 1830.

Turn R through the hamlet (The Street) to reac **Litlington** (49km, 8m) (refreshments). Follow roa winding past marshy flood plain of river Cuckmere with White Horse carved into hillside above to reac T-junction with main road at **Exceat**. Turn R (A259) fo lowing causeway with Cuckmere haven L and cros Exceat bridge to reach Cuckmere Inn pub (52km, 4m (refreshments).

To avoid rough track, continue on A259 and turn L at beginning of Seaford..

Turn L through pub carpark and continue throug gate on rough cycle track beside salt marsh L. ◀ Ju before entrance to Cuckmere Valley nature reserve, tur R through gate uphill through fields on grassy trac Turn L at top of hill and R after 80 metres. At begin ning of built-up area turn L on gravel road (Chyngto Lane). Pass through barrier and turn R (Chyngton Wa with fields L and housing R. Bear R and L at elongate roundabout (Chyngton Rd) past golf course L. At en

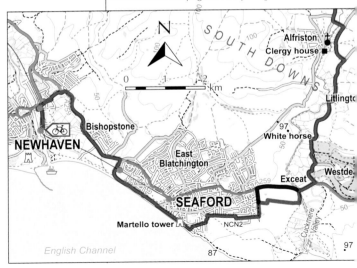

Litlington white horse on the South Downs escarpment

f golf course turn L uphill (Southdown Rd) then turn R Corsica Rd) and continue along Cliff Gardens (gravel) o reach seashore. Turn R along Esplanade and immedi- ely after **Martello tower** L bear L onto concrete track eside beach. ▶ Continue past The Salts, an open grassy rea near centre of **Seaford** (57km, 0m) (accommoda- on, refreshments, camping, tourist office, cycle shop, ation). ▶

Where route beside beach becomes pedestrian only, ear R on asphalt cycle track beside Marine Parade and ollow this bearing R away from beach. Pass Bishopstone ation R (station) and cycle under railway bridge to reach -junction. Turn L (A259) on cycle track L and follow oad past **Bishopstone** on hillside R. Pass through car ark, continuing beside main road, then fork R beside narled tree stump following cycle track as it winds long more or less parallel to road. Continue ahead at rst roundabout (A259, first exit) and go ahead again A2109, second exit) at second roundabout. Cross rail- ay level crossing beside Newhaven Town station, then ear L beside bus stop and turn L into **Newhaven** docks 2.5km, 2m) (accommodation, refreshments, camping, ycle shop, station). Go ahead over mini-roundabout and ollow signs to ferry terminal.

For information about Martello towers see the classic route, Stage 3.

To reach Seaford centre, turn right (Dane Road) just before The Salts.

There are two or three sailings daily depending c the season connecting Newhaven with Dieppe in north ern France. The crossing takes four hours.

Newhaven (pop 12,500) developed around the mouth of the river Ouse after a breakwater was constructed to prevent longshore drift of shingle blocking the river mouth. A cut was dug below Castle hill and from 1850 the London, Brighton and South Coast railway started to develop harbour facilities. Cross-channel shipping from Newhaven reached its zenith during the two world wars when facilities were greatly expanded to handle military traffic. Since the opening of the Channel Tunnel, services have declined with a reduced service operating to Dieppe in France.

Newhaven fort on Castle hill was built between 1864–1871 to defend the harbour. It was the largest military construction in Sussex and the use of concrete for part of the defences was the first use of this material in British military architecture. The fort was vacated by the army in 1962 and is now open as a preserved monument.

REVERSE ROUTE: NEWHAVEN TO ERIDGE

At exit from **Newhaven** docks (accommodation, refreshments, camping, cycle shop, station) turn R on cycle track R beside Grove Rd (B2109). Cross railway and continue to roundabout. Go ahead beside A259 (second exit) and continue over second roundabout onto cycle track winding beside saltmarsh R of road. Pass **Bishopstone** L (station) and follow cycle track turning R beside Marine Parade under railway. Bear L along Esplanade beside beach past **Seaford** (5.5km, 0m) (accommodation, refreshments, camping, tourist office, station).

Pass **Martello Tower** R and turn second L on gravel road. Continue on Corsica Rd and turn L at end (Southdown Rd). Turn R at crossroads (Chyngton Rd) beside golf course then continue over roundabout into Chyngton Way. Turn L at end on gravel track past farm R and pass through barrier. Turn R through fields then zigzag L and R and descend on grassy track. Turn L

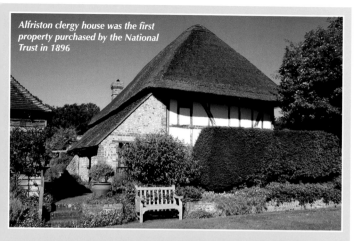

Alfriston clergy house was the first property purchased by the National Trust in 1896

before river Cuckmere to reach Cuckmere Inn beside Exceat bridge (10.5km, 4m) (refreshments).

Turn R over river then L (Litlington Rd) at **Exceat**. Follow road winding through **Litlington** (13.5km, 8m) (refreshments) and continue to Lullington. Turn L (sp Alfriston) and follow road bearing L over Cuckmere to reach T-junction. Turn R (sp Berwick station) then continue past **Drusillas zoo** and amusement park R (17km, 15m) and go ahead over roundabout. Turn R at crossroads before **Berwick station** (refreshments, station), pass under railway and follow winding road to **Arlington** (21km, 12m) (refreshments).

Turn R by Yew Tree Inn through fields then R again (sp Polegate). At triangular junction turn L (Thornwell Rd) and L again at next junction (Robin Post Lane). Where this ends continue ahead on gravel track and after 250 metres turn R at crossing of tracks. Cycle through woodland, doglegging L and R beside entrance to Cophall farm. Bear R beside A22 to reach rear entrance of farm (26km, 14m) (accommodation, refreshments in Polegate service area; camping, cycle shop, station in Polegate).

Bear L beside slip road to pass under A22 then follow cycle track bearing R beside A27 embankment R to reach T-junction of cycle tracks. Turn L onto **Cuckoo Trail** (NCN21). *Cuckoo Trail cycle track is followed for the next 16km.* In **Hailsham** (30.5km, 23m) (accommodation, camping, refreshments), bear R and L onto Station Rd. Cycle past built-over old station site then turn L beside carpark and R under road bridge to regain Cuckoo Trail.

Fork L at junction of tracks passing under bridge. Further on in Upper Horsebridge, follow route winding between houses built over old railway then turn L beside house 1A to continue on Cuckoo Trail past **Hellingly** (33.5km, 23m) (camping). In **Horam** (39km, 63m) (camping) again wind between houses then pass site of old station and continue past **Maynard's Green** (refreshments, camping). Dogleg across two road junctions then follow cycle track between houses to end of Cuckoo Trail in **Heathfield** (43km, 132m) (accommodation, refreshments, camping, cycle shop).

Turn R (Newnham Way) and immediately L (Station Rd). Turn R (Gibraltar Rise) and R again (Highcroft Cres) to reach T-junction. Turn R (Marshlands Lane) then L (Cuckmere Rise) and R (Downs View). At end turn L (Tower St) then continue ahead over traffic lights and fork R (Marklye Lane) downhill into open country. *This route is rough and can be muddy when wet. For the alternative route turn right at the traffic lights (A265) and then turn left (Newick Lane); follow this for 3km to rejoin the main route at the bottom of the descent.* Continue ahead on track winding downhill. Fork L (sp Tigers Haven) and just before gate turn L again on rough track through trees and fields to reach main road. *The alternative route rejoins here.* Turn L and follow road over small hill then descend to T-junction in **Mayfield** (50km, 109m) (accommodation, refreshments).

Turn R uphill (Stone Cross) and after 200 metres turn L (Fir Toll Cl). Follow cycle track zigzagging down to cross A267 and continue on Fir Toll Rd opposite, descending to cross river. Ascend and fork R at triangular junction (sp Rotherfield) continuing uphill. Turn R at T-junction (Five Ashes Rd) and R again at next T-junction (Cottage Hill). Descend to reach **Rotherfield** (55km, 156m) (refreshments).

Go ahead through village (High St) then bear R (North St) beside Catts Inn. Continue on Eridge Lane, first descending through woodland then ascending on Blackdon Hill. Continue onto Sham Farm Rd at first descending then ascending for short distance to reach triangular junction. Turn L (Old Eridge Rd) and continue into lay-by beside A26. Just before end of lay-by, fork L descending on narrow track between trees. At end, turn R under main road then L by Huntsman pub to reach **Eridge station** (62.5km, 57m) (refreshments, station). *The route into Eridge is private road with permissive use.*

STAGE 4

Dieppe to Neufchâtel-en-Bray

Start	Dieppe ferry terminal (0m)
Finish	Neufchâtel-en-Bray, old station (78m)
Distance	37km (23 miles)
Ascent	90m
Waymarking	Avenue Verte (yellow provisional signs to Arques-la-Bataille, then green signs)

After leaving Dieppe on quiet roads, the route follows a voie verte along the course of a disused railway line, ascending very gently all the way to Neufchâtel-en-Bray.

From **Dieppe ferry terminal** follow exit road to reach roundabout at port entrance. Turn sharply R (Quai de la Marne, first exit, sp centre ville) and follow road back past port with white chalk cliffs rising L. Go ahead (first exit, sp centre ville) at roundabout and follow road (still Quai de la Marne) bearing L beside entrance to inner harbour. Continue into Quai de la Somme and turn R over Pont Colbert swing bridge. Continue ahead (Quai du Carénage, D925) and turn fifth L (Rue Guillaume Terrien) immediately after digital signboard L. Pass carpark L and

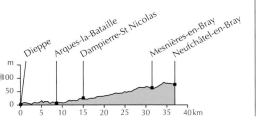

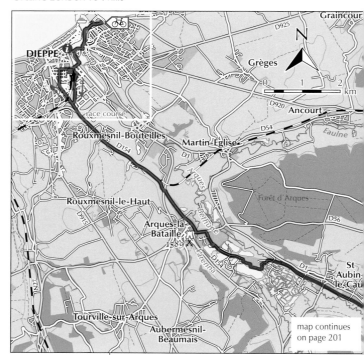

map continues
on page 201

at end go ahead R over staggered crossroads into Rue
Edouard Lavoine with old dock L. Bear R and continue
along quayside R to reach complicated road junction
near to centre of **Dieppe** (2.5km, 5m) (accommodation,
refreshments, tourist office, station).

DIEPPE

Dieppe (pop 30,000) grew up around an 11th-century castle and a small
port that provided a connection between Normandy and Norman Britain.
After a lengthy period under English control during the Hundred Years' War
(1337–1453), the town was captured by the French in 1435. The Norman

castle was replaced by the current castle in 1443. Subsequent development of the harbour made Dieppe a leading port for trans-oceanic exploration and trade with the Americas, Africa and Asia. Over the years, the port was steadily expanded and industries such as shipbuilding, tobacco and ivory developed. During the 19th century Dieppe became an upmarket resort with hotels, theatre, casino and race track frequented by the cream of European nobility. This reached a peak before the First World War, after which decline began in both industry and tourism. After capture by the Germans in 1940, Dieppe was the site of a failed Allied landing in August 1942 during which over 2000 Canadian soldiers perished. A memorial in the old theatre is dedicated to this landing. Afterwards many buildings were cleared from the seafront and the beaches were mined to prevent further landings. Decline continued post-war. Unable to handle container ships, commercial shipping came to an end. High unemployment and low wages made Dieppe one of the most depressed towns in France. Subsequent regeneration has renovated much of the centre and improved tourist attractions including the golf course and leisure pools.

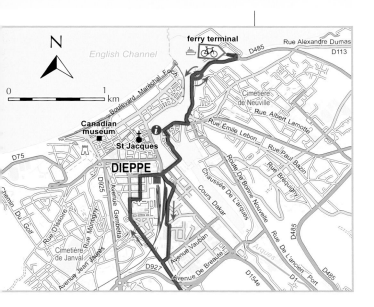

Arques-la-Bataille castle, site of a victory for Henri IV during the religious wars

Turn L through barrier marked 'bus', then cross road, passing station R, into Ave Normandie Sussex. After 200 metres, fork R (Rue de Stalingrad), soon joining cycle track R, and continue ahead past roundabout. At end, turn R (Ave Vauban) over railway crossing then L (Rue du Général Chanzy) at T-junction. Pass under road bridge and continue ahead (D154, Rue du Champ de Courses) past racecourse behind houses L and through **Rouxmesnil-Bouteilles** (5km, 9m) (accommodation, refreshments, camping, cycle shop). Continue on Rue de la Croix de Pierre (D154) ahead over roundabout into **Arques-la-Bataille** (8.5km, 11m) (accommodation, refreshments, camping).

The **Battle of Arques** (1589) was fought during the French Wars of Religion between the mainly Protestant forces of King Henri IV and those of the Catholic League commanded by the Duke of Mayenne. Despite a large inferiority in numbers (8000 versus 35,000), Henri's forces held on for 14 days until relief arrived in the form of troops sent by Queen Elizabeth I of England, after which Mayenne withdrew leaving Henri victorious. Both sides suffered heavy losses. Before he left Arques,

Henri scratched a message with his diamond ring *'Dieu gard de mal ma mie'* (God protects my heart from evil).

Fork L beside calvary cross (Rue St Julien, D54), passing parish church R, then follow road bearing L. Just before railway crossing turn R on cycle track R of Pl de la Gare, passing sports club R and carpark L. Turn L beside lake and bear immediately R between Ch des Prairies L and lake R. Pass sailing club R and bear R before entrance to aggregates depot. Follow cycle track winding between trees L and lake R. Dogleg R and L across approach road of aggregates depot to reach voie verte cycle track along

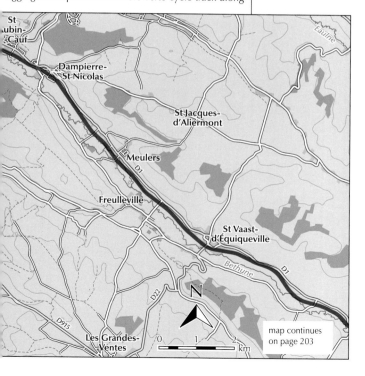

map continues on page 203

201

Voie verte is followed for 40km to Serqueux in the next stage.

course of disused railway. ◄ Turn R and follow voie verte past **St Aubin-le-Cauf** (13km, 16m).

Continue past old station in **Dampierre-St Nicolas** (15km, 24m), then past **Meulers** (18km, 25m) (accommodation) and old station at **St Vaast-d'Équiqueville** (21.5km, 37m) (refreshments). Route continues through open country passing **Osmoy-St Valery** (26.5km, 50m) and **Bures-en-Bray** (28.5km, 63m) to reach old station in **Mesnières-en-Bray** (32km, 62m) (accommodation, refreshments).

> The 16th-century chateau in **Mesnières-en-Bray** (pop 1000) really looks the part, being built in the style of a Loire château with pepperpot towers, central courtyard, moat and formal gardens. Used as a prison during the revolution it fell into decay, but afterwards was renovated by its former owners. In the late 19th century it became a boys' school run by a monastic order and later a horticultural college. Badly damaged by fire in 2004, it is undergoing restoration with the completed parts open to visitors.

Voie verte continues through open country and crosses side road leading to St Martin-l'Hortier R (accommodation). Pass under road bridge to reach old station in **Neufchâtel-en-Bray** (37m, 78m) (accommodation, refreshments, camping, tourist office).

> Most of the buildings in the small Norman town of **Neufchâtel-en-Bray** (pop 4750) were destroyed by German bombing during the Battle of France in June 1940. Some, including Notre Dame church and the Mathon-Durrand museum, were restored to original designs but the main administrative and cultural buildings (town hall, courthouse, theatre and meeting hall) were replaced by four new buildings, each in a distinctive style, grouped beside the old castle mound. Traditional materials were used, applied in innovative ways. The district is best known for Neufchâtel cheese, a soft creamy cheese with a bloomy rind produced in a distinctive heart shape.

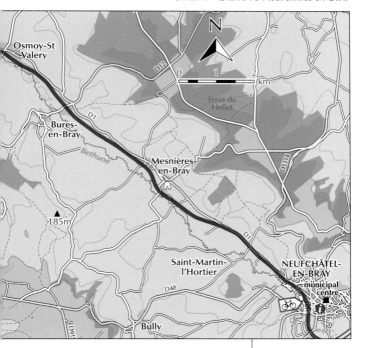

REVERSE ROUTE: NEUFCHÂTEL-EN-BRAY TO DIEPPE

From old station in Neufchâtel-en-Bray, cycle N on voie verte along old railway trackbed passing under road bridge. Continue past side road leading to St Martin-l'Hortier L (accommodation) and **Mesnières-en-Bray** (5.5km, 62m) (accommodation, refreshments) with attractive château R.

Voie verte continues past **Bures-en-Bray** (9km, 63m), **Osmoy-St Valery** (11km, 50m), **St Vaast-d'Équiqueville** (16km, 37m) (refreshments), **Meulers** (19.5km, 25m) (accommodation), **Dampierre-St Nicolas** (22.5km, 24m) and **St Aubin-le-Cauf** (24.5km, 16m).

Where voie verte ends, turn L and dogleg across main road to follow cycle track winding alongside series of old aggregate pits. Pass aggregates depot R and bear L beside access road (Ch des Prairies). Zigzag L and R past

The Avenue Verte at Mesnières-en-Bray

sports club and continue into Pl de la Gare. Turn L on main road (Rue de la Chaussée, D54) and follow this bearing R through **Arques-la-Bataille** (29km, 11m) (accommodation, refreshments, camping).Go ahead over roundabout and through **Rouxmesnil-Bouteilles** (32,5km, 9m) (accommodation, refreshments, camping, cycle shop). Pass racecourse R and go under road bridge, continuing ahead on Rue du Général Chanzy. Cross railway and go ahead over roundabout (Rue Thiers) then turn R (Rue Jules Porte) past hospital R. Turn L at roundabout (Ave Pasteur) and R at third crossroads (Bvd Georges Clémenceau) past **Dieppe station** R (35km, 5m) (accommodation, refreshments, tourist office, station).

Continue ahead (Quai du Tonkin) beside inner harbour L then bear L (Quai Guynemer) between arms of harbour. Turn R at end (Quai de Carénage) and pass over Pont Colbert swing bridge. Turn immediately L (Quai de la Somme) and continue into Quai de la Marne. Go ahead at roundabout by business centre L and continue to roundabout at entrance to **Dieppe ferry terminal** L (37km, 0m).

STAGE 5

Neufchâtel-en-Bray to
Gournay-en-Bray

Start	Neufchâtel-en-Bray, old station (78m)
Finish	Gournay-en-Bray, Pl Nationale (99m)
Distance	45km (28 miles)
Ascent	265m
Waymarking	Avenue Verte (yellow provisional signs after Serqueux)

This stage, which crosses the Bray (a region similar to the Sussex Weald), starts by following a cycle track ascending gently along an old railway trackbed to Serqueux and the spa town of Forges-les-Eaux. From here minor roads are followed undulating across rolling limestone hills through a succession of small hamlets before descending into Gournay-en-Bray.

From old station in **Neufchâtel-en-Bray**, follow cycle track S along old railway trackbed. Pass under motorway and through **La Béthune** (2.5km, 92m). ▶ Continue past **St Saire** (6km, 99m) (accommodation, refreshments) and **Beaubec-la-Rosière** (accommodation) to reach railway junction on edge of **Serqueux** (14km, 164m) (station).

The right turn at the railway crossing leads to Neuville-Ferrières (refreshments).

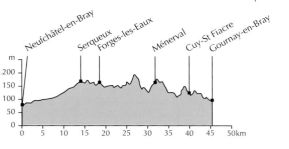

205

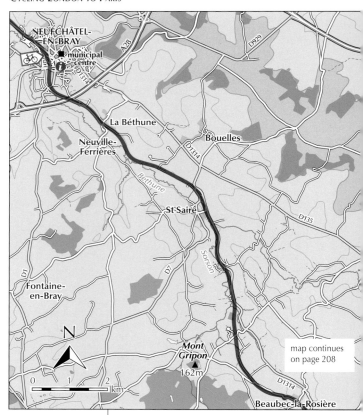

map continues
on page 208

Bear R beside railway, dropping down to T-junction
then turn L (D83) under railway and R through barrier
onto cycle track parallel with railway. Follow track bear
ing L away from railway, then turn R at T-junction ascend
ing on quiet country road (D13). Cross railway bridge
and bear L through barriers onto cycle track. Follow thi
curving L and descending. Bear R then go ahead acros
main road. Zigzag L and R downhill then turn L ont
cycle track along route of another old railway. Follow thi

escending through trees. After 1.25km, take small turn L
off cycle track to reach road. Turn R (Rue des Coquerels)
nd go ahead at crossroads (Rue du Dr François le Roy)
nd over another crossroads into Rue Jules Ferry. Turn R
t end (Rue Marette, D13) and continue to T-junction.
Turn L (Rue de la République) to reach centre of **Forges-
es-Eaux** (18.5km, 163m) (accommodation, refreshments,
amping, tourist office, cycle shop).

As its name implies, **Forges-les-Eaux** (pop 4250) is
a town of iron and water. In Roman and medieval
times, local ore deposits were used to produce iron.
Later in the 17th and 18th centuries the town's hot
springs made it a popular spa resort patronised by
French monarchs and the royal court. The waters
from four springs have a high iron content and are
said to be good for many maladies. The casino's
popularity is due to its proximity to Paris, the result
of a law prohibiting casinos being built closer to
the capital.

Bear R ahead (D915, sp Gaillefontaine), passing
own hall L, and after 75m fork L (Rue du Maréchal

*Forges-les-Eaux
casino is the
nearest to Paris*

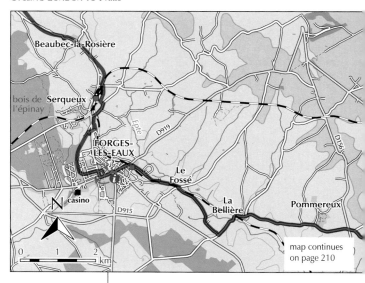

map continues
on page 210

Rue des Laitiers is a one-way street with contra-flow cycling allowed.

Leclerc, D919, sp Gaillefontaine). Cross railway crossing and turn R (Pl de la Gare), parallel with railway. Go ahead on quiet country road (Rue des Laitiers becoming Rue de la Voie). ◀ Continue to T-junction in hamlet of **Le Fossé** (20.5km, 148m) (accommodation, refreshments). Turn R across railway and immediately L beside railway (Rue du Pont Bain, sp La Bellière) to reach T-junction. Turn L (Rte de la Haie, D61) and follow road winding through fields then across railway to pass church L at **La Bellière** (23.5km, 141m) (accommodation).

Continue ahead past **Pommereux** (25.5km, 146m) L then ascend steeply to reach crossroads near brow of hill. Go straight ahead then fork R (Rue Artus de Fricourt, D120, sp Haussez) winding downhill through open fields to reach T-junction. Turn R and immediately fork R (D130, sp Saumont la Poterie) to reach road junction in **Haussez** (29.5km, 132m).

Turn R (D41, sp Ménerval) then pass under railway and fork L (Rue du Moulin, D130, sp Ménerval). Cross ver Epte then follow road winding through fields and scending past church L to reach **Ménerval** (31.5km, 55m). Turn L (Rte de Gournay, D16) then fork L (sp ampierre-en-Bray) and descend through open country. fter 2.5km, turn R on small unmarked sideroad. ▶ After 0 metres, turn L at T-junction (Ch des Planques) and llow road to reach T-junction in **Dampierre-en-Bray** 5.5km, 123m) (accommodation).

The right turn is easy to miss; it is opposite a left turning sp Hyaumet.

Turn R and immediately L (D84), then con-nue through fields to roundabout. Turn R (D16, sp uy-St Fiacre) and continue descending to cross river esangueville. Ascend then turn first L (Rue du Mort) inding and ascending over ridge before descending to ossroads in **Cuy-St Fiacre** (39.5km, 124m).

Go ahead past church R (Rue St Martin) then fork L ut of village to reach T-junction in hamlet of **Le Ménillet**. rn R (Rue de l'Epte, D916) and continue through elds. Turn L on quiet country road (sp Vieux-St Clair), en follow road bearing R by derelict farm and pass rough hamlet of **Vieux-St Clair** (43km, 101m). Turn L T-junction passing industrial estate L. Follow road curv-g R to reach main road and bear L (Rue de l'Abreuvoir, 916). Go ahead over traffic lights and continue into Rue es Bouchers to reach Pl Nationale in centre of **Gournay-n-Bray** (45km, 99m) (accommodation, refreshments, urist office).

Gournay-en-Bray (pop 6400) developed around a collegiate church, built in the 12th century to house the relics of St Hildevert, a former bishop of Meaux. The River Epte runs through the town in three streams along which several mills developed. The principal industry however is the production of dairy products, as evidenced by the Butter Hall of 1821, which is nowadays used as a cinema. In the adjoining town of Ferrières-en-Bray, a major dairy operated by Danone was the original factory of Charles Gervais who developed a cylindrical shaped cream cheese enriched with extra cream which he branded as Petit-Suisse.

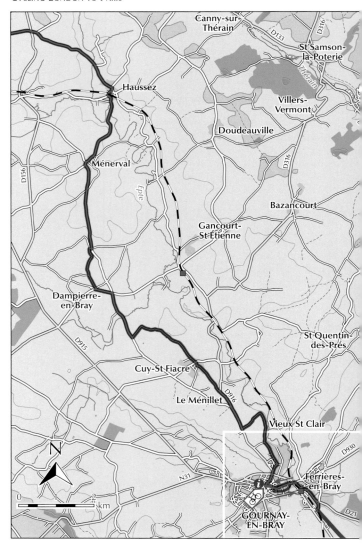

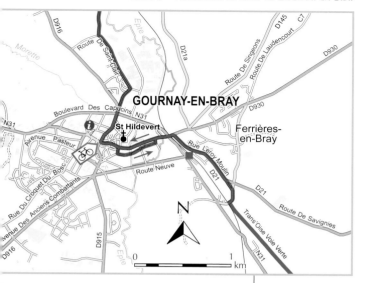

REVERSE ROUTE: GOURNAY-EN-BRAY TO NEUFCHÂTEL-EN-BRAY

Many villages have an old lavoir *(laundry-house) like this one in Haussez*

From Pl Nationale in **Gournay-en-Bray**, follow Rue des Bouchers NE (D916), continuing into Rue de l'Abreuvoir. Cross N31 and fork R (Rte de St Clair). Bear L past industrial area R then turn R (sp Vieux-St Clair). Follow this bearing L and turn R at T-junction (D916). Pass first fork L to Cuy-St Fiacre, then take second fork L (in Le Ménillet) and continue through **Cuy-St Fiacre** (5.5km, 124m), bearing R past church L into open country.

Follow road bearing L and turn R at T-junction (D16). Turn L at roundabout (D84) to **Dampierre-en-Bray** (9.5km, 123m) (accommodation). Turn R and immediately L, then fork R after end of village. Turn R and L onto D16 to **Ménerval** (13.5km, 165m).

Fork R (D130) through fields then turn R (D41) under railway into **Haussez** (15.5km, 132m). Turn L in village (D130) and L again (D120). Bear L (D61), then go ahead over crossroads and through **Pommereux** (19.5km, 146m). Go across railway in **La Bellière** (21.5km, 141m) (accommodation) and cross river Epte. Turn R (C2) to reach beginning of **Le Fossé** (24.5km, 148m) (accommodation, refreshments).

Turn R (D9) across railway and immediately L (Rue de la Voie) beside railway. Continue on Rue des Laitiers, past old station L, to T-junction and turn L (D919) across railway into **Forges-les-Eaux** (26.5km, 163m) (accommodation, refreshments, camping, tourist office, cycle shop).

Turn R at T-junction (D919) beside tourist office and L at crossroads in town centre (D915). Turn R (Rue de Verdun) passing church R, then turn L at T-junction and R (Rue Marette) at second T-junction. Turn immediately L (Rue Jules Ferry) and continue over two crossroads. Follow road bearing R and turn L on cycle track into trees. Turn R on voie verte along old railway trackbed. Follow this zigzagging R and L, then cross main road. Continue on cycle track bearing L and at end turn R (Rue de Compainville) over railway. Continue downhill and turn L through barrier onto cycle track. Turn L under railway and R onto start of voie verte in **Serqueux** (31km, 164m) (station). Voie verte runs for 40km to Arques-la-Bataille on next stage.

Continue past **Beaubec-la-Rosière** (accommodation), **St Saire** (39km, 99m) (accommodation, refreshments) and **La Béthune** (42.5km, 92m) (refreshments in Neuville). Pass under motorway and continue to old station in **Neufchâtel-en-Bray** (45km, 78m) (accommodation, refreshments, camping, tourist office).

STAGE 6

Gournay-en-Bray to Gisors

Start	Gournay-en-Bray, Pl Nationale (99m)
Finish	Gisors, Pl de Blanmont (68m)
Distance	35.5km (22 miles)
Ascent	190m
Waymarking	Avenue Verte

This stage follows the Epte valley from Gournay-en-Bray to Gisors, but not always on the valley floor. A voie verte on an old railway trackbed and minor roads are used to reach Neuf-Marché, then the route climbs steeply onto a chalk ridge west of the valley before descending to Gisors.

rom NE corner of Pl Nationale in **Gournay-en-Bray**, fol-
w Rue du Dr Duchesne E into Pl Alain Carment. Turn
(Passage Bourgeois) then L through barriers onto tree-
ned track (Bvd des Planquettes), crossing river Epte. At
nd turn L (Rue Athanase Caux) then R at T-junction (Rue
e Ferrières). Go ahead over main road at traffic lights
nd cross railway. Turn R (Rue Leroy Moulin, D21, sp
illers-sur-Auchy) parallel with railway, passing station in
errières-en-Bray R (refreshments, station).

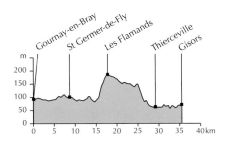

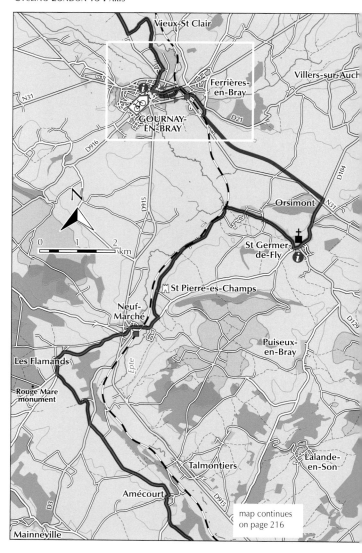

map continues
on page 216

214

Pass Allo Auto Service car scrapyard R and fork R on
named road. Bear R at end (Rue Charles Gervais) then
st before railway crossing, fork L on Trans'Oise cycle
ack beside railway. This soon bears L away from railway
rough fields on voie verte along trackbed of old rail-
ay. Go ahead over first road crossing to reach second
nction (where sp ahead shows Beauvais 24km). Turn R
)104) to reach crossroads in **Orsimont** (refreshments).
o ahead over crossroads (D129, sp St Germer-de-Fly)
nd continue to reach Pl de l'Abbaye in **St Germer-de-
y** (8km, 105m) (accommodation, refreshments, tourist
ffice).

The huge parish **church** of St Germer-de-Fly (pop
1750) was the basilica of a Benedictine abbey
that became a church during the revolution when
monastic properties were confiscated. Built in the
1230s in Romanesque-Gothic transitional style, its
light airy design presaged the great Gothic cathedrals of northern France. The Marian chapel closely
resembles the Saint-Chapelle in Paris built a few
years earlier, although it has lost its original painted
interior. The rest of the abbey was destroyed in
1414 during the Hundred Years' War, then subsequently rebuilt only to be pulled down again during
the Revolution.

Pass abbey R and turn R at roundabout (Douce Rue).
ear L at triangular junction (Rue de Boisville) and con-
nue into Rue du Moulin l'Evêque. Just before railway
rossing, turn L (Rue de Brétel) parallel with railway
nd continue to pass old château and church (both L) in
t Pierre-es-Champs (13.5km, 101m).
Continue ahead (Rue de l'Irompha) to reach
-junction and turn R (Rue de Montel, D104, sp Neuf-
Marché). Cross river Epte and continue (now on D1)
nder railway bridge to reach crossroads in centre of
Neuf-Marché (15km, 86m) (refreshments).
Go straight ahead (D1, sp Les Flamands) then fork L
t triangular junction with tree in middle (Rue de Corval,

215

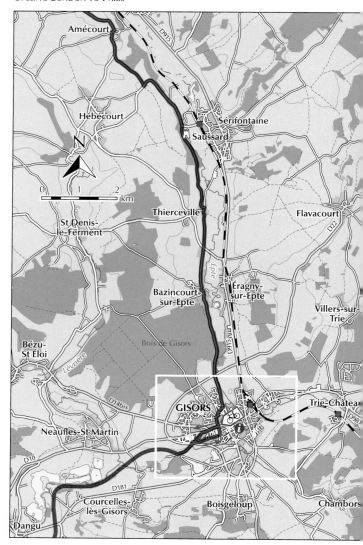

Poppies bloom on the chalk downland in spring

19, sp Les Flamands). Road now climbs steeply to pass
rough hilltop hamlet of **Les Flamands** (17.5km, 187m)
ccommodation). ▶ At end of village, fork L and imme-
ately L again on quiet country road (C7, sp Le Camp â
an), descending gently across open plateau. Zigzag L
d R past farm and continue ahead across road junc-
on (C10, sp Amécourt). Pass series of farms on road
ong top of escarpment to reach triangular junction with
adonna statue in middle in **Amécourt** (23km, 149m)
ccommodation).

Turn R through village, then L (D660, sp Gisors)
ssing small brick chapel L and continue into open
untry. Fork L (C11, sp Sérifontaine) through fields then
rn sharply L (D17) at T-junction. Follow road curv-
g R and descending steeply through trees past metal-
rgical factory below L on opposite side of river Epte.
here road turns L downhill into **Sérifontaine** (station),
ar R on quiet road ascending through trees and con-
ue past **Château du Saussard** behind trees L. Descend
to open country and continue through houses, bear-
g L to reach T-junction in **Thierceville** (29.5km, 63m)
ccommodation).

A monument
at Rouge Mare,
in the forest a
kilometre southwest,
commemorates a
shoot-out (1914)
between local
gendarmes and
German saboteurs
operating behind
French lines.

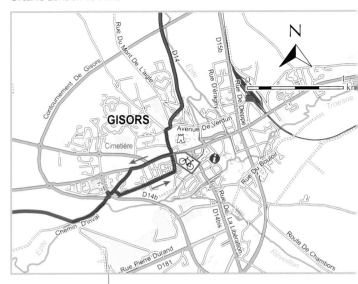

Turn R and continue ahead out of village betwee
fields then cross main road to reach **Bazincourt-sur-Ep**
(32km, 66m) (accommodation, refreshments). Follc
road (D14) winding through village and into **Bois**
Gisors forest. Pass under road bridge and continue in
built-up area. Follow road bearing R (Rue Louis Malla
to reach T-junction and turn R (Ave de Verdun). Turn L
traffic lights (Rue Albert Leroy, sp centre ville) and cyc
past fortifications L to reach Pl de Blanmont mini-roun
about in **Gisors** (35.5km, 68m) (accommodation, refres
ments, camping, tourist office, cycle shop, station).

GISORS

In medieval times, Gisors (pop 11,250), a border town between Normandy
and France, was a frequent meeting point between the rulers of these countries when negotiating treaties. The ruined 11th-century Norman motte and
bailey castle was originally just a round tower atop an earth mound, but was

later surrounded by a ditch and walls flanked by towers. After its military role declined, the castle became a prison with its most famous inmates being members of the Knights Templar interred here between 1310–1314. The Templars were a wealthy order and legend has it that when the order was proscribed they buried their immense treasure in tunnels beneath the castle. A dig in the 1950s to test this legend led to cracks appearing in the dungeons making the castle unsafe and the excavations were filled in with concrete to stabilise the site. However, it is claimed that before the site was sealed 10 medieval caskets were seen far below ground but could not be reached. A book by Gérard de Sède (1962) popularised this myth.

REVERSE ROUTE: GISORS TO GOURNAY-EN-BRAY

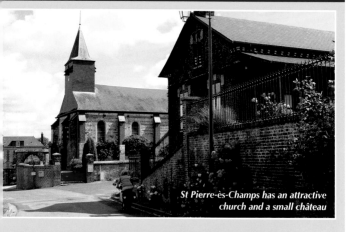

St Pierre-ès-Champs has an attractive church and a small château

From Pl de Blanmont in **Gisors** follow Rue Albert Leroy N. Turn R at crossroads then L (D14). Follow this bearing R out of town. Continue under road bridge and through Bois de Gisors forest to **Bazincourt-sur-Epte** (3.5km, 66m) (accommodation, refreshments). At end of village go ahead at crossroads to **Thierceville** (6km, 63m) (accommodation).

Turn second L in village (Rte du Château Saussard) and pass Château du Saussard in woods R. Bear L on D17 and continue past **Sérifontaine** R (station). Road climbs steeply through woods onto plateau. At top of hill turn R to **Amécourt** (12.5km, 149m) (accommodation).

Follow D660 zigzagging R and L through village. Pass through **Bouchevilliers**, then cross main road and zigzag L and R past farm to reach **Les Flamands** (18km, 187m) (accommodation). Pass through village on D19 and cycle downhill. Bear R (D1) through **Neuf-Marché** (20.5km, 86m) (refreshments).

Cross main road and go under railway, passing through Montel on D104. At end of village turn L (C3) ascending to **St Pierre-es-Champs** (22.5km, 101m) then descend past church and château (both R). Continue parallel with railway L to reach T-junction and turn R through Boisville. Bear R on Rue Douce Rue to reach roundabout and turn L into **St Germer-de-Fly** (28km, 105m) (accommodation, refreshments, tourist office).

Follow D129 past abbey L and continue out of village and over N31 at Orsimont (refreshments). Turn L on Trans'Oise cycle track along old railway trackbed. Where this ends, turn R then fork L beside scrapyard. Bear L (D21) past station in **Ferrières-en-Bray** L (refreshments, station) to reach T-junction. Turn L across railway and continue ahead (D21) to reach Pl Nationale in **Gournay-en-Bray** (35.5km, 99m) (accommodation, refreshments, tourist office).

Start	Gisors, Pl de Blanmont (68m)
Finish	Neuville-sur-Oise bridge (22m)
Distance	60.5km (37.5 miles)
Ascent	275m
Waymarking	Avenue Verte, V33 (Bray-et-Lu to Neuville-sur-Oise)

The stage starts by following the Voie Verte de la Vallée de l'Epte south along an old railway trackbed on a level grade to Bray-et-Lû. It then turns east on quiet country roads, climbing onto and undulating across the Vexin, a limestone plateau that forms the northern rim of the Paris basin, before descending on another old railway line through the new-town of Cergy-Pontoise to end beside the river Oise. There is very little accommodation on this stage.

om Pl de Blanmont in **Gisors**, cycle W on Rue du ubourg de Neaufles. Where main road bears R, con- ue ahead (still Rue du Faubourg de Neaufles), then here houses end fork L downhill (Ch Noir). At end, ar R on cycle track and follow this turning sharply L reach roundabout. Go straight ahead following cycle ick passing L of roundabout, into Ch d'Inval. Continue rallel with river Epte L, then fork R onto Voie Verte

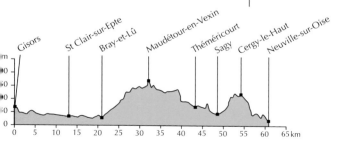

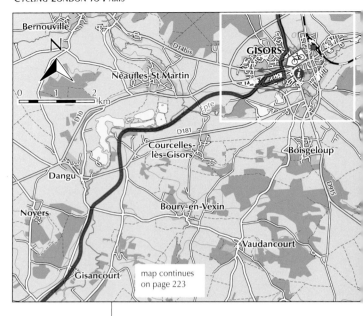

map continues on page 223

Voie verte is followed for 19km.

de la Vallée de l'Epte cycle track along course of ol railway. ◀ Pass turn-off for Neaufles-St Martin R, the cycle through hamlet of Beausséré to reach turn-off fe **Dangu** (6km, 42m) (refreshments, camping).

Continue through **Gisancourt** (9.5km, 41m then pass Guerny R and cycle under motorway. Pa Château-St Clair-sur-Epte station (12.5km, 38m) (refresh ments) and ruined **Château-sur-Epte** on hillside R, the continue past **Berthenonville** (15.5km, 32m), **Aven** (17.5km, 33m) and **St Rémy** (19km, 32m), all R. Cro main road to reach road junction in **Bray-et-Lû** (21kn 29m) (accommodation, refreshments).

Turn sharply L (D86A) past zinc factory R and imme diately R (Grande Rue, D86, sp Ambleville) passir church R and crossing Epte. Follow road bearing R (Ru de l'École) then go ahead over roundabout (D142, thir exit). Go ahead over staggered crossroads ascendir

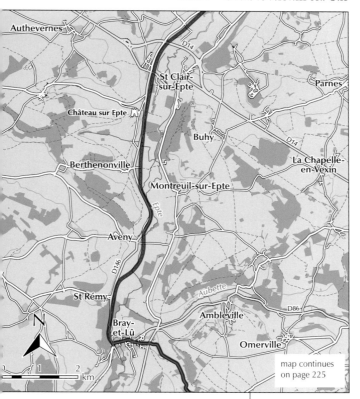

map continues
on page 225

rough open country to reach **Chaussy** (24.5km, 82m)
ccommodation, refreshments).

Bear L (Grande Rue, D142, sp Villers-en-Arthies)
en continue through main square past church L. At
d of village, fork R (Rte de Villers, D142) and continue
cending past parkland of **Domaine de Villarceaux** L
6km, 100m).

The demesne of **Villarceaux** includes a medieval
French castle, a 17th-century manor house and an

The impressive Domaine de Villarceaux

18th-century château in the style of Louis XV. The surrounding park has several water features and formal gardens including a rare vertugadin Italian garden surrounded by statues.

Turn L through park, passing between lake L and golf course R, then ascend steeply through forest and into open country of Vexin plateau. At point where route reaches main road, turn L on quiet road through fields. Go ahead over crossroads onto gravel track to reach T-junction and turn R into hilltop village of **Maudétour-en-Vexin** (32km, 169m) (accommodation).

Turn L in front of church and pass impressive gate of **château** R. At end of village, where road bears L, fork R onto gravel track between fields. Pass between barns to reach road on edge of **Arthies** (33.5km, 154m). Turn L (do not enter village) and immediately fork R (D159 sp Wy-dit-Joli-Village) on road across plateau. Go ahead over roundabout and continue through fields to **Wy-dit-Joli-Village** (36.5km, 126m).

In village, fork R and immediately L (Rue Henri IV C4, sp Gadancourt) then bear R at mini-roundabout and follow road through fields to **Gadancourt** (38.5km,

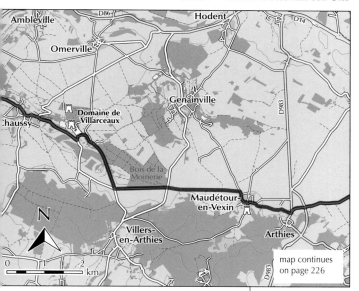

map continues
on page 226

7m). ▶ Go ahead at crossroads (Rue de Faubourgs, sp
ernes) to reach T-junction at end of village and turn
 through woods. Follow road descending to **Avernes**
0km, 90m).

Turn L at T-junction (Grande Rue, D43) then fork R
side house 68 into Rue du Clos Prigent. Where this
ds, continue ahead on gravel track between fields. Turn
at T-junction and R at crossing of tracks. Emerge onto
iet road and cycle past cemetery L into **Théméricourt**
2.5km, 79m) (refreshments, tourist office).

Théméricourt château was built in the 15th century
and remodelled in 1721. In 1986 it was bought by
the exiled dictator of Haiti, Jean-Claude Duvalier,
known as Baby Doc, after he was forced to leave
Haiti. He arrived with an estimated fortune of
US$900million plundered from the Haitian excheq-
uer, but much of this disappeared as the result of an

The dry stone-lined
depression to the
right of the road by
the crossroads is
the remains of an
old pond that held
water for livestock.

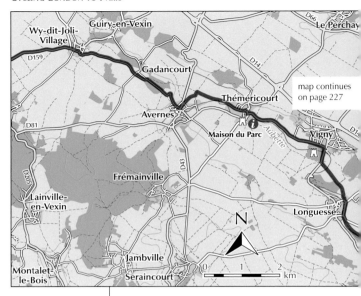

map continues
on page 227

acrimonious divorce settlement. After being refused
asylum in France and declared an illegal immigrant,
he left Théméricourt and went into hiding before
returning to Haiti in 2011, dying there three years
later. During his stay, he disposed of the château's
collection of historic furniture. In 1994 the château
was bought by the local council and is now the HQ
of the Vexin regional park. In front of the château,
the Maison du Parc houses the museum of the Vexin
and information centre.

Pass church and **Maison du Parc** (both R) and con
tinue through village on Rue Achim d'Abos. Turn secon
R (Rue du Puits de la Ville) to reach T-junction. Turn
(Rue d'Orléans) and L (Rue du Pont aux Bois, D81, s
Vigny). Continue through fields to reach **Vigny** (44.5kr
72m) (refreshments). Pass château R then turn R
T-junction (Pl d'Amboise, D169, sp Longuesse). Contin

ast church R into Rue de la Comté. At end of village turn
on gravel track through fields that rises over a small
dge before descending to edge of **Longuesse** (46.5km,
6m) (refreshments).

Emerge onto road (Rue du Moulin) and bear L (do
ot enter village) then after 75 metres turn R (Ch des
Marais). Continue over crossroads onto 4WD gravel
ack. Emerge onto road and bear L, then keep ahead
Rue de l'Abreuvoir). Continue ahead (Rue de la Mairie)
ast town hall R to reach centre of **Sagy** (49km, 50m)
efreshments).

Turn R at T-junction into Grande Place (D81, sp
aillancourt) and L at crossroads (Rue des Deux Granges,
81). Follow road bearing R out of village and go ahead
cross main road to reach square in centre of **Saillancourt**
0.5km, 68m). Pass old *lavoir* (wash house) R and bear
. At end of village, fork L at mini-roundabout (sec-
nd exit) uphill through woods. Continue ascending to

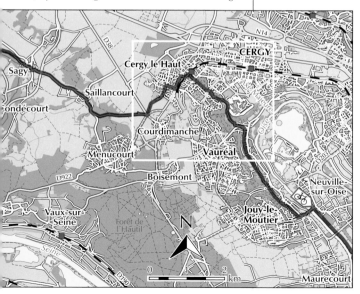

From Cergy-le-Haut there is a first distant view of La Défense and central Paris 20km away (photo: Christine Gordon)

At this point the route enters Cergy-Pontoise new town.

roundabout and turn L taking cycle track through barrier between third and fourth exits. At junction of tracks, bea R to reach road. ◀ Continue on Bvd des Chasseurs pas sports centre L. Turn R at traffic lights (Bvd Ste Apolline to reach large roundabout. Follow cycle track aroun roundabout and turn L (Bvd de la Crête, fourth exit

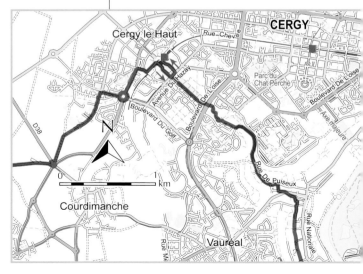

urn R at crossroads (Rue du Désert aux Nuages) then ear R (Bvd de l'Evasion) using contra-flow bus lane, and nmediately L (Rue de l'Embarquement) to reach station Cergy-le-Haut (54.5km, 119m) (refreshments, station).

> **Cergy-Pontoise** (pop 200,000) is one of five new towns that have been built around Paris since the 1970s. The community has been formed by expanding the historic town of Pontoise and creating a new centre around Cergy, previously only a small village.

Turn R before station (Rue de la Destinée) and con-nue between carpark L and apartment buildings R. At nd, dogleg L and R onto cycle track with parkland L and ollow this passing series of crossing tracks. At sixth cross-ng, bear L through parkland to reach tunnel under main ɔad. Continue winding through parkland, then fork R to ass under wooden bridge. After more parkland, emerge n road (Rue de Puiseux) and turn L, at first through oodland and then between houses. Turn R immediately efore old railway viaduct (Rue des Bardoulais) and fol-w this bearing L (Rue du Marais) under bridge through dge of **Vauréal** (cycle shop). Cross main road at traffic ghts (Rue Neuve). At end turn R (still Rue Neuve) then ɔ ahead over staggered crossroads into Rue de Caix ɛ St Aymour. ► Where road turns R, continue ahead ɪrough barriers on gravel track. Emerge onto road (Rue ɛ la Gare) and continue ahead past site of old station. Vhere road bears R, fork L on gravel track along old ɑilway embankment, keeping above road and cross gh railway bridge. Continue through woods onto Ch ɛs Miettes and pass above parish church L of **Jouy-le-ɪoutier** (accommodation).

Just before reaching main road, turn L on cycle track inding downhill and bear L to cross road at pedes-ian crossing. Turn R, passing roundabout R, then cross ɛxt road and turn L on cycle track beside road (D48E). ɔntinue across river Oise and bear R past roundabout to ɛach Rue du Pont in **Neuville-sur-Oise** (60.5km, 22m) ɛfreshments).

Rue de Caix de St Aymour follows the route of an old railway.

REVERSE ROUTE: NEUVILLE-SUR-OISE TO GISORS

From Neuville-sur-Oise cycle SW (D48E) over Oise. Turn R across road before roundabout then cross side road and follow cycle track zig-zagging up embankment. Turn R on cycle track along old railway trackbed and pass **Jouy-le-Moutier** (accommodation). Where cycle track ends continue on Rue de Caix de St Aymour past **Vauréal** (cycle shop). Where track divides, fork R. Go ahead over staggered crossroads (Rue Neuve) and follow this bearing L. Cross main road into Rue des Marais then bear R (Rue des Bardoulais) and turn L (Rue de Puiseux). At end continue uphill on cycle track. Just before houses start R, turn R on cycle track winding uphill. Pass under three bridges and continue past grassy area R. At end, turn R and L past **Cergy-le-Haut station** R (6km, 119m) (refreshments, station).

Bear L past bus station L. Turn R at end, then fork L and turn L on cycle track beside Bvd de la Crête. Turn R at roundabout (Bvd Ste Apolline) then L (Bvd des Chasseurs). At end continue on cycle track through fields and fork L to roundabout. *The left fork is easy to miss.* Take second exit (C2, sp Sagy). Bear R onto D81 through **Saillancourt** (10km, 68m) and continue over main road to **Sagy** (11.5km, 50m) (refreshments).

Follow D81 winding through village centre then fork L (sp La Gaule de Sagy). At end bear R on cycle track out of village. At beginning of **Longuesse** (14km, 56m) (refreshments) cross main road into Ch des Marais, passing

Despite its classic elegance, Vigny château is empty and unused

village L. Turn L at T-junction (Rue du Moulin) and after 75 metres fork R on cycle track. Continue to beginning of **Vigny** (16km, 72m) (refreshments) and turn R (Rue de la Comté) into village. Turn L (Rue Beaudouin, D81) past château L and continue to **Thémericourt** (18km, 79m) (refreshments, tourist office).

Turn R (Rue d'Orleans) and L, then L again at T-junction. Pass château L and continue out of village, with surface becoming gravel. Turn L at wayside cross, then soon fork R. Go ahead over crossroads and bear L on D43 into **Avernes** (20.5km, 90m). Turn R (Rue de l'Audience) and continue through woodland. Fork L in second wood (sp Wy-dit-Joli-Village) past **Gadancourt** R (22km, 127m).

Continue ahead to **Wy-dit-Joli-Village** (24km, 126m). Fork L at mini-roundabout, then go ahead at staggered crossroads. Follow D159 ahead over roundabout to beginning of **Arthies** (27km, 154m), then bear L and turn R (Rue aux Ours). Do not enter village. Continue on track between fields to reach T-junction and turn L into **Maudétour-en-Vexin** (28.5km, 169m) (accommodation).

Turn R (sp Genainville) and fork L to follow Rte des Moines winding through village. By village end sign turn L on track between fields and continue across minor road to reach crossroads. Turn R on minor road (sp Villarceaux) then fork L (sp Chaussy). Pass entrance to **Domaine de Villarceaux** R (34.5km, 100m) and turn R (D142) at triangular junction to reach **Chaussy** (36km, 82m) (accommodation, refreshments). Bear R in village and continue through open country. Go ahead over crossroads (D142) into **Bray-et-Lû** (39.5km, 29m) (accommodation, refreshments).

Go ahead over roundabout (D86), crossing river Epte, to T-junction. Turn L then immediately turn sharply R along Voie Verte de la Vallée de l'Epte cycle track. Follow this past **St Rémy** (41.5km, 32m), **Aveny** (43km, 33m) and **Berthenonville** (45km, 32m). Pass below ruined **Château-sur-Epte** on hillside L, then continue past Château-St Clair-sur-Epte station (48km, 38m) (refreshments), Guerny, **Gisancourt** (51km, 41m) and turn-off for **Dangu** L (54.5km, 42m) (refreshments, camping).

Where track ends at T-junction, turn L (Ch d'Inval) to reach roundabout. Go straight ahead, then turn sharply R and immediately fork R (Rue de la Reine Blanche). Go ahead over first crossroads then turn L at second (Rue de Preslay) to reach Pl de Blanmont in **Gisors** (60.5km, 68m) (accommodation, refreshments, camping, tourist office, cycle shop, station).

STAGE 8

Neuville-sur-Oise to St Denis station

Start	Neuville-sur-Oise bridge (22m)
Finish	St Denis station (32m)
Distance	44km (27.5 miles)
Ascent	51m
Waymarking	Avenue Verte

This level stage first uses forest tracks through the woodland of St Germain-en-Laye to reach the edge of Greater Paris. It then continues through the conurbation, mostly on riverside cycle tracks or towpaths. The river Seine is crossed four times before the stage ends in St Denis.

From Rue du Pont in **Neuville-sur-Oise**, cycle SE across car park then turn R on cycle track along tree-lined avenue. Bear L on rough track and turn L along gravel tow-path beside Oise. Pass under road viaduct and continue past sewerage works L. Emerge onto Quai du Confluent and turn R, passing series of aggregates quays R, then go under railway bridge. Pass below multi-story carpark for Fin d'Oise station L and under road bridge. Follow road bearing L passing **monument** R at confluence of rivers Oise and Seine R. Continue on cycle track beside Seine and pass under railway bridge, high-level road bridge and smaller girder bridge into **Conflans-Ste Honorine** (4.5km, 22m) (accommodation, refreshments, tourist office, station).

Turn sharply L and L again to cross Seine on St Nicholas girder bridge. At end of bridge continue ahead on Ave de St Germain beside main road R. Where road ahead becomes no entry, fork L between bollards. After 50 metres, turn R through barrier (Allée des Prunus) and fork L (Allée des Tamaris). Follow road bearing L then turn

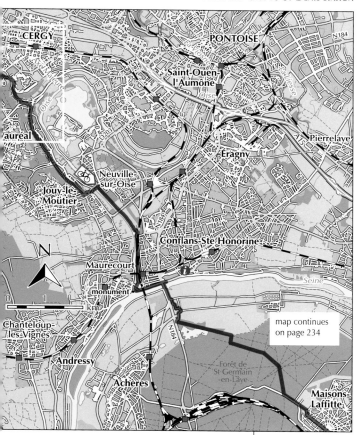

away from houses. Where this road becomes no entry,
ork R on gravel track and bear R beside Rte Centrale.
ust before reaching motorway slip road, turn L and R
cross road to continue on cycle track L of road. Before
his reaches motorway, turn L through barrier on gravel
rack (Rte Madame) beside wall of **St Germain-en-Laye**
orest R.

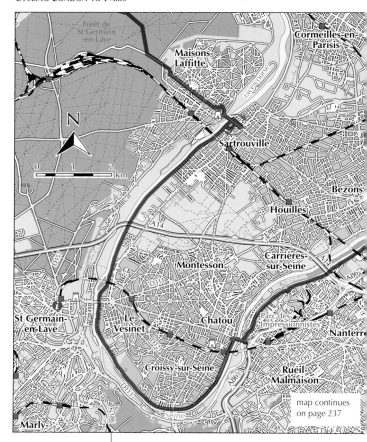

map continues
on page 237

Forêt de St Germain-en-Laye (3500 hectares) is a
largely undeveloped area of natural woodland. For
many years it was a hunting forest for French kings,
who resided at the royal château of St Germain-
en-Laye, surrounded by a wall to prevent poach-
ing. Over half the trees are oak and the habitat is
actively maintained to encourage regrowth and

sustainability. The forest is crossed by a network of straight trails used for leisure cycling, riding and walking by Parisiens and for racehorse and military training from stables and barracks in the forest.

After 1.5km, turn R over cattle grid into forest and after another 200 metres, turn L (Rte du Corra) at first junction of forest tracks. Continue straight ahead over next two crossing tracks and bear R to reach 10-way crossing of forest tracks. Go ahead R (Rte de la Vente Brûleuse, fourth track anti-clockwise) and continue through forest to reach road. Turn L (Rte des Pavillons) on cycle track L. Where road bears R, continue ahead on cycle track soon leaving forest through stone gateway pillars. ▶ Fork R (Ave Bourdaloue) and where road forks again, bear R and turn L along R side of dual carriageway (Ave Albine) with wide expanse of grass between carriageways. Pass through Pl Marine and go ahead again at Pl du Château into Ave du Général Leclerc to reach **Château de Maisons-Laffitte** (12.5km, 34m) (accommodation, refreshments, cycle shop, station).

These pillars held the original gateway into the park surrounding Château de Maisons-Laffitte.

The baroque-style château at Maisons-Laffitte

Château de Maisons-Laffitte was built in baroque style between 1630 and 1649, the time taken being caused by architect François Mansart's desire for perfection. It is claimed that after completing the first floor he pulled it down and started again as he was unhappy with the outcome. During the revolution, the château was appropriated by the state and sold-off. In 1818 banker Jacques Lafitte purchased the property and sold the surrounding park as building lots. Acquired by the state in 1905 it has been preserved as a national monument.

Turn L in front of château (Ave Carnot) then R (Ave du Louvre). Follow this bearing L into Ave Henry Marce then turn R at crossroads (Ave Louvois) and fork R (Ave François Mansart) to reach roundabout with view of front of château through gardens R. Take third exit (Ave de Verdun, D308, sp Sartrouville) on cycle lane R and cross bridge over Seine into **Sartrouville** (cycle shop).

On opposite bank, turn first R (Rue de la Constituante and after 200 metres R again (Rue Léon Fontaine, sp MJC) to reach riverside road (Quai de Seine). ◀ Cross road and turn L along riverside cycle track. Continue beside Quai du Pecq and pass under railway bridge. Road becomes Quai George Sand and, where this ends, continue ahead through barriers on gravel track along towpath. Pass large childrens' psychiatric hospital L and go under motorway bridge. Emerge beside road (Bvd Folke Bernadotte) and continue under railway bridge, passing St Germain-en-Laye on opposite side of Seine.

Road becomes Quai de l'Orme de Sully and passes under road bridge. Dogleg around sailing club R and continue beside Bvd de la Libération. Where this turns away from river, cycle ahead on towpath to reach Quai de l'Écluse. ◀ Continue under road bridge onto Berge de la Prairie. Road becomes Berge de la Grenouillère passing pastel coloured riverside houses L and going under railway bridge to reach main road (Quai Jean Mermoz) Continue beside river, then just before road overbridge turn L across road at traffic light controlled crossing

For the next 13km the route follows the towpath on the *rive droite* (right bank) of the Seine.

Quai de l'Écluse is a one-way street with contra-flow cycling permitted.

ontinue away from river on cycle track winding uphill
rough Sq Realier Dumas and turn R through barrier
 reach road leading to bridge in **Chatou** (27km, 31m)
efreshments).

Cross two bridges over main and Marly arms of Seine,
sing cycle lane R. Once over bridges, bear R then turn
arply downhill and R again beside Rue des Martinets to
ass back under bridge into **Rueil** (refreshments). ▸ Fork
 (Quai Adolphe Giquel) on cycle track beside river.
urn L past pumping station R and continue on towpath
eside river (Promenade Bad Soden) passing **Parc des
npressionnistes** R and series of industrial quays L. Cross
nodern curved bridge over entrance to Nanterre port
en cross Ave Jules Quentin. ▸ Turn L and R to continue
eside river, following towpath past more factories and
uays. Dogleg R and L past Pavillon des Berges R (refresh-
ents) and go under motorway and railway bridges then
ass site of old paper mills R and go under second railway
ridge. Pass series of housing developments R, then just
efore next road bridge (Pont de Bezons) follow towpath
oglegging L and R under bridge. Follow towpath past
arkland and under Pont de Colombes bridge to emerge
n Quai du Petit Gennevilliers and reach T-junction
eside Argenteuil-Gennevilliers bridge (36.5km, 33m).

For the next 9km
the route follows
the towpath on the
rive gauche (left
bank) of the Seine.

The bridge has steps
with steep ramps for
pushing cycles and
lifts on both sides.

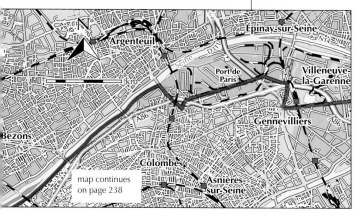

map continues
on page 238

237

The Seine chemin de halage (towpath) is followed for 23km

Turn R (Ave d'Argenteuil, D909), passing SAFRAN aircraft engine factory R. Pass over motorway and under railway bridges into Ave de Stalingrad and turn L across road at light controlled crossing by apartment no175. Continue ahead away from main road (sp Gennevilliers Port) on cycle track along middle of dual carriageway (Rte

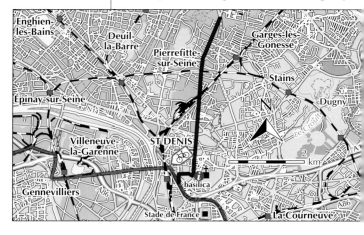

Principale du Port), recrossing motorway. Go ahead over roundabout (second exit) on cycle track R and continue through industrial area of Gennevilliers Port over second roundabout (accommodation, refreshments). Pass under motorway and at third roundabout turn R (first exit) under railway bridge. Continue to T-junction and turn R (Ave Marcel Paul, D911, sp Gennevilliers Village) on cycle lane R. Cross motorway for third time then go ahead over middle of first roundabout and pass Gennevilliers University R. Just before second roundabout turn L across road at pedestrian crossing and continue beside tram tracks R parallel with Ave Général de Gaulle (D986) past **Gennevilliers station** L (41.5km, 29m) (accommodation, refreshments, station).

Continue under railway bridge and pass Chanteraines regional park L. Just before motorway overbridge, turn R cross tram tracks and road at light controlled crossing and continue under bridge on cycle lane R of road (Ave de Verdun, sp Villeneuve la Garenne) with tram tracks in middle of dual carriageway. Continue following tram tracks through **Villeneuve-la-Garenne**. Pass over bridges crossing two branches of Seine and under railway bridge to reach **St Denis station** R (44km, 32m) (accommodation, refreshments, tourist office, cycle shop, station). ▶

For a description of St Denis see Stage 10, classic route.

REVERSE ROUTE: ST DENIS STATIOIN TO NEUVILLE-SUR-OISE

From **St Denis station** (accommodation, refreshments, tourist office, cycle shop, station) cycle W under railway bridge, parallel with tramway R. Cross to R of road and continue over two arms of Seine, then under motorway. Pass Chanteraines park R and go under railway with **Gennevilliers station** R (3km, 31m) to reach roundabout (accommodation, refreshments, station).

Turn R (D911), then cross motorway and turn L (sp Gennevilliers Port). Pass under railway and bear L at roundabout (Rte Principale du Port). Go under motorway and continue ahead over two roundabouts (accommodation, refreshments). After second roundabout, cycle track runs down middle of road over another motorway bridge to reach T-junction. Turn R (D909, sp Argenteuil) then pass under railway and over motorway to reach Argenteuil bridge (8km, 28m).

Conflans-Ste Honorine stands on a small hill overlooking the Oise

Turn L beside Seine (do not cross bridge) and follow riverside cycle track for 9km, passing under five bridges. Immediately after fifth bridge (refreshments), turn R and L to continue beside river. Cross curved footbridge over sidestream and pass **Park des Impressionnistes** L. *Curved bridge has steep ramps for pushing cycles and lifts on both sides.* Cycle past **Rueil** (refreshments) then pass under bridge and bear L on cycle track climbing to bridge (17.5km, 31m) and turn L over two arms of Seine to **Chatou** (refreshments).

Now on opposite bank, follow cycle track curving L beside slip road to reach riverside and turn R on cycle track beside riverside road. Continue for 13km beside river on quiet roads and cycle tracks, going under six bridges. After seventh bridge, turn R through gates (sp Maisons-Laffitte) and follow cycle track winding through Parc du Dispensaire. Emerge beside roundabout in **Sartrouville** (cycle shop) and turn R (D308) across bridge over Seine to roundabout in front of château in **Maisons-Laffitte** (31.5km, 34m) (accommodation, refreshments, cycle shop, station).

Turn half-R (Ave François Mansart) on tree-lined avenue beside château, then fork L (Ave Louvois) and turn second L (Ave Carnot). Opposite main entrance to château, turn R (Ave du Général Leclerc) and continue ahead through Pl du Château into Ave Albine then continue across Pl Marine. Where road ends, bear R (Ave Bourdaloue) and turn L through stone pillars into **St Germain-en-Laye forest**.Continue ahead to emerge on road (Rte des Pavillons) then bear R on cycle track in forest beside road, eventually doglegging R, L and R again into forest on Rte de la Vente Frileuse. At 10-way junction of tracks, fork L taking fourth track clockwise (Rte du Corra). Go ahead over two crossing tracks and turn R at third. *The right turn is easy to miss.* Pass through gate out of forest and turn L to reach T-junction. Turn R beside motorway slip road and after motorway junction turn L across road to continue on cycle track on opposite side. Bear L away from road and turn L (Allée des Tamaris). Follow this bearing R through houses and continue on Allée des Prunus. At end turn L and R through barriers onto road and where this bears L under motorway, continue ahead over Seine on girder bridge to **Conflans-Ste Honorine** (39.5km, 22m) (accommodation, refreshments, tourist office, station).

At end of bridge, turn R and R again to pass under bridge on riverside cycle track. Follow this under railway bridge and bear R past **monument** L at confluence of Seine and Oise. Continue beside Oise under two bridges and past industrial quays. Continue into woods and fork L, passing waterworks R. Follow towpath under road bridge and continue to just before blue arch Neuville bridge. Fork R away from river, then turn L and L again to reach bridge over Oise in **Neuville-sur-Oise** (44km, 22m) (refreshments).

STAGE 9

St Denis station to Notre Dame cathedral

Start	St Denis station (32m)
Finish	Notre Dame cathedral (35m)
Distance	13km (8 miles)
Ascent	16m
Waymarking	Avenue Verte (occasional), N-S Véloroute

From St Denis the route follows urban canal towpaths, city sidestreets through the Marais and cycle tracks beside grand boulevards to reach the centre of Paris, where the ride ends in front of Notre Dame cathedral. It is level and busy, with Parisien cyclists everywhere.

Cycle E over **canal St Denis** then turn R (do not ente centre of St Denis) and bear R past tram station L ont cycle track parallel with canal. Pass first lock (lock 6) an join canal towpath. Continue under series of bridges an curve L round huge bulk of **Stade de France** stadium c opposite side of canal R.

> **Stade de France** (capacity 81,000) was built on the site of a former gasworks for the 1998 FIFA World Cup finals. As the French national stadium, it stages international football and rugby matches and finals of national competitions. It also hosts major music concerts. The most noticeable features are the roof which although it weighs 13,000 tonnes appears to float above the stadium and the lower tier of seats which retract to reveal an athletics track.

The first bridge carries the Bvd Périphérique motorway ring road that surrounds central Paris.

Follow towpath past more locks and bridges. Pas lock 2, where cycle track becomes Quai de l'Allier, an go under two road bridges. ◄ Then bear L up cobble ramp passing under railway bridge to reach major roa

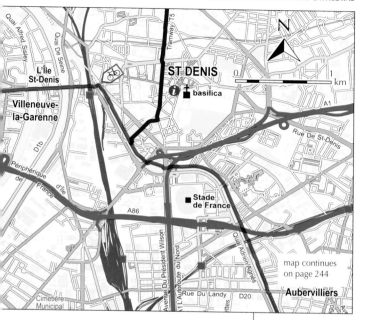

junction above Pont de Flandre bridge. Go ahead across
road and turn R on cycle track on opposite side. Cross
bridge and turn L to continue on Quai de la Gironde
beside canal now on opposite bank, with futuristic
buildings of **Science and Industry museum** in Parc de la
Villette L across canal. Follow cycle track bearing R and
continue on Quai de l'Oise beside Villette canal basin L.
Where this ends, turn R beside Rue de Crimée (cobbled)
and immediately L (Quai de la Seine) on cycle track L.
Continue parallel with canal basin L to reach T-junction
and follow cycle track L to reach square with fountains in
front of **Rotonde de la Villette** (8km, 53m).

Cycle past La Rotonde R and follow cycle track
bearing R under railway. Cross side road and continue
ahead for short distance on cycle track down middle of
Rue Lafayette. Follow cycle track forking L beside Quai

CYCLING LONDON TO PARIS

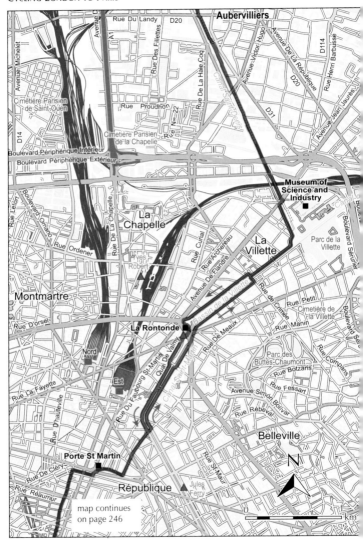

Rotonde de la Villette was originally a toll station collecting taxes on goods entering Paris

…e Valmy and continue over crossroads following Canal … Martin L. Pass two locks and immediately after second …ck turn R beside number 85 (Rue de Lancry) away from …anal. ▶ Cross dual-carriageway Bvd Magenta and con…nue to T-junction in front of bust of Johann Strauss. Turn … (Rue René Boulanger) on cobbles and follow street to …quare with **Porte-St Martin** archway in centre.

Rue de Lancry is a one-way street with contra-flow cycling permitted.

Porte-St Martin is a triumphal arch standing on the line of the medieval city walls which was commissioned by Louis XIV in 1674 to commemorate French victories on the Rhine. It is heavily ornamented with three of the four reliefs featuring Louis as Mars, Hercules and Fame.

Turn R and L opposite arch into Rue St Martin then …rst R (Rue Ste Apolline). At end, turn L (Rue St Denis) …nd follow this ahead across series of crossroads. Pass …quare R with Fontaine des Innocents fountain in centre …nd continue for 100 metres, turning third R into narrow …lleyway (Rue Courtalon) between buildings 23 and 21. …merge into Pl Ste Opportune and go ahead across Rue …es Halles into Rue des Lavandières Ste Opportune.

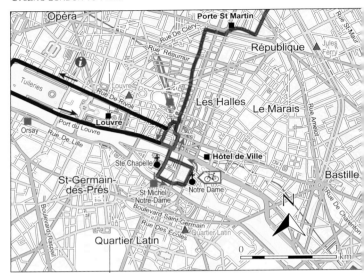

Cross Rue de Rivoli and continue through no entry signs into Rue Edouard Colonne to emerge on R bank of Seine. Turn L (Quai de la Mégisserie) and then R over Pont au Change bridge onto Île de la Cité. Continue ahead (Bvd du Palais) past Conciergerie and Ste Chapelle (both R) then turn L (Quai du Marché Neuf) alongside second branch of Seine and L again into square in front of **Notre Dame cathedral** to end by bronze plaque set in road marking zero km point for French road network (13km, 35m).

NOTRE DAME

Although neither the largest (that is Amiens) nor the most spectacular (that is Chartres), Notre Dame de Paris is the most well-known cathedral in France. Occupying a site on the Île de la Cité, between two branches of the river Seine, it lies at the heart of Paris. Indeed, the zero kilometre plaque, from which all distances to Paris are measured, is set in the square in front of the

Notre Dame cathedral is the end point of Avenue Verte

cathedral. Built in Gothic style, it was constructed between 1163–1345 and was among the first buildings in the world to use flying buttresses, although these were not part of the original plan. As the walls grew higher, cracks and bowing started to appear and the buttresses were added for support. These were enhanced with stone-carved gargoyles and chimera, which were originally brightly painted but are now bare stone, and give the outside of the cathedral its distinctive appearance. Of three rose windows, that on the north transept is the most spectacular. Much of the ornamentation was damaged during the revolution. When restoration began, many of the most flamboyant Gothic elements were ignored, in particular the stained-glass windows which were replaced by clear panes. This annoyed the author Victor Hugo, a strong supporter of Gothic architecture, who in 1831 published his novel *Notre Dame de Paris* (the English translation was subsequently renamed *The Hunchback of Notre Dame*) which emphasised the importance of maintaining the Gothic appearance of the cathedral. The stained-glass windows were eventually restored in the first half of the twentieth century.

REVERSE ROUTE: NOTRE DAME CATHEDRAL TO ST DENIS STATION

From front of **Notre Dame cathedral** (35m), cycle N (Rue d'Arcole) and turn L beside Seine (Quai de la Corse). Turn R over river on second bridge (Pont au Change) then go ahead R through Pl du Châtelet.

Continue into Bvd de Sébastopol past Tour St Jacques R, then turn L (Rue de Rivoli). Turn first R into pedestrianised Rue St Denis and follow this through square past Fontaine des Innocents L and continue across series of streets and boulevards. With Porte-St Denis gateway just ahead, turn R beside no246 into Rue Ste Apolline. Turn second L beside Rue St Martin then follow cycle track winding R and L past Porte-St Martin gateway into Rue René Boulanger. *Rue René Boulanger can be found behind Théâtre de la Renaissance.* Emerge into Pl Johann Strauss and turn L (Rue de Lancry). After this crosses canal turn L beside Canal St Martin (Quai de Jemmapes). Pass two locks and where road ends continue under railway and turn L (Bvd de la Villette). Cycle ahead over road junction and bear L beside canal L (Quai de la Loire) with **Rotonde de la Villette** (4.5km, 53m) visible across canal L.

Continue beside canal basin and turn L (Rue de Crimée) over second bridge then R (Quai de l'Oise) along opposite bank. Follow cycle track bearing L beside Canal St Denis, with **Museum of Science and Industry** behind lock R, to reach complicated road junction on next bridge. Turn R then L across tram tracks to join cycle track along opposite bank. Follow this along towpath past three locks and under ten bridges to pass **Stade de France** L.

Continue past lock 6, then pass tram station R and turn second L over canal to reach railway bridge beside **St Denis station** L (13km, 32m) (accommodation, refreshments, tourist office, cycle shop, station).

APPENDIX A

Facilities summary tables

	Stage distance (km)	Cumulative (km)	Altitude (m)	Accommodation	Refreshments	YH	Camping	Tourist office	Cycle shop	Station
Classic route										
Stage 1										
London			18	x		x	x			x
Greenwich	7	7	6	x	x			x	x	x
Charlton	10	10	4						x	x
Woolwich	12.5	12.5	6	x	x				x	x
Plumstead	14	14	6							x
Abbey Wood	16.5	16.5	2		x					x
Erith	21.5	21.5	10		x					x
Dartford	27	27.5	4	x	x					x
Gravesend Cyclopark	38.5	38.5	43		x				x	
Strood					x					
Rochester	50	50	4	x	x	x		x	x	x
Stage 2										
Borstal					x					

	Stage distance (km)	Cumulative (km)	Altitude (m)	Accommodation	Refreshments	YH	Camping	Tourist office	Cycle shop	Station
Blue Bell	9	59	183	×	×					
Detling	16	66	119	×	×					
Thurnham	17.5	67.5	119	×	×					
Hollingbourne	22.5	72.5	91		×					×
Lenham										×
Charing	35	85	142	×	×					×
Westwell	39.5	89.5	89	×	×		×			
Ashford	47.5	97.5	37	×	×			×	×	×
Stage 3										
Hythe	25.5	123	6	×	×				×	×
Sandgate	30.5	128	11	×	×					
Folkestone	33.5	131	8	×	×		×	×	×	×
Capel-le-Ferne	38	135.5	166		×					
Dover	49.5	147	10	×	×		×	×	×	×
Stage 4										
Calais	3.5	150.5	5	×	×	×	×	×	×	×
Coulogne	7	154	2		×					
Guînes	14	161	10	×	×		×	×		

	Stage distance (km)	Cumulative (km)	Altitude (m)	Accommodation	Refreshments	YH	Camping	Tourist office	Cycle shop	Station
Fiennes	19.5	166.5	105	x	x					
Hardinghen	22.5	169.5	115	x	x		x			
Le Wast	31	178	53	x	x					
Desvres	41	188	92	x	x			x		
Stage 5										
Courset	3	191	156	x						
Doudeauville	7.5	195.5	87	x						
Zérables	15	203	45		x					
Beussent	16.5	204.5	32	x	x		x			
Inxent	18	206	29	x	x					
Recques-sur-Course	19.5	207.5	25	x						
La Ballastière				x						
Estréelles				x						
Estrée	22	210	10	x	x					
Neuville-sous-Montreuil	26	214	15	x	x	x	x	x		x
Marles-sur-Canche	30	218	17	x	x					

	Stage distance (km)	Cumulative (km)	Altitude (m)	Accommodation	Refreshments	YH	Camping	Tourist office	Cycle shop	Station
Marenla	33.5	221.5	18				x			
Beaurainville	37.5	225.5	16	x	x		x			x
Aubin-St Vaast	43.5	231.5	23							x
Guisy	46	234	26	x			x			
Huby-St Leu	48.5	236.5	28	x	x					
Hesdin	49.5	237.5	29	x	x			x	x	x
Stage 6										
Crécy-en-Ponthieu	20.5	258	40	x	x			x		
Domvast	27	264.5	59	x						
Caours	35.5	273	16	x	x				x	
Abbeville	40	277.5	15	x	x		x	x	x	x
Stage 7										
Épagnette					x					
Pont-Remy	9	286.5	11	x	x					x
Long	15.5	293	12	x	x		x			
Hangest-sur-Somme	25	302.5	12	x	x					x
Picquigny	32	309.5	13		x		x			x

	Stage distance (km)	Cumulative (km)	Altitude (m)	Accommodation	Refreshments	YH	Camping	Tourist office	Cycle shop	Station
Samara park					x					
Ailly-sur-Somme	37.5	315	14	x	x			x		x
Dreuil-lès-Amiens	40	317.5	16		x					x
Montières					x		x			
Amiens	46.5	324	32	x	x	x		x	x	x
Stage 8										
Neuville-lès-Lœuilly	15.5	339.5	45		x					
Lœuilly	17.5	341.5	48	x	x		x			
Conty	22.5	346.5	60	x	x			x		
Croissy-sur-Celle	28.5	352.5	79	x						
Fontaine-Bonneleau	32.5	356.5	88				x			
Crèvecœur-le-Grand	41.5	365.5	178		x					
Regonval	46	370	127	x						
Blicourt	47.5	371.5	123	x						
Troissereux	57	381	80	x	x				x	
Beauvais	65	389	69	x	x			x	x	x

	Stage distance (km)	Cumulative (km)	Altitude (m)	Accommodation	Refreshments	YH	Camping	Tourist office	Cycle shop	Station
Stage 9										
Rochy-Condé				x						
Hermes	16.5	405.5	51	x	x					x
Heilles	20	409	54		x					x
Mouy	24.5	413.5	50	x	x					x
Balagny-sur-Thérain	28	417	42		x		x			x
Cires-les-Mello					x		x			x
Mello	32.5	421.5	45	x	x					x
Cramoisy	36	425	57		x					
St Leu d'Esserent	40.5	429.5	31	x	x		x	x		x
Chantilly	46	435	52	x	x			x		x
Stage 10										
Gouvieux	3.5	438.5	35	x	x					
Domaine du Lys				x	x					
Chaumontel				x	x				x	
Luzarches	13.5	448.5	69		x			x		x
Villiers-le-Bel	29.5	464.5	82	x	x					

	Stage distance (km)	Cumulative (km)	Altitude (m)	Accommodation	Refreshments	YH	Camping	Tourist office	Cycle shop	Station
Sarcelles-Lochères	33.5	468.5	70		x					
Pierrefitte-sur-Seine					x					
St Denis	38.5	473.5	30	x	x			x	x	x
Stage 11										
Paris	16.5	490	36	x	x	x	x	x	x	x
Avenue Verte										
Stage 1										
London			10	x	x	x	x	x	x	x
Coulsdon	29	29	88	x	x				x	x
Nutfield	37.5	37.5	85		x					
Redhill	40.5	40.5	78	x	x				x	x
Stage 2										
Horley	9.5	50	57	x	x				x	x
Gatwick	11.5	52	60	x	x			x	x	x

	Stage distance (km)	Cumulative (km)	Altitude (m)	Accommodation	Refreshments	YH	Camping	Tourist office	Cycle shop	Station
Three Bridges/ Crawley	18	58.5	68	x	x				x	x
Crawley Down	25	65.5	116							
East Grinstead	30.5	71	132	x	x			x	x	x
Forest Row	35	75.5	64	x	x		x		x	
Hartfield	41	81.5	47	x	x					
Groombridge	46	86.5	48		x					
Eridge	49	89.5	59		x					x
Stage 3										
Rotherfield	7.5	97	156		x					
Mayfield	12.5	102	109	x	x					
Heathfield	19.5	109	132	x	x		x		x	
Maynard's Green					x		x			
Horam	23.5	113	63				x			
Hellingly	29	118.5	23				x			
Hailsham	32	121.5	23	x	x		x			
Polegate (off-route)				x	x		x		x	x
Arlington	41.5	131	12		x					

	Stage distance (km)	Cumulative (km)	Altitude (m)	Accommodation	Refreshments	YH	Camping	Tourist office	Cycle shop	Station
Berwick station					x					x
Alfriston (off-route)				x	x		x			
Litlington	49	138.5	8		x					
Cuckmere Haven	52	141.5	4		x					
Seaford	57	146.5	0	x	x		x	x	x	x
Bishopstone										x
Newhaven	62.5	152	2	x	x		x	x	x	x
Stage 4										
Dieppe	2.5	154.5	5	x	x			x		x
Rouxmesnil-Bouteilles	5	157	9	x	x		x		x	
Arques-la-Bataille	8.5	160.5	11	x	x		x			
Meulers	18	170	25	x						
St Vaast d'Équiqueville	21.5	173.5	37		x					
Mesnières-en-Bray	32	184	62	x	x					
St Martin-l'Hortier				x						

CYCLING LONDON TO PARIS

	Stage distance (km)	Cumulative (km)	Altitude (m)	Accommodation	Refreshments	YH	Camping	Tourist office	Cycle shop	Station
Neufchâtel-en-Bray	37	189	78	x	x		x	x		
Stage 5										
Neuville-Ferrières (off-route)					x					
St Saire	6	195	99	x	x					
Beaubec-la-Rosière				x						
Serqueux	14	203	164							x
Forges-les-Eaux	18.5	207.5	163	x	x		x	x	x	
Le Fossé	20.5	209.5	148	x	x					
La Bellière	23.5	212.5	141	x						
Dampierre-en-Bray	35.5	224.5	123	x						
Gournay-en-Bray	45	234	99	x	x			x		
Stage 6										
Ferrières-en-Bray					x					x
Orsimont					x					
St Germer-de-Fly	8	242	105	x	x			x		

	Stage distance (km)	Cumulative (km)	Altitude (m)	Accommodation	Refreshments	YH	Camping	Tourist office	Cycle shop	Station
Neuf-Marché	15	249	86		x					
Les Flamands	17.5	251.5	187	x						
Amécourt	23	257	149	x						
Sérifontaine										x
Thierceville	29.5	263.5	63	x						
Bazincourt-sur-Epte	32	266	66	x	x					
Gisors	35.5	269.5	68	x	x		x	x	x	x
Stage 7										
Dangu	6	275.5	42		x		x			
Château-St Clair-sur-Epte	12.5	282	38		x					
Bray-et-Lû	21	290.5	29	x	x					
Chaussy	24.5	294	82	x	x					
Maudétour-en-Vexin	32	301.5	169	x						
Théméricourt	42.5	312	79		x			x		
Vigny	44.5	314	72		x					
Longuesse	46.5	316	56		x					
Sagy	49	318.5	50		x					

	Stage distance (km)	Cumulative (km)	Altitude (m)	Accommodation	Refreshments	YH	Camping	Tourist office	Cycle shop	Station
Cergy-le-Haut	54.5	324	119		x					x
Vauréal (off-route)									x	
Jouy-le-Moutier (off-route)				x						
Neuville-sur-Oise	60.5	330	22		x					
Stage 8										
Conflans-Ste Honorine	4.5	334.5	22	x	x			x		x
Maisons-Laffitte	12.5	342.5	34	x	x				x	x
Sartrouville									x	
Chatou	27	357	31		x					
Rueil					x					
Pavillon des Berges					x					
Gennevilliers Port				x	x					
Gennevilliers	41.5	371.5	29	x	x					x
St Denis	44	374	32	x	x			x	x	x
Stage 9										

APPENDIX B
Tourist information offices

Classic route

Stage 1
City of London
St Paul's churchyard
EC4M 8BX
tel 0207 332 1456
www.visitthecity.co.uk

Greenwich
Pepys House
2 Cutty Sark Gdns
SE10 9LW
tel 0870 606 2000
www.visitgreenwich.org.uk

Rochester
95 High St
ME1 1LX
tel 01634 338141
www.visitmedway.org

Stage 2
Maidstone (off route)
Bentlif art gallery
St Faith's St
ME14 1LH
tel 01622 602168
www.visitmaidstone.com

Ashford
Ashford Gateway Plus
Church Rd
TN23 1AS
tel 01233 330316
www.visitashfordandtenterden.co.uk

Stage 3
Folkestone
Town Hall
1–2 Guildhall St
CT20 1DY
tel 01303 257946
www.folkestonetouristinformation.co.uk

Dover
Dover museum
Market Sq
CT16 1PH
tel 01304 201066
www.whitecliffscountry.org.uk

Stage 4
Calais
12 Bvd Clemenceau
62100
tel +33 321 96 62 40
www.calais-cotedopale.com

Guînes
14 Rue Georges Clemenceau
62340
tel +33 321 35 73 73
www.paysdopale-tourisme.fr

Desvres
1 Rue du Louvre
62240
tel +33 321 92 09 09
www.cc-desvressamer.fr

Stage 5
Montreuil
21 Rue Carnot
62170
tel +33 321 06 04 27
www.tourisme-montreuillois.com

Hesdin
Hôtel de Ville
Place d'Armes
62140
tel +33 374 20 00 13
www.tourisme-7vallees.com

Stage 6
Crécy-en Ponthieu
32 Rue du Maréchal Leclerc
80150
tel +33 322 23 93 84
www.crecyenponthieu.com

Abbeville
1 Pl de l'Amiral Courbet
80100
tel +33 322 24 27 92
www.abbeville-tourisme.com

Stage 7
Ailly-sur-Somme
Maison Éclusière
11 Rue du Pont
80470
tel +33 322 51 46 85
www.amiens-ouest-tourisme.fr

Amiens
40 Place Notre Dame
80000
tel +33 322 71 60 50
www.amiens-tourisme.com

Stage 8
Conty
Pl du 8 Mai
194580160
tel +33 322 41 08 18
www.cccconty.com

Beauvais
1 Rue Beauregard
60000
tel +33 344 15 30 30
www.beauvaistourisme.fr

Stage 9
St Leu d'Esserent
7 Ave de la Gare
60340
tel +33 344 56 38 10
www.pierresudoisetourisme.fr

Chantilly
73 Rue du Connétable
60500
tel +33 344 67 37 37
www.chantilly-tourisme.com

Stage 10
Luzarches
6 Rue St Damien
95270
tel +33 134 09 98 48
www.tourisme-luzarches.org

St Denis
1 Rue de la République
93200
tel +33 155 87 08 70
www.tourisme-plainecommune-paris.
com

Stage 11
Paris
25 Rue des Pyramides
75001
tel +33 149 52 42 63
www.parisinfo.com

Avenue Verte

Stage 2
Horsham (off-route)
Causeway
RH12 1HE
tel 01403 211661
www.horsham.gov.uk/tourismpages

East Grinstead
Library Buildings
West St
RH19 4SR
tel 01342 410121
www.eastgrinstead.gov.uk/tourism

Tunbridge Wells (off-route)
Corn Exchange
The Pantiles
TN2 5TE
tel 01892 515675
www.visittunbridgewells.com

Stage 3
Eastbourne (off-route)
Cornfield St
BN21 4QA
tel 01323 415415
www.visiteastbourne.com

Seaford
37 Church St
BN25 1HG
tel 01323 897426
www.seaford.co.uk

Stage 4
Dieppe
Pont Jehan Ango
76200
tel +33 232 14 40 60
www.dieppetourisme.com

Neufchâtel-en-Bray
6 Pl Notre Dame
76270
tel +33 235 93 22 96
www.tourisme.braywy.fr

Stage 5
Forges-les-Eaux
Rue Albert Bochet
76440
tel +33 235 90 52 10
www.forgesleseaux-tourisme.fr

Gournay-en-Bray
9 Pl d'Armes
76220
tel +33 235 90 28 34
www.gournayenbray-tourisme.fr

Stage 6
St Germer-de-Fly
11 Pl de Verdun
60850
tel +33 344 82 62 74
www.ot-paysdebray.fr

Gisors
4 Rue du Général de Gaulle
27100
tel +33 232 27 60 63
www.tourisme-gisors.fr

Stage 7
Théméricourt
Maison du Parc
Rue Achim d'Abos
95450
tel +33 134 48 66 10
www.pnr-vexin-francais.fr

Cergy-Pontoise (off-route)
Pl de la Piscine
95300
tel +33 134 41 70 60
www.ot-cergypontoise.fr

Stage 8
Conflans-Ste Honorine
2 Rue René Albert
78700
tel +33 134 90 99 09
www.conflans-tourisme.fr

St Germain-en-Laye (off-route)
38 Rue au Pain
78100
tel +33 130 87 20 63
www.saintgermainenlaye-tourisme.fr

Stage 9
Paris
25 Rue des Pyramides
75001
tel +33 149 52 42 63
www.parisinfo.com

APPENDIX C
Youth hostels

Classic route

Stage 1
London
St Pauls (213 beds)
38 Carter Lane
EC4V 5AB
tel 0845 371 9012

London Rotherhithe (320 beds)
20 Salter Rd
SE16 5PR
tel 0845 371 9756

Stage 2
Medway (52 beds) (off-route)
351 Capstone Rd
Gillingham
ME7 3JE
tel 0845 371 9649

Stage 4
Calais (146 beds)
Rue du Maréchal de Lattre de Tassigny
62100
tel +33 321 34 70 20

Stage 5
Montreuil (FUAJ) (40 beds)
La Hulotte Citadelle, Rue Carnot
62170
tel +33 321 06 10 83

Stage 7
Amiens (FUAJ) (186 beds)
30 et 46 Sq Friant les 4 Chênes
80000
tel +33 322 33 27 30

Stage 11
Paris Louvre (BVJ)
20 Rue Jean-Jacques Rousseau
75001
tel +33 153 00 90 90

Paris Quartier Latin (BVJ)
44 Rue des Bernardins
75005
tel +33 143 29 34 80

Paris Opéra-Montmartre (BVJ)
1 Rue de la Tour des Dames
75009
tel +33 142 35 88 18

Paris Jules Ferry (FUAJ) (78 beds)
8 Bvd Jules Ferry
75011
tel +33 143 57 55 60

Paris Champs Elysées-Monceau (BVJ)
(130 beds)
12 Rue Léon Jost
75017
tel +33 142 67 20 40

Paris Yves Robert (FUAJ) (116 beds)
20 Rue Pajol
75018
tel +33 140 38 87 90

Paris Le d'Artagnan (FUAJ) (440 beds)
80 Rue Vitruve
75020
tel +33 140 32 34 56

Avenue Verte

Stage 1
London Earl's Ct (186 beds)
38 Bolton Gdns
SW5 0AQ
tel 0845 371 9114

London Oxford St (104 beds)
14 Noel St
W1F 8GJ
tel 0845 371 9133

London Central (274 beds)
104 Bolsover St
W1W 5NU
tel 0845 371 9154

London St Pancras (186 beds)
79–81 Euston Rd
NW1 2QE
tel 0845 371 9344

Stage 3
Eastbourne (30 beds) (off-route)
East Dean Rd
BN20 8ES
tel 0845 371 9316

Southease (66 beds) (off-route)
Itford Farm
Beddingham
BN8 6JS
tel 0845 371 9574

Stage 5
Forges-les-Eaux (gîte d'étape) (20 beds)
Pl de l'Ancienne Gare Thermale
78440
tel +33 235 09 68 37

Stage 9
For details of Paris hostels, see above
(Stage 11, classic route)

APPENDIX D
Useful contacts

Transport
P&O Ferries
Dover Ferry Terminal travel centre
Eastern docks
Dover,
Kent
CT16 1AJ

tel 0800 130 0030
www.poferries.com

DFDS Ferries
www.dfdsseaways.co.uk

SNCF (French Railways)
tel 0844 848 4064
https://uk.voyages-sncf.com

Eurotunnel
01303 282201
(UK cycle reservations on Le Shuttle)
tel +33 (0)3 21 00 22 01
(F cycle reservations on Le Shuttle)
www.eurotunnel.com

Eurostar
tel 0343 218 6186 (UK reservations)
tel +33 (0)8 92 35 35 39 (F reservations)
tel 0344 822 5822 (UK baggage)
tel +33 (0)1 55 31 68 33 (F baggage)
www.eurostar.com

European Bike Express
tel 01430 422111
info@bike-express.co.uk
www.bike-express.co.uk

The Man in Seat 61
(rail travel information)
www.seat61.com

Cycling organisations
Cycle Touring Club (CTC)
tel 0844 736 8450
cycling@ctc.org.uk
www.ctc.org.uk

Maps and guides
Avenue Verte route guide
www.avenuevertelondonparis.co.uk

Open Street Maps (on-line mapping)
www.openstreetmap.org

Stanford's
12/14 Long Acre
London
WC2E 9LP
tel 0207 836 1321
sales@stanfords.co.uk
www.stanfords.co.uk

The Map Shop
15 High St
Upton upon Severn
Worcs
WR8 0HJ
tel 08000 854080 or 01684 593146
themapshop@btinternet.com
www.themapshop.co.uk

Accommodation
Websites such as www.booking.com can be useful for finding accommodation. Local tourist offices (listed in Appendix D) provide accommodation lists either directly or on their websites.

Youth Hostels Association
tel 08000 191700
customerservices@yha.org.uk
www.yha.org.uk

Hostelling International
(youth hostel bookings)
www.hihostels.com

Gites d'étape guide
www.gites-refuges.com

Hostel Bookers
(independent hostel bookings)
www.hostelbookers.com

APPENDIX E

Language glossary

English	French
hello	bonjour
goodbye	au revoir
yes	oui
no	non
please	s'il vous plait
thank you	merci
watch out!	attention!
left	à gauche
right	à droite
straight on	tout droit
abbey	la abbaye
barrier	la barrière
bed & breakfast	les chambres d'hôte
bicycle	le vélo/la bicyclette
brake	le frein
bridge	le pont
castle	le château
cathedral	la cathédrale
chain	la chaîne
church	l'église
cycle track	la vèloroute/la piste cyclable
cyclist	le/la cycliste
diversion	la déviation
ferry	le bac/le ferry

English	French
field	le champ
flood	l'inondation
forest/wood	la forêt/le bois
handlebar	le guidon
inner tube	la chambre à air
lock (anti-theft)	l'antivol
lock (canal)	l'écluse
marsh	le marais
monastery	le monastère
motorway	l'autoroute
no entry	entrée interdite
one-way street	sens unique
puncture	la crevaison
railway	le chemin de fer
river	le fleuve/la rivière
riverbank	la rive
road closed	route barrée
station	la gare
tourist information office	l'office de tourisme
town hall	l'hôtel de ville/la mairie
tyre	le pneu
wheel	la roue
youth hostel	l'auberge de jeunesse

DOWNLOAD THE ROUTES
IN GPX FORMAT

All the routes in this guide are available for download from:

www.cicerone.co.uk/914/GPX

as GPX files. You should be able to load them into most formats of mobile device, whether GPS or smartphone.

When you go to this link, you will be asked for your email address and where you purchased the guide, and have the option to subscribe to the Cicerone e-newsletter.

www.cicerone.co.uk

LISTING OF CICERONE GUIDES

Walking on the Gower
Welsh Winter Climbs

DERBYSHIRE, PEAK DISTRICT AND MIDLANDS

Cycling in the Peak District
Dark Peak Walks
Scrambles in the Dark Peak
Walking in Derbyshire
White Peak Walks:
  The Northern Dales
White Peak Walks:
  The Southern Dales

SOUTHERN ENGLAND

20 Classic Sportive Rides
  in South East England
20 Classic Sportive Rides
  in South West England
Cycling in the Cotswolds
Mountain Biking on the
  North Downs
Mountain Biking on the
  South Downs
North Downs Way Map Booklet
South West Coast Path Map
  Booklet – Minehead to St Ives
South West Coast Path Map
  Booklet – Plymouth to Poole
South West Coast Path Map
  Booklet – St Ives to Plymouth
Suffolk Coast and Heath Walks
The Cotswold Way
The Cotswold Way Map Booklet
The Great Stones Way
The Kennet and Avon Canal
The Lea Valley Walk
The North Downs Way
The Peddars Way and Norfolk
  Coast Path
The Pilgrims' Way
The Ridgeway Map Booklet
The Ridgeway National Trail
The South Downs Way
The South Downs Way
  Map Booklet
The South West Coast Path
The Thames Path
The Thames Path Map Booklet
The Two Moors Way
Walking in Cornwall
Walking in Essex
Walking in Kent
Walking in London
Walking in Norfolk
Walking in Sussex
Walking in the Chilterns
Walking in the Cotswolds
Walking in the Isles of Scilly
Walking in the New Forest

Walking in the North
  Wessex Downs
Walking in the Thames Valley
Walking on Dartmoor
Walking on Guernsey
Walking on Jersey
Walking on the Isle of Wight
Walking the Jurassic Coast
Walks in the South Downs
  National Park

BRITISH ISLES CHALLENGES, COLLECTIONS AND ACTIVITIES

The Book of the Bivvy
The Book of the Bothy
The C2C Cycle Route
The End to End Cycle Route
The End to End Trail
The Mountains of England and
  Wales: Vol 1 Wales
The Mountains of England and
  Wales: Vol 2 England
The National Trails
The UK's County Tops
Three Peaks, Ten Tors

ALPS CROSS-BORDER ROUTES

100 Hut Walks in the Alps
Across the Eastern Alps: E5
Alpine Ski Mountaineering
  Vol 1 – Western Alps
Alpine Ski Mountaineering Vol 2
  – Central and Eastern Alps
Chamonix to Zermatt
The Tour of the Bernina
Tour of Mont Blanc
Tour of Monte Rosa
Tour of the Matterhorn
Trail Running – Chamonix and
  the Mont Blanc region
Trekking in the Alps
Trekking in the Silvretta and
  Rätikon Alps
Trekking Munich to Venice
Walking in the Alps

PYRENEES AND FRANCE/SPAIN CROSS-BORDER ROUTES

The GR10 Trail
The GR11 Trail – La Senda
The Pyrenean Haute Route
The Pyrenees
The Way of St James – France
The Way of St James – Spain
Walks and Climbs in the Pyrenees

AUSTRIA

The Adlerweg
Trekking in Austria's Hohe Tauern
Trekking in the Stubai Alps

Trekking in the Zillertal Alps
Walking in Austria

SWITZERLAND

Cycle Touring in Switzerland
The Swiss Alpine Pass Route –
  Via Alpina Route 1
The Swiss Alps
Tour of the Jungfrau Region
Walking in the Bernese Oberland
Walking in the Valais
Walks in the Engadine –
  Switzerland

FRANCE

Chamonix Mountain Adventures
Cycle Touring in France
Cycling the Canal du Midi
Écrins National Park
Mont Blanc Walks
Mountain Adventures in
  the Maurienne
The Cathar Way
The GR20 Corsica
The GR5 Trail
The GR5 Trail – Vosges and Jura
The Grand Traverse of the
  Massif Central
The Loire Cycle Route
The Moselle Cycle Route
The River Rhone Cycle Route
The Robert Louis Stevenson Trail
The Way of St James –
  Le Puy to the Pyrenees
Tour of the Oisans: The GR54
Tour of the Queyras
Tour of the Vanoise
Vanoise Ski Touring
Via Ferratas of the French Alps
Walking in Corsica
Walking in Provence – East
Walking in Provence – West
Walking in the Auvergne
Walking in the Cevennes
Walking in the Dordogne
Walking in the Haute Savoie:
  North
Walking in the Haute Savoie:
  South
Walks in the Cathar Region
Walking in the Ardennes

GERMANY

Hiking and Biking in the
  Black Forest
The Danube Cycleway Volume
The Rhine Cycle Route
The Westweg

For full information on all our
guides, books and eBooks,
visit our website:
www.cicerone.co.uk

Walking – Trekking – Mountaineering – Climbing – Cycling

Over 40 years, Cicerone have built up an outstanding collection of over 300 guides, inspiring all sorts of amazing adventures.

Every guide comes from extensive exploration and research by our expert authors, all with a passion for their subjects. They are frequently praised, endorsed and used by clubs, instructors and outdoor organisations.

All our titles can now be bought as **e-books**, **ePubs** and **Kindle** files and we also have an online magazine - **Cicerone Extra** – with features to help cyclists, climbers, walkers and trekkers choose their next adventure, at home or abroad.

Our website shows any **new information** we've had in since a book was published. Please do let us know if you find anything has changed so that we can publish the latest details. On our **website** you'll also find great ideas and lots of detailed information about what's inside every guide and you can buy **individual routes** from many of them online.

It's easy to keep in touch with what's going on at Cicerone by getting our monthly **free e-newsletter**, which is full of offers, competitions, up-to-date information and topical articles. You can subscribe on our home page and also follow us on **Facebook** and **Twitter** or dip into our **blog**.

Cicerone – the very best guides for exploring the world.

CICERONE

Juniper House, Murley Moss, Oxenholme Road, Kendal, Cumbria LA9 7RL
Tel: 015395 62069 info@cicerone.co.uk
www.cicerone.co.uk